UNIVERSITY COLLEGE BIRMINGHAM
COLLEGE LIBRARY, SUMMER ROW
BIRMINGHAM. B3 1JB
Tel: (0121) 243 0055

DATE OF RETURN		
26/06/09		

Please remember to return on time or pay the fine

Handbook of
Tourist Behavior

Routledge Advances in Tourism

EDITED BY STEPHEN PAGE, *University of Stirling, Scotland*

Handbook of
Tourist Behavior
Theory & Practice

Edited by Metin Kozak and
Alain Decrop

Routledge
Taylor & Francis Group
New York   London

First published 2009
by Routledge
270 Madison Ave, New York, NY 10016

Simultaneously published in the UK
by Routledge
2 Park Square, Milton Park, Abingdon, Oxon OX14 4RN

Routledge is an imprint of the Taylor & Francis Group, an informa business

© 2009 Taylor & Francis

Typeset in Sabon by IBT Global.
Printed and bound in the United States of America on acid-free paper by IBT Global.

Library of Congress Cataloging in Publication Data
Handbook of tourist behavior : theory & practice / edited by Metin Kozak and Alain Decrop.
    p. cm.—(Routledge advances in tourism)
    Includes bibliographical references and index.
    1. Consumer behavior. I. Kozak, M. (Metin), 1968– II. Decrop, Alain.
G155.A1.H356 2009
    910.68'8—dc22
    2008038498

ISBN10: 0–415–99360–1 (hbk)
ISBN10: 0–203–88180–X (ebk)

ISBN13: 978–0–415–99360–9 (hbk)
ISBN13: 978–0–203–88180–4 (ebk)

Contents

Part VII: Environmental Determinants of Tourist Behavior

Figures

Tables

Preface

In today's highly competitive and global economy, understanding tourist behavior is imperative to success. Understanding tourists/travelers is even more important as they appear to be still more demanding and changeable, and to show complex preference structures and decision patterns. In brief, tourist behavior has become a cornerstone of any marketing strategy and action. Choosing, buying, and consuming tourism/travel products and services involves a range of psychosocial processes and a number of personal and environmental influences that researchers and managers should take into account. This book aims at providing an overview of such processes and influences, and at explaining the basic concepts and theories that underlie tourist decision making and behavior. It also incorporates a number of short case studies in order to aid readers to better appraise the application of those concepts and theories. The *Handbook of Tourist Behavior* will be of significant interest to researchers and students in tourism, leisure, marketing, and psychology, and also to practitioners of the tourism industry.

Consumer behavior generally focuses on the activities people undertake when obtaining, consuming, and disposing of products and services. In line with such a focus, most consumer behavior models consist of three stages: prepurchase, consumption, and postconsumption (e.g., Engel, Blackwell, and Miniard, 1995). In the first stage, potential tourists recognize the need and feel some motivation to go on holiday; they search for information about various destinations and evaluate those alternatives in order to choose one destination to vacation (Klenosky and Gitelson, 1998; Um and Crompton, 1990). A variety of supply- and demand-related factors influence whether to go on holidays and the choice of destinations, including psychological, economic, social, political, geographical, and demographic factors (Crompton and Ankomah, 1993). The consumer behavior literature makes a general distinction between individual and environmental influences on tourist behavior. The former involve determinants that make each of us unique as an individual (including consumers' demographics, personality traits, lifestyles and values, emotions, involvement, etc.), whereas the latter pertain to external factors (including social, cultural, business, and media variables) that shape one's behavior and have an impact on decisions and choices.

In the second stage, tourists experience the destination and its products or services. This stage is made up of a series of events or activities (Smith, 2003) which help consumers to give meaning and to convey symbolic value to their choices and actions (Kim, 2001; Uriely, 2005). Consumer experience is highly subjective and is based on sensations, emotions, and social interaction to a large extent. It involves participation in activities and results in learning or knowledge acquisition. In the last stage, after having completed their holiday experiences, tourists evaluate their experiences by matching the outcome not only with the information received from various sources such as media and relatives but also with their own expectations (Pizam, Neumann, and Reichel, 1978). Their evaluation typically results in feelings of dis/satisfaction, which has ramifications of intentions to come back or switch to other domestic or international destinations and tell others about favorable or unfavorable aspects of their experiences (Baker and Crompton, 2000; Kozak, 2001).

This book follows the rationale of the abovementioned decisional and behavioral stages and applies them in the context of tourist behavior. The work is laid out in seven parts containing sixteen chapters. The first five parts describe the three stages depicted in traditional consumer decision-making and behavior models while the last two chapters deal with personal and environmental influences on tourist behavior, respectively.

With two specific chapters, Part I begins with introducing the concept of motivation and need recognition. The first chapter, coauthored by *Blichfeldt* and *Kessler*, tries to illustrate the necessity for more qualitative approaches in tourism research, by analyzing the nature of tourist behavior and then presenting a selection of representative examples of interpretive research. The examples are chosen to demonstrate the range of surprising and in-depth knowledge that can be achieved by applying qualitative approaches to tourism research. In the second chapter, *Correia* and *Moital* contribute to the growing body of knowledge on tourist motivation by reviewing existing research in the field of the prestige motivation and by developing an analytical model of prestige tourism motivation. Motivation is conceptualized from an expectancy-value perspective and the model emphasizes the antecedents and consequences of prestige motivation. This chapter also identifies a number of research opportunities in that field.

Part II addresses an overall view of how tourists form their perceptions and process the information they acquire by tracing various internal and external sources. In this respect, the first contribution here is offered by *Govers* and *Go,* who examine the deconstruction of the tourism destination image-formation paradigm as a consequence of the influence of twin forces: information technology and glocalization. It contributes to the advancement of theory through multidisciplinary insights by mining various conceptual perspectives, including perceptions, beliefs, feelings, and attitudes. The analytical three-gap image-formation model provides insight into the way in which tourism destinations' identities are constructed, imagined, and experienced. Next, *Hyde* focuses on a popular topic of tourist behavior that has been extensively studied in tourism research, particularly over the past decade. His chapter presents a contextual framework for tourist information search based on the purposes of travel, first-time versus repeat visits to a destination, and pretrip versus on-trip information search. Research evidence is presented on the sources of information utilized most often by tourists, on the extensiveness of information search tourists undertake, and on the determinants of such a search. The chapter concludes by presenting a list of suggested areas for future research.

Part III specifically presents the ways tourists evaluate alternative products and plan their choices. Such subjects as decision making and exploratory behavior have a long tradition in psychology and consumer research, but have received limited attention from tourism scholars. First, *Decrop* and *Kozak* draw on the application of decision strategies by potential tourists while evaluating their alternative tourism products and making the final decision to purchase. The chapter introduces a set of strategies that tourists are likely to apply in their decision processes and also addresses various practical examples to support their validity in tourism research. In a subsequent chapter, *Teichmann* and *Zins* follow the framework of exploratory buying behavior outlined by Raju (1980) and investigate the existing tourism behavior literature along seven different types of motivating deeds: innovativeness, risk taking, interpersonal communication, information seeking, exploration through shopping, brand switching, and repetitive behavior proneness.

Part IV focuses on the tourism experience, which is the cornerstone of tourist behavior, as it is the point where consumers can enjoy the benefits and emotions of their choices. The consumption experience is both relevant for tourism practice and research (Uriely, 2005). The aim of the first chapter of Part IV is to present the mindfulness construct, borrowed from applied social psychology, and to use this theory to set out a series of principles for the better design and management of tourist settings and activities. *Moscardo* first reviews the concept of experience in tourism before describing mindfulness theory and its relationship to other concepts that have been linked to tourist experiences. She then examines the use of mindfulness in tourism research before setting out a preliminary mindfulness theory of tourist experiences. In the second chapter, *Morgan* and *Watson* try to "unlock the shared experience" by enhancing the major challenges of consumer experience research. They first set up a research agenda and next describe a few problems related to experience research (e.g., time consumption and the nonrepresentativeness of samples). Third, the authors show the usefulness of online communities and Internet-based methods (netnography) as a rich source of material for the study of consumer experiences. Finally, they examine how research into the outputs of such online communities can be used to understand the elements of the consumer experience and to reveal consumers' satisfactions, benefits, experiences, and meanings.

Consumption is followed by the postconsumption stage where consumers are expected to live their experiences. This is the purpose of Part V in this book. The first chapter of this part, contributed by *Foster*, aims to respecify tourism dis/satisfaction research and proposes a new approach to how tourists evaluate their holidays. Rather than understanding tourist dis/satisfaction as an evaluative judgment made at any specific point in time, she argues that tourist dis/satisfaction should be understood as an evaluative process which takes place over time. Numerous studies have demonstrated that failures in any one of these elements can lead to dissatisfaction, which may stimulate tourists' intentions of complaining. Hence, as the focal part of the elaboration of tourists' post-choice or consumption processes, *Duman* and *Kozak* discuss service failure, customer complaints, and factors that identify complaining behavior in services. Later in the chapter, they also deliberate service recovery and its effects on tourist behavior. Finally, *Li* and *Petrick* attempt to identify a useful theory that may lead to a theoretical explanation of loyalty development. After reviewing and conceptually comparing several theoretical frameworks on commitment, the authors suggest that the Investment Model (IM) in social psychology may lend a theoretical foundation to future discussion on loyalty formation.

Once the major stages of tourist decision making and behavior have been outlined, the last two parts of the Handbook focus on the individual and environmental variables that influence such decisions and behaviors. Part VI includes two chapters that deal with a series of individual determinants of tourist behavior. The first contribution, by *Dolnicar* and *Kemp,* focuses on the consumer-based variables that may be used in tourism segmentation. The chapter aims at analyzing market segmentation studies in tourism research over the past decade, at reviewing recent varying examples of segmentation approaches, and at discussing a range of theoretical and methodological dangers associated with market segmentation studies. Emotions and affective states are the topic of the second chapter of Part VI. Emotions have gained increasing interest amongst tourism researchers and managers, which is not very surprising as tourism is all about recreating, feeling better both mentally and physically. *Gnoth* and *Zins* detail the phenomenon of emotions and related constructs (including affect, feeling states, mood, and traits). They then discuss emotion and affective response in tourism research. The authors close their chapter with a brief outline of further related constructs that are of importance to cross-cultural emotion research, including the link of emotions to schemata, values. and acculturation.

Coming after the presentation of individual variables, the environmental determinants of tourist behavior are the focus of the last part of the Handbook. Three chapters describe how a series of environmental factors, including information technology (IT), media products and culture, may influence the way tourists behave and make their decisions. E-tourist behavior represents the core of a first chapter in which *Petr* outlines the influence of IT on consumers. The chapter aims at a better understanding and forecasting of the changes brought about by the digital revolution through looking at the main features of the online vacation decision-making process. The second chapter of Part VII deals with the role of media products in tourism behavior. *Månsson* elaborates upon the role and effect of intertwined media products on tourism behavior. The author begins with an overview of some popular cultural media products like photographs and film in relation to tourist behavior. Following Morgan and Pritchard (1998), she suggests that tourists' decisions and consumption of destinations are no longer primarily influenced by promotion material such as brochures and advertisements but are affected by media products like literature and film to a much higher degree. In the very last chapter of the Handbook, *Reisinger* shows how culture may strongly affect tourist behavior. In the author's eyes, the continued growth in international tourism and the changes in travel patterns have significant implications for the tourism industry. After enhancing the difficulty for operators to meet the needs of culturally different tourists, she reviews studies about cultural differences in tourism and outlines the major cultural differences in tourist behavior, partly referring to Hofstede's four-dimensional taxonomy.

All the seven parts included in this Handbook show how consumer behavior is central to tourism managerial decisions and to academic research. It is pleasing to see that, in the last few decades, many studies in tourism have empirically looked into consumer decisions and behaviors from various perspectives. However, the literature still lacks a collection of consumer-related topics in a book form from a more conceptual and theoretical perspective. This book attempts to fill such a gap by proposing a series of chapters on topics related to consumer behavior in tourism. More specifically, the Handbook features papers using theoretical approaches and synthesis to building and examining theory of how consumers think and act within the context of tourism consumption. Each contribution is organized in line with this direction. Again, our target was not to produce a collection of empirical studies but to generate a conceptual work based on the synthesis of earlier studies published in the general consumer research literature as well as in more specific tourism journals. This book is likely to serve as a state-of-the-art enterprise to assist with future tourism research in the area of consumer decision making and behavior.

Metin Kozak and Alain Decrop
The Editors
August 2008

REFERENCES

Baker, D. A. & Crompton, J. L. (2000). Quality, satisfaction and behavioural intentions. *Annals of Tourism Research*, 27(3): 785–803.

Crompton, J. L. & Ankomah, P. K. (1993). Choice set propositions in destination decisions. *Annals of Tourism Research*, 20(1): 461–75.

Engel, J. F., Blackwell, R. D. & Miniard, P. W. (1995). *Consumer behavior*, 8th Edition, Florida: The Dryden Press.

Kim, Y.-K. (2001). Experiential retailing: An interdisciplinary approach to success in domestic and international retailing. *Journal of Retailing and Consumer Services*, 8: 287–89.

Klenosky, D. & Gitelson, R. E. (1998). Travel agents' destination recommendations. *Annals of Tourism Research*, 25(3): 661–74.

Kozak, M. (2001). Repeaters' behavior at two distinct destinations. *Annals of Tourism Research*, 28(3): 785–808.

Morgan, N. & Pritchard, A. (1998). *Tourism, Promotion and power: Creating images, creating identities*. Chichester, UK: Wiley.

Pizam, A., Neumann, Y. & Reichel, A. (1978). Dimensions of tourist satisfaction area. *Annals of Tourism Research*, 5: 314–22.

Raju, P. S. (1980). Optimum stimulation level: Its relationship to personality, demographics, and exploratory behavior. *Journal of Consumer Research*, 7(December): 272–82.

Smith, W. A. (2003). Does B & B management agree with the basic ideas behind experience management strategy?. *Journal of Business and Management*, 9(3): 233–47.

Um, S. & Crompton, J. L. (1990). Attitude determinants in tourism destination choice. *Annals of Tourism Research*, 17: 432–48.

Uriely, N. (2005). The tourist experience: Conceptual developments. *Annals of Tourism Research*, 32(1): 199–216.

Part I

Motivation and Need Recognition

1 Interpretive Consumer Research
Uncovering the "Whys" Underlying Tourist Behavior

Bodil Stilling Blichfeldt and Inès Kessler

INTRODUCTION

Most consumer research in tourism is quantitative in nature as well as destination-based (e.g., Mehmetoglu and Altinay, 2006; Riley and Love, 1999). A number of good reasons have led to the dominance of destination-based, quantitative studies. Especially, the reliance on destination-based studies ensures that the researcher generates knowledge of relevance to practitioners. Hence, the outcome of a destination-based study is likely to directly contribute to practitioners as this type of study clarifies what tourists like and dislike about the destination and how destination marketers can improve their "product" in order to better fulfill the needs of their customers. Thus, this kind of study is excellent insofar as the purpose of research is to generate *normative* theory (Hunt, 1976) that offers suggestions as to how destination marketers may improve their situation (e.g., how to attract more visitors; how to make visitors revisit the destination; or how to improve customer satisfaction).

Apart from their ability to form the basis for generating normative theory, quantitative studies are excellent at producing knowledge on the what, when, how, who, and where questions, the answering of which is crucial to destination marketers. After all, destination-based quantitative studies are the basis for generating the statistics desperately needed in order to assess the extent, nature, and development in destinations' bonds with tourists. Thus, quantitative studies (if conducted properly) generate knowledge that transcends the respondents and hence, knowledge that relates to the entire population of visitors in question. As such, quantitative studies are the means of choice when uncovering the what, where, when, who, how much, and how relating to all of the topics that are discussed in the various chapters of this book.

Most hotels, for example, conduct quantitative studies in order to reveal whether guests are (dis)satisfied with their stay as well as with various elements of this stay (the room, the restaurant, Internet facilities, front desk personnel, etc.). As another example, a variety of quantitative studies address tourist motivations by means of a series of questions relying on extant typologies of motivations. Furthermore, quantitative studies are excellent at uncovering the types of activities visitors engage in during their stay as well as their satisfaction with the different kinds of activities and experiences the destination has to offer. Thus, destination-based quantitative studies hold a series of valuable advantages. However, destination-based quantitative studies are also characterized by a number of drawbacks. The key advantages and drawbacks of quantitative consumer research in tourism can thus be summarized as (Powell and Watson, 2006: 299): "A survey is a practical and efficient way of gaining data from a large number of people but is not so effective at discovering the meanings and the motives that form the basis of social action."

Hence, especially quantitative studies are not only practical and efficient, but often superior, when the purpose is to get an overview of who our guests are; what they do while visiting us; and how satisfied they are with our tourism offer. However, quantitative studies have one major drawback as they are not especially good at generating knowledge on the 'whys' underlying tourist behavior. Accordingly, although quantitative studies, if conducted properly, give excellent overviews of our visitors, they are not very good at uncovering what goes on in the minds of these visitors. As such, quantitative studies are not especially valuable insofar as we wish to gain insight into the tourists' lines of reasoning that make them behave in certain ways.

Several philosophers of science (e.g., Denzin, 2001; Denzin and Lincoln, 1994; Guba, 1990; Miles and Hubermann, 1994) argue that if we wish for a research area to prosper, we should rely on *both* quantitative and qualitative research methods. Accordingly, if we wish for consumer research in tourism to be a research area characterized by continuous evolvement and refinement, then it is crucial that such research makes the best possible use of both qualitative and quantitative methods. Hence, the key reason why quantitative research is necessary is that it can uncover the answers to the focal who, what, when, where, how much, and how questions. However, the argument substantiated in this chapter is that qualitative research is a necessary supplement as this kind of research is especially fruitful when we wish to uncover the 'whys' underlying consumer behavior. However, at the moment, the vast majority of consumer research in tourism is quantitative in nature, thus often neglecting the "whys" of tourist behavior.

In order to make a contribution to a prosperous future for consumer research in tourism, the objective of this chapter is firstly to illustrate the necessity for more qualitative approaches in tourism research, by analyzing the very nature of tourism consumer behavior and decision making. By describing the complexities as well as constant evolution of tourism consumer behavior, we hope to achieve an understanding for the necessity of applying a method matching the research object, that is, a complex and ever-developing approach. Further, we would like to introduce the reader to qualitative methods in tourism and especially to the types of insights that such additional research generates, by using some examples from existing research, representing different settings, preconditions, and therefore different variations of qualitative research.

NATURE OF TOURIST BEHAVIOR AND THE NEED TO ASK "WHY"

Due to the fact that quantitative research is not especially good at uncovering the "whys" underlying consumer behavior in tourism, Mehmetoglu and Altinay (2006: 13) argue that "There is thus a need for theory-generating approaches, namely qualitative research, to hospitality and tourism research."

In the same vein, in regard to tourism research, Cohen (1988: 30) argued that

> The most significant and lasting contributions have been made by researchers who employed an often loose, qualitative methodology . . . The much more rigorous and quantitative "touristological" studies often yielded results of rather limited interest.

Especially, the call for more qualitative research in tourism originates from the fact that several researchers (e.g., Henderson and Bedini, 1995; Hollinshead, 1996; Walle, 1997) argue that quantitative research is not especially good at generating understanding and uncovering meaning. However, as pointed out by Denzin and Lincoln (1994: 2), interpretative approaches relying on qualitative methods are especially relevant when we wish to investigate the "whys" underlying behavior, as they define qualitative research as:

> Multi-method in focus, involving an interpretive, naturalistic approach to its subject matter. This means that qualitative researchers study things in their natural setting, attempting to make sense of, or interpret, phenomena in terms of the meanings people bring to them.

Around twenty years ago, interpretive research adhering to qualitative methods gained acceptance within consumer behavior research (e.g., Anderson, 1989; Deshpande, 1983; Hirschman, 1986, 1994; Hirschman and Holbrook, 1992; Holbrook and O'Shaughnessy, 1988; Peter and Olson, 1989). Despite the fact that interpretive research has become an integral part of consumer behavior research, nonetheless, in their review of tourism research methods, Riley and Love (1999) argue that quantitative research methods still dominate consumer research in tourism. This may be a problem as it seems that interpretive research has much to offer to the study of tourists, as researching, for example, tourist/consumer behavior and decision making mostly means researching more than mere preferences, dislikes, past experiences, and expectations. Researching tourist/consumer behavior and decision making mostly means looking at complex and multifaceted processes evolving over time, very often a rather long period of time.

Even more than most other "conventional" consumer goods, the tourism product and related purchasing decisions are subject to influences that are difficult to quantify and that are constantly changing. As a consequence, this means that " . . . the behavior patterns during purchase are not routine and every purchase occasion will show different approaches" (Swarbrooke and Horner, 2007: 72). Another predominant characteristic of the tourism product is that the purchasing decision is highly emotional as well as influenced by other people, which adds an extra difficulty to researching the subject matter, as "the people who influence decision[s] will also change their views over time" (Swarbrooke and Horner, 2007: 73).

Middleton and Clarke (2002) even compare consumers' minds with computers, where the outcome is preconditioned by two factors: the program run on the computer and the input fed into it. Information can only be processed, both by computers and consumers, if the input occurs and occurs at the right time, that is to say, when required. Therefore, when the objective is to understand the "output" (i.e., the purchase decision), marketers and researchers alike have to understand the "program" processing that information. To make sense of the *factual* information given "it is necessary for marketers to have some understanding of how information is likely to be received and

---

Case Study 1. "Freed from Experience" as a Reason to Go on Holiday

Although we tend to emphasize people's needs for memorable, out-of-the-ordinary experiences, some people (exemplified by Danes who spend their summer vacations at a Danish caravan site) choose vacations that, from the outside, appear *not* to incorporate "extraordinary" experiences. A study at a Danish caravan site (comprised of observations and thirty-one in-depth interviews with sixty-one informants) revealed that a key reason why people choose to spend their vacations at a caravan site is that it offers them many opportunities to "do" things *whilst* they feel no obligation to do so. Hence, these people immerse in life at the caravan site freed from tasks and pressures of everyday life as well as from pressures to experience (e.g., visiting attractions). The study thus indicates that individuals choose to stay at a nearby caravan site because it offers *opportunities* for making "good" use of valuable spare time (i.e., engaging in experiences) while it will be perfectly all right, once immersed in life at the caravan site, to spend the vacation experiencing nothing out of the ordinary—and that this is an experience in itself. Hence, these people suggest that being "freed from experience" is a key reason why they choose this kind of vacation.

Care to read more? http://www.sam.sdu.dk/ime/PDF/blichfeldt7.pdf.

processed" (Middleton and Clarke, 2002: 76). In other terms, in order to understand and eventually analyze, classify, describe, and possibly predict the decisions made by tourists, one has to try to understand the underlying rationale, the "program," in short, the *whys* underlying tourist behavior.

Gaining insight into tourists' rationale and uncovering motivation have become even more crucial over the past decade or two than ever before. Crucial for the researcher who wants to find valid and consistent answers, but also crucial for practitioners who need to market their products or even re-create what they have "on display." This heightened need for actually understanding tourist decision-making processes is due to a change in tourism and thus tourist behavior as well as an even more drastic change in the way tourism is marketed, sold, and bought. Already in 1993, Auliana Poon described a shift within tourism and tourist behavior. From the "old tourism," the mass tourism of the 70s and 80s, largely dominated by economical factors, the market moved forward toward an increasing demand for individually tailored holidays. "New tourism" thus is described as "flexible, segmented, customized and diagonally integrated" (Poon, 1993).

A pivotal part in this changing tourism behavior is of course played by modern technologies and the opportunities they create for both providers and consumers. As early as 1997, the Travel Industry Association of America claimed that the travel and tourism market will be one of the predominant markets for online sales. Time has proved this notion to be true. And along with new technologies, the notion of "new tourism" has been refined and defined more clearly. The new technologies are more than a means to an end (e.g., information search, comparisons of price, offer, etc.). These new opportunities have not only changed the kind of information sought by consumers—an increase in the amount, specifics, and detail of information provided. These changes also work "the other way round"—the consumer is influenced by amount, specifics, and detail of information as well. As Buhalis (2003: 54) puts it, "The Internet has enabled the 'new' type of tourist to become more knowledgeable and to seek exceptional value for money and time. New consumers are more culturally and environmentally aware and they often like a greater involvement with the local society."

In other words, not only have circumstances and markets changed, but also consumers have changed considerably. This change in consumers is not only due to the new technological possibilities. There are other factors deriving from society's development as a whole. Cooper and Buhalis (1998, quoted in Buhalis, 2003: 128) point out, for example, that "the new, sophisticated traveler has emerged as a result of experience" and that this new type is also more linguistically skilled. This means, amongst other things, that an even wider part of the market is accessible to them and that they have much better opportunities for understanding other cultures, at least those cultures they share a language with. But not only linguistic skills bring other cultures and formerly remote places and people closer to each other and to the (potential) tourist. The modern world offers means and opportunities enough to get to know, visit, and stay in touch with other cultures and their members.

In one word, globalization has altered tourism, the tourist, and tourist behavior as it has altered the world as a whole. And with these alterations, many of our concepts of the world and the subjects and objects in it are forever changed. This affects not only our choices and ways in travel and tourism; it also affects the impressions these travels make on us—and we make on the places visited. Tourism is to a great extent a question of "mind over matter," the factual *who, what, when, where, how much, and how*; the abovementioned "classical" questions for a quantitative research setting thus take second place only. Circumstances of setting, time frame, and so on do not stand on their own any longer but are firmly rooted in the mind's preconceived notions and expectations, derived from past experiences as well as from ideas formed from information by the self, from others, or by means of modern technologies.

In other words, experiences as well as places are set into relation to each other, or as Urry (2007: 259) puts it: "A place is not so much a place with its own associations and meanings for those dwelling or even visiting there, but each is a combination of abstract characteristics, that mark it out as more scenic or cosmopolitan or cool or exotic or global or environmentally degraded than other places . . . This is a consumption of movement, of bodies, images and information, moving over, under and around the globe and subjecting it to abstract characterizations." For researchers and marketers of tourism, this emphasizes the need to pose questions other than who, what, when, where, how much, and how. Not necessarily instead of them, but in addition to investigating the factual, a complex, sophisticated and multifaceted "why" has to be asked. This means asking why a certain choice was made, but also why others were not.

Therefore, the abovementioned structure of the "processing program" within the consumer has to be mapped as clearly as possible; its elements have to become visible. It has by now become clear that it is a rather complex undertaking and that a merely quantitative approach will not suffice. Preconceived categories will not cover all aspects and, therefore, research has to be *both* inductive and deductive. To practically illustrate what qualitative research can do for tourism, the following section introduces the reader to the world of qualitative research in tourism, drawing on some of the most influential pieces of interpretive consumer research as well as discussing the main advantages of this kind of research.

CONTRIBUTION OF INTERPRETIVE CONSUMER RESEARCH TO TOURISM

One of the pieces of interpretive consumer research that has had a very deep impact on academia is probably Hirschman's study of consumers and their companion animal, published in the *Journal of Consumer Research* in 1994. Due to the fact that Hirschman (1994) anticipated that consumers might react defensively to questions indicating that their pets perform human roles in their lives, she conducted a series of "nondirective" phenomenological interviews. One key result of her study was that animal companions may act as either friends, extensions of consumer selves, or as family members. Hirschman's (1994) study is an excellent example of how interpretive research enables us to transcend extant knowledge. Hence, the identification of the three "roles" that companion animals may be assigned by consumers would probably not be revealed by more quantitative studies.

Hirschman's (1994) study is an "archetype" of interpretive studies that generate new theory. Some would argue that interpretive studies do not easily translate into normative theory. However, a study such as Hirschman's (1994) is actually of value to tourism and hospitality practices. In recent years, many hotels have moved into the niche market comprised of consumers who take their companion animals along on holidays and/or consumers who are willing to pay "top dollar" for accommodation for their dogs (e.g., when these consumers go on holiday without their companion animals). In this respect, Hirschman's (1994) findings are valuable as the three roles that pets may perform seem to be an excellent starting point for segmentation and tailoring of the offerings of "dog hotels" to their key target market.

Another conclusive example of interpretive consumer research was published in *Annals of Tourism Research* in 2007. In this article, White and White (2007) offer highly significant insights into ways in which the use of communication services influences tourists' concepts of the notions of "home" and "away" while traveling. Hence, this study presents various, complex, and valuable insights in the interwoven network of feelings, fears, and fantasies that are created by the ubiquitous possibility to use modern forms of long-distance communications by modern times' travelers. The main focus of White and White's (2007) research is on how tourists' use of communication services influences social connections and, as a consequence, how it influences the tourists' understanding of what "home" means and what, interrelated, the notion of "away" stands for.

Although White and White only interviewed twenty-seven people, their purposively sampling (which is facilitated by the fact that they were touring in circumstances similar to those of the interviewees) enables them to paint a very strong picture of how the use of communication services affects the traveler. All interviewees were traveling outside their country of residence and for a longer time span than the usual holidaymaker; the shortest duration being six weeks, the rest traveling between three months and two years. Further, a critical criterion underlying choice of informants was that, during traveling, interviewees stayed frequently in touch with family, friends, or colleagues at their place of origin either by mobile phone or by using the Internet (or, in same cases, also by use of landline telephones). By choosing these "sampling" criteria, the authors could be certain that each of the informants was sure to develop a sense of home and away that could be examined in depths.

Even though the twenty-seven travelers had different ideas of the concepts of home and away while traveling, the authors succeeded in categorizing the findings in a meaningful way, showing similarities and repetitive patterns. They were thus able to show that the constant contact with the place of origin was mostly motivated by a need to belong and by a need for security and stability. However, they also found a rather unpredictable angle. One interviewee from Israel, traveling with partner and children, reported that being away mostly meant peace for them. In their home country, death was present all the time. So while away, the family refrained from watching the news or reading newspapers. Therefore, the contact with the people "left behind" for this family meant a reminder of the "bliss" of their current situation, a situation qualifying as a period free from the anxieties of home life.

Another unforeseeable effect of the constant contact with their home was, for some of the interviewees, a reminder of "bad feelings" lived through at home. This means that the process of deliberately leaving a situation or problem behind is stopped or decelerated and henceforth the concept of "away" gets challenged and interacts with the concept of "home." White and White's (2007) interpretive study thus sheds light on the fact that a sense of closeness and belonging can be achieved without physical proximity by the use of modern communication services. It is doubtful whether this rather complex knowledge could have been obtained by more traditional means. It also suggests a need to reexamine existing knowledge and challenges preconceived notions of traveling as a means of breaking free from everyday life back home or the idea of escapism as the main reason for traveling.

White and White (2007: 101) conclude that "recurrent communication and contact reinforced tourists' sense of connection with those at home. The tourists were both home and away." White and White thus offer the interesting new insight that today's vast opportunities for long-distance communication may challenge traditional conceptions of "away" and, henceforth, tourism.

Interpretive consumer research also proves adequate when studying *groups* of consumers. In their 2003 article, Johns and Gyimóthy account for the results of a study of family groups and their consumption processes in relation to a visit to an amusement park (i.e., the child-oriented theme park Legoland in Denmark). Drawing on MacCannell (1976) and Urry (1995), the authors claim that groups (and especially family groups) rather than individual consumers are at the core of most tourist consumption and that the dynamics of such groups therefore "must play a key part in the motivation and behavior of tourists" (p. 8). The researchers conducted a

Case Study 2. Holidays and Saturday Evening are the Same

In his seminal article on the tourism-leisure behavioral continuum, Carr (2002) argues that the concepts of tourism and leisure are highly inter-related. A series of phenomenological interviews which focused on *informants'* definitions of nice vacations suggested that although people differ in their definitions of holidays and leisure, a majority of informants argued that these two concepts are so interrelated that they do not discriminate between them in ways that resemble traditional definitions. To these informants the distinction between tourism and leisure behavior (including vacationing at home) is actually rather arbitrary because these entities are simply perceived as not-so-different means to the same end; i.e., to make best possible use of the scarce leisure time that is available. Consequently, the informants accounted for ways in which they form coherent wholes of the entire spectrum of "ways to spend scarce leisure time"; wholes that include both Friday evenings, vacationing at home, and "real" holidays. One key result of this study is thus that it seems far too simplistic to define "home" as that which people wish to escape from during their holidays. Hence—along with "away," "home" may also be a place that relates to relaxation, etc.

Care to read more? http://www.sam.sdu.dk/ime/PDF/blichfeldt8.pdf .

series of unstructured interviews, the objective of which was to "obtain vacationers' stories of their expectations and experiences" (p. 10).

One extremely interesting aspect of Johns and Gyimóthy's study is that they both interviewed adults and children on the subject of prevalence of push-and-pull factors. This led to their conclusion that "for adults several of the push factors were clearly relevant, but very few of the pull factors. This picture was reversed for the children, who experienced most of the pull factors, but very few of the push factors" (p. 18). Johns and Gyimóthy thus raise the question whether future tourism research studies could benefit from further studies of children—something which seems far more possible to do by means of qualitative research methods than by means of questionnaires. Thus, the study conducted by Johns and Gyimóthy (2003) inspires the questioning of traditional research methods in tourism which (1) focus on the individual tourist and (2) let the answers given by one member of the family group (i.e., mostly one of the spouses) generalize across all family members.

As to the all-important question of the "why" underlying the decision to go to Legoland, Johns and Gyimóthy (2003) conclude that there is a clear schism between the families' "actual" lives and the parents' idea of the "ideal family," which they try to live up to. As a result of this schism, the authors suggest that the time spent at Legoland had more to do with the adults' "penance for aspiring to (child-free) lives of their own" (p. 21) and less to do with an enjoyable joint tourist activity for the whole family.

Whereas Johns and Gyimóthy (2003) conducted a destination-based study, Alain Decrop conducted a qualitative, longitudinal study of vacation decision making in a number of Belgian decision-making units (i.e., families, singles, couples, and groups of friends). The study is described in his book *Vacation Decision Making* (2006). Decrop applies the "grounded theory approach" (Glaser and Strauss, 1967; Strauss and Corbin, 1990) and hence he used a highly inductive method as existing literature and theories were primarily enfolded during and/or after the data-gathering process. Grounded theory thus represents a rather emic view of the subject matter, as theory is developed on the basis of the informants' accounts for decision-making processes.

One result of Decrop's study is his presentation of a comprehensive list of criteria for vacation decision making that has actually been used within the "decision-making units." Furthermore, Decrop (2006) generated a new typology of vacationers on the basis of his data. Although some of the vacationer types that Decrop identified (e.g., the [bounded] rational vacationer and the hedonic vacationer) resemble traditional typologies, Decrop also identified types of vacationers that have not been revealed by previous research. This is especially the case in relation to the habitual vacationer, for whom vacation decision making is characterized by (1) habit and hence brand loyalty or inertia; (2) little or no information search; and (3) little or no evaluation of alternatives. The identification of this type of vacationers seems to be of utmost importance as it questions our traditional conception of tourists' decision-making processes as characterized by high involvement, complexity, extensive information search, and/or elaborate evaluation of alternatives.

A quantitative study drawing on predefined categories and variables would probably only be able to account for the prevalence of decision-making criteria already known to the researcher from earlier studies, thus perhaps failing to include some of the "new" decision-making processes and criteria identified by Decrop. Furthermore, a key strength of Decrop's (2007) study is the longitudinal perspective. Apart from the identification of habitual vacationers, the longitudinal character of the study enabled Decrop to make a couple of (perhaps breakthrough) discoveries. The most important of these discoveries is probably that Decrop followed a series of decision-making processes, the end result of which was a decision *not* to go on vacation, thus enabling Decrop to question the assumption that the generic decision "to go" is the first decision to be made (Mansfeld, 1994; Um and Crompton, 1990). This finding is extremely valuable as it suggests that vacation decision-making processes may be far more iterative, adaptable, "messy," and subject to change than traditional models of consumer decision making (e.g., Engel, Kollat, and Blackwell, 1973, 1990) indicate.

Albeit the studies introduced earlier (i.e., Decrop, 2007; Hirschman, 1994; Johns and Gyimóthy, 2003; White and White, 2007) are but four examples of the kind of results that interpretive consumer research generates, they do generalize across the world of interpretive consumer research insofar as they reveal what this kind of research has to offer in relation to the study of tourist behavior, that is, the uncovering of the "whys" underlying tourist behavior and generation of (perhaps "radically") new knowledge.

CONCLUSION AND IMPLICATIONS

Obviously, the intention with this chapter is *not* to suggest that consumer researchers in tourism should not do quantitative research. On the contrary, a series of good reasons suggests that quantitative studies should still be focal to the study of how consumers think, feel, and act within the context of tourism consumption. Especially, quantitative studies should still be conducted because these studies are excellent at painting a portrait of the population of tourists as well as of the various subgroups (or segments) that exist within the context of tourism consumption. A number of the chapters in this book reveal the critical contribution of quantitative research to the study of consumer behavior in tourism.

However, when all comes to all, in quantitative research the tourist is a *respondent* who answers a series of questions that are derived from our extant pool of knowledge, or, as Powell and Watson (2006: 299) put it: "The survey gives answers only to those questions asked."

Thus, quantitative studies foremost test existing knowledge whereas qualitative research especially enables us to generate *new* theory as informants may raise unexpected issues (Powell and Watson, 2006). Consequently, the key advantage of interpretive consumer research is that inductive analysis uncovers realities that could not be predicted a priori. Hence, if we wish for consumer research in tourism to prosper, we need to do *both* quantitative and qualitative studies. Consequently, this chapter closes with the suggestion that more qualitative research is needed insofar as we wish to ensure that our research indicates the "whys" underlying how tourists think and act.

Holbrook and O'Shaughnessy (1988: 400) reminded us that

> The recognition that people in general and human consumers in particular differ from atoms and molecules in their endless quest for meaning dictates the need for interpretation in our attempt to explicate the meanings embedded in consumer behavior.

The need for interpretive research seems to be especially critical because postmodern tourists are extremely aware of the reasons why they act, feel, and think in certain ways and why they consume special kinds of tourism products. Hence, as consumers qualify as excellent "disseminators" of the whys underlying their behavior, there seems to be no valid reason why the future of consumer research in tourism should not rely on both traditional research and more interpretive, qualitative approaches.

REFERENCES

Anderson, P. F. (1989). On relativism and interpretivism—with a prolegomenon to the 'why' question. In E. C. Hirschman (Ed.), *Interpretive Consumer Research*, pp. 10–23. Provo, UT: Association for Consumer Research.

Buhalis, D. (2003). *eTourism*, Harlow, UK: Prentice Hall.

Carr, N. (2002). The tourism-leisure behavioral continuum. *Annals of Tourism Research*, 29(4): 972–86.

Cohen, E. (1988). Traditions in the qualitative sociology of tourism. *Annals of Tourism Research*, 15(1): 29–46.

Cooper, C. & Buhalis, D. (1998) (quoted in Buhalis 2003). The future of tourism. In C. R. Cooper et al., Eds, *Tourism: Principles and practices*. London: Addison Wesley Longman.

Decrop, A. (2007). *Vacation decision making*. Oxfordshire, UK: CABI.

Denzin, N. (2001). The reflective interview and a performative social science. *Qualitative Research*, 1(1): 23–46.

Denzin, N. & Lincoln, Y. S. (1994). *Handbook of qualitative research*. Thousand Oaks, CA: Sage.

Deshpande, R. (1983). Paradigms lost: On theory and method in research in marketing. *Journal of Marketing*, 4: 101–10.

Engel, J. F., Blackwell, R. D. & Miniard, P. W. (1990). *Consumer behavior*. Chicago, IL: The Dryden Press.

Engel, J. F., Kollat, D. T. & Blackwell, R. D. (1973). *Consumer behavior*. New York: Holt, Rinehart & Winston.

Glaser, B. G. & Strauss, A. L. (1967). *The discovery of grounded theory: Strategies for qualitative research*. Chicago: Aldine.

Guba, E. G. (1990). *The paradigm dialog*. London: Sage.

Henderson, K. A. & Bedini, L. A. (1995). Notes on linking qualitative and quantitative data. *Journal of Therapeutic Recreation*, 29: 124–30.

Hirschman, E. C. (1986). Humanistic inquiry in marketing research: Philosophy, method and criteria. *Journal of Marketing Research*, 21: 237–49.

———. (1994). Consumers and their animal companions. *Journal of Consumer Research*, 20: 616–32.

Hirschman, E. C. & Holbrook, M. B. (1992). *Postmodern consumer research: The study of consumption as text*. Newbury Park, CA: Sage.

Holbrook, M. B. & O'Shaughnessy, J. (1988). On the scientific status of consumer research and the need for an interpretive approach to studying consumer behavior. *Journal of Consumer Research*, 15: 398–402.

Hollinshead, K. (1996). The tourism researcher as bricoleur: The new wealth and diversity in qualitative inquiry. *Tourism Analysis*, 1: 67–74.

Hunt, S. D. (1976). The nature and scope of marketing. *Journal of Marketing*, 40(3): 17–28.

Johns, N. & Gyimóthy, S. (2003). Postmodern family tourism at Legoland. *Scandinavian Journal of Hospitality and Tourism*, 3(1): 3–23.

MacCannell, D. (1976). *The tourist: A new theory of the leisure class*, 2nd ed. New York: Schocken Books.

Mansfeld, Y. (1994): The 'value stretch' model and its implementation in detecting tourists' class-differentiated destination choice. In R. V. Gasser & K. Weiermair (Eds.), *Spoilt for choice, decision making processes and preference change of tourists: Intertemporal and intercountry perspectives*, pp. 60–79. Thaur, Germany: Kulturverlag.

Mehmetoglu, M. & Altinay, L. (2006). Examination of grounded theory analysis with an application to hospitality research. *International Journal of Hospitality Management*, 25: 12–33.

Middleton, V. & Clarke, J. (2002). *Marketing in travel and tourism*. Oxford/ Woburn, UK: Butterworth-Heinemann.

Miles, M. B. & Hubermann, M. A. (1994). *Qualitative data analysis: An expanded sourcebook*. London: Sage.

Peter, J. P. & Olson, J. C. (1989). The relativist/constructionist perspective on scientific knowledge. In E. Hirscman (Ed.), *Interpretive consumer research*, pp. 24–28. Provo, UT: Association for Consumer Research.

Poon, A. (1993). *Tourism, technology and competitive strategies*. Oxon, UK: CABI.

Powell, P. H. & Watson, D. (2006). Service unseen: The hotel room attendant at work. *International Journal of Hospitality Management*, 25: 297–312.

Riley, R. W. & Love, L. L. (1999). The state of qualitative tourism research. *Annals of Tourism Research*, 27(1): 164–87.

Strauss, A. L. & Corbin, J. (1990). *Basics of qualitative research: Grounded theory procedures and techniques*. Thousand Oaks, CA: Sage.

Swarbrooke, J. & Horner, S. (2007). *Consumer behavior in tourism*. Oxford/Burlington, UK: Butterworth-Heinemann.

TIA. (1997). *Travel and interactive technology: A five year outlook*. Washington, DC: The Travel Industry Association of America.

Ums, S. & Crompton, J. L. (1990). Attitude determinants in tourism destination choice. *Annals of Tourism Research*, 17: 432–48.

Urry, J. (1995). *Consuming Places*. London: Routledge.

———. (2007). *Mobilities*. Cambridge/Malden, MA: Polity Press.

Walle, A. H. (1997). Quantitative versus qualitative tourism research. *Annals of Tourism Research*, 24(3): 524–36.

White, N. R. & White, P. B. (2007). Home and away: Tourists in a connected world. *Annals of Tourism Research*, 34(1): 88–104.

2 Antecedents and Consequences of Prestige Motivation in Tourism

An Expectancy-Value Motivation

Antónia Correia and Miguel Moital

INTRODUCTION

Motivation appears in existing literature as a construct underpinning human action, which is largely guided by the individual's goals. This perspective defines motivation as an internal drive which pushes the individual to do things in order to achieve something (Harmer, 2001). According to Seaton (1997), motivation is a state of arousal of a drive or need which impels people to activity in pursuit of goals that leads to temporary equilibrium. Motivation theory as the basis for action posits that human behavior is driven by the goal of satisfying one or more needs. One underlying assumption is that human behavior is guided by two types of needs: needs that are inherently independent of others (personal needs) and needs that pertain to the relationship between the individual and the members of his/her social system (interpersonal needs). The interpersonal needs appear in the literature as the desire to achieve the goal of prestige/status. Tourism motivation is no exception, and research has demonstrated that tourists' motivations originate from personal and interpersonal needs (Krippendorf, 1987; Woodside, Caldwell and Spurr, 2006). The dimension that explains the interactions and relations individuals establish with others is perhaps one of the main drivers of tourism consumption in a consumer-oriented society, eager to enhance their prestige among peers (Vigneron and Johnson, 1999).

Motivation is possibly one of the most researched areas in the field of tourism research (e.g., Beard and Ragheb, 1983; Cohen, 1972; Correia and Crouch, 2004; Crompton, 1979; Dann, 1977, 1981; Fodness, 1994; Gnoth, 1997; Iso-Ahola, 1982; Kozak, 2002; Pearce and Caltabiano, 1983). However, the vast majority of these studies have focused on a comprehensive understanding of what motivates the individual as a whole. In contrast, the in-depth study of the individual motivations of tourists in general, and particularly the prestige motivation, is virtually nonexistent. The end result is a thorough understanding of what motivates the individual and the relative importance of each motive, but scant in-depth understanding of the nature, structure, and implications of one of the main drivers of tourism motivations: prestige. The number of studies devoted to the systematic examination of prestige in the context of tourism motivation is rather limited and an integrative model is lacking. Therefore, this chapter aims to contribute to the growing body of knowledge on tourist motivation (1) by reviewing existing research in the field of prestige motivation and (2) by developing an analytical model of prestige tourism motivation. This model is supported by current knowledge on prestige consumption, both within and outside the tourism literature, resulting in a detailed understanding of the motivation and expectation formation process. A number of research opportunities in the field of prestige tourism motivation are also identified.

MOTIVATION THEORIES

Part of what a theory of motivation tries to do is to explain and predict who has which motivations. For that purpose, several theories of motivation have been put forward. The main theoretical approaches to the study of motivation can be grouped into content theories and process theories. Content theories explain what the human needs are and how these needs change over time (Maslow, 1943; McClelland, 1988). Process theories, on the other hand, attempt to explain the mechanisms by which human needs are formed and could change. Locke and Latham (1990) cited expectancy theory (Vroom, 1964), equity theory (Adam, 1963), and goal setting (Locke, 1968) as some of the most influential process motivation theories. The content motivation theories emphasize what actually motivates consumers. Examples of content theories in tourism include, for instance, Pearce (1988), Crompton (1979), and Iso-Ahola (1982). In tourism, one of the most frequently used content theories is push-and-pull motivations (Crompton, 1979). Push factors refer to the internal forces that push individuals to travel. Pull factors are external forces of the destination which are concurrently attractive in the choice of a particular destination (Crompton, 1979). In general, push motives explain the decision to travel and pull motives justify the options when faced with the travel destinations chosen.

Process theories of motivation focus on the interaction between the variables influencing motivation and how they influence behavior. A number of process theories have been developed, including the theory of goal setting (Locke, 1968, cited in Locke and Latham, 1990) and the equity theory (Adams, 1963, cited in Locke and Latham, 1990). However, one of the most frequently used process theories of motivation is the expectancy-value theory (Vroom, 1964). This theory expresses the idea that motivation is a function of the extent to which the person believes that making a purchase is feasible (expectancy), the attractiveness of the outcome (valence), and the expectancy of achieving that outcome (instrumentality). According to Vroom's theory, these three factors interact psychologically, and the resulting motivational force drives the individual towards the maximization of pleasure and minimization of punishment. This theory is meant to bring many of the elements of previous theories together. It combines the perceptual aspects of equity theory with the behavioral aspects of the other theories (Kay, 2003).

Several authors have adopted an expectancy-value perspective to model tourism motivation, suggesting that the theory provides an appropriate framework for analyzing tourist motivation (e.g., Witt and Wright, 1992; Sparks, 2007). The advantages of the expectancy-value model lie on its comprehensive account of the factors influencing motivation. However, the large number of factors influencing motivation makes it difficult to use the model to predict individual behavior (Witt and Wright, 1992) and to measure (Kay, 2003).

PRESTIGE MOTIVATION

Prestige and status have usually been employed interchangeably when it comes to illustrate the social comparison aspects of events consumption. Yet, it can be argued that these are different, although closely interrelated, concepts. Neuman, Pizam, and Reichel (1980) argued that prestige refers to respect and standing, and is an intrinsic motive that is different from status. In a similar vein, Burn (2004: 10) defined status as "a group member's standing in the hierarchy of a group based on the prestige, honour, and deference accorded to him or her by other members," thus emphasizing the cause-effect relationship between prestige and status. Others (e.g., Weiss and Fershtman, 1998; Clark, Zboja, and Goldsmith, 2007) further noted the difference between the two. Therefore, instead of treating prestige and status at the same level, status should be viewed as a probable consequence of prestige. In this context, status is the position or rank in a society or group awarded to an individual by others, and the consumption of prestigious tourism products could facilitate going up in the status ladder. This separation between the two concepts implies that status (or social standing) may be achieved through means other than the consumption of prestigious tourism, such as social or professional achievements.

In order to provide a tentative definition of prestige consumption that incorporates the distinction between status and prestige, Eastman, Goldsmith, and Flynn's (1999: 42) definition of status consumption and Riley's (1995) definition of prestige were adapted. Prestige tourism consumption is defined as "the motivational process by which individuals strive to improve their regard or honour through the consumption of travel experiences that confer and symbolises prestige both for the individual and surrounding others." The importance of treating the two concepts distinctively has also the added benefit of facilitating the association of prestige consumption to other important tourism consumption outcomes (or consequences), as will be shown in the next section. This implies that

Case Study 1. Space Tourism

Space tourism is one of the most recent experiences available to tourists. This experience contains many of the values associated with prestigious consumption. Due to the rarity of the experience, the unique value is, presumably, the most important one. Therefore, for an individual seeking to achieve prestige through the consumption of this value, space tourism is likely to be chosen. Yet, if an individual seeks to achieve prestige through the consumption of social value, then selecting this experience is unlikely. This example illustrates the importance of matching the values underlying instrumentality and valence. However, even when the instrumentality and valence match (i.e., are both high), the expectancy will dictate whether an individual will be motivated to chose the space travel experience. An individual who perceives that the benefits of traveling to space are worth the effort (e.g., time, money, physical) is more likely to be motivated than one who believes that no matter the effort put in, he/she will not be able to do it. For example, if an individual perceives that he/she will never have the money or that he/she will not pass the fitness test required to participate in the experience, motivation will decrease. This example illustrates the influence of expectancy on the motivation to chose a specific form of travel, providing another opportunity for research.

consumers seek prestigious tourism experiences to satisfy not only status needs but also other needs.

The motivations for traveling have been extensively researched over the years, leading to a comprehensive understanding of what motivates tourists. A number of these studies have highlighted prestige as a tourism motivation (Crompton, 1979; Dann, 1977; Fodness, 1994; O'Reilly, 2006; Riley, 1995; Sørensen, 2003; Tiefenbacjer, Day, and Walton, 2000). Dann (1977) was one of the earliest to focus on prestige as a reason for traveling. He argued that the desire to be recognized drives humans to look for "ego-enhancement" activities and behaviors. Two years later, Crompton (1979) also identified prestige as a primary motivating factor. However, he also found that respondents were reluctant to recognize prestige as an underlying motive for tourism. Riley (1988) studied budget travelers and concluded that much of the tourism decisions during their journey were driven by status objectives. A number of recent studies, mostly of a qualitative nature, have also provided valuable information regarding the prestige tourism motivation (O'Reilly, 2006; Sørensen, 2003).

Papers specifically devoted to exploring the prestige motive in tourism are virtually nonexistent. Riley (1995) is one of the few who have focused on the topic. He employed a qualitative methodology to study the underlying dimensions of prestigious tourism consumption. Yet, despite the frequent references to prestige as one important dimension of tourism motive, the attention paid to the understanding of prestige tourism motivation is scant, a fact that has been pointed out before (Laing and Crouch, 2005). One of the possible reasons for the limited interest in the study of the prestige in tourism could be the lack of a model that could guide researchers. The next section presents and explains a prestige motivation model.

PRESTIGE MOTIVATION MODEL

Based on the analysis of existing work on motivation and prestige consumption, a model of prestige tourism motivation was developed (Figure 2.1). Motivation is conceptualized from an expectancy-value perspective (Vroom, 1964). That is, motivation is viewed as a result of the interplay between the expectancy about the instrumentality and the valence of prestige within the context of travel consumption. In other words, the model assumes that motivation (needs and desires) are the main drives of a purposive action (goals) to achieve an expected outcome that is valued by the individual. In addition to the prestige-related motivation, the model emphasizes the antecedents and consequences of prestige-related motivation. This model implies that tourism products can be perceived as featuring different levels of prestige and that the level of importance of this attribute will vary from individual to individual. An underlying difference between the three components of motivation is that while instrumentality refers to a characteristic of the product (i.e., tourism attributes), the expectancy refers to a characteristic of tourism experience and the value refers to a characteristic of the individual (i.e., the tourist).

The Antecedents of Prestige

The antecedents refer to those reasons why a destination would be perceived as prestigious, and these are established on the basis of the perceived value offered by the product. In their review of prestige-seeking consumer behavior, Vigneron and Johnson (1999) argued that a brand's prestige is determined by five types of perceived value associated to the brand. In line with Vigneron and Johnson's model, the prestige-related motivation model suggests that the prestige of destinations and tourism products are determined by five categories of values: conspicuous, unique, social, emotional, and quality.

The *conspicuous value* is associated to a 'Veblenian' motivation and refers to the extent to which the tourism product signals wealth (Vigneron and Johnson, 1999). Price is the single most important determinant of conspicuous value. Papatheodorou (2001) documented the existence of this type of value in tourism, giving the example of Myconos, which is able to attract more tourists than other equally attractive islands which are more inexpensive. Interestingly, however, certain forms of tourism may appear prestigious due to the "inconspicuous" nature of the consumption. In other words, prestige is conferred not to those who spend the most money but to those who are able to travel inexpensively (Sørensen, 2003; Riley, 1988). The "unconspicuous" valence is usually associated with budget tourists or backpackers.

The *unique value* is associated to the "snob" motivation and is determined by the limited availability of the product and rests on the assumption that rarity creates value (Vigneron and Johnson, 1999). In other words, inherent scarcity (or exclusivity) satisfies an individual's need for uniqueness. Scarcity may be related to the cost of the product, the limited number of units available (e.g., space tourism), other restrictions that make it inaccessible to the vast majority of people in a social system (e.g., only a few qualify to experience the product). The tourism literature has emphasized that the tourist's ability to use a skill that is rare among, and valued by, those who confer prestige is of particular relevance to creating uniqueness (Sørensen, 2003; Riley, 1995).

The *unique value* is common in new destinations or tourism products, whereby innovators adopt the product before everyone else in order to benefit from the prestige associated with owning a product not owned by many other individuals in the social system (Rogers, 1995). Several examples could be found illustrating how rarity could lead to a perception of prestige. Riley (1988) and O'Reilly (2006) pointed out that for certain types of tourism it is the nontouristic experience, or the "off-the-beaten-track" locations, that are not readily available to "mainstream" tourists that made the budget tourist's journey prestigious. Hanqin and Lam (1999) suggested that the restrictions placed on traveling to Hong Kong by the Chinese government was the reason why traveling to the region was perceived as prestigious.

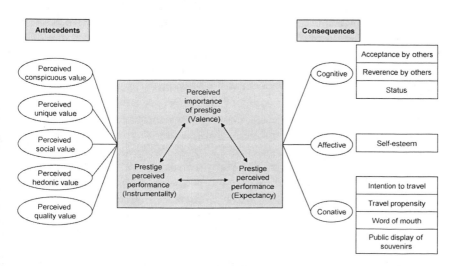

Figure 2.1 An expectancy-value model of prestige-related travel motivation.

Case Study 2. Golf in the Algarve

Algarve is one of the leading golf destinations in the world. Why do golfers choose the Algarve as a golf destination? The choice is very likely associated to the sense of prestige the tourists get at this destination. This is because the Algarve is perceived to contain certain values (pull factors—instrumentality). In 2006, the IAGTO (International Association of Golf Tourism Operators) recognized the Algarve as the golf destination of the year (unique value). The destination has also managed to ensure that golf courses are designed by some of the best experts in golf course design (quality value). Moreover, the destination is made up by challenging golf courses, leading golfers to feel a strong sense of achievement once they successfully finish playing there (hedonic). Some of the top players in the world and celebrities have played and endorsed the Algarve as a golf destination (social value). Finally, the Algarve has positioned itself as an expensive golf destination, which enables the satisfaction of prestige motivations through conspicuous value. This example illustrates how destinations can be managed in order to be perceived as prestigious. While it appears that the Algarve has managed to develop each of the five values, their relative contribution to the perceived prestige of the Algarve as a golf destination could be an issue for future research.

Laing and Crouch (2005) focused on the "frontier traveler" and found that prestige was conferred by the rarity and difficulty of their experience.

The *social value* is associated with the bandwagon motivation and is related to the snob motivation (Vigneron and Johnson, 1999). The difference lies in the fact that whereas the "snob" motivation is driven by a need for differentiation, the bandwagon is driven by a need for group affiliation. Social value is determined by the extent to which the consumption of the product is perceived as a facilitator to, or a requirement for, reference group membership. In other words, some products may have an important social function in that purchasing a product that certain (prestigious) referents purchase (or have purchased) will result in enhanced prestige (Chao and Schor, 1998; Vigneron and Johnson, 1999). There is evidence that this type of value is relevant in a tourism context too. Tiefenbacjer, Day, and Walton (2000) found that there was a group of tourists who traveled to places that their friends went to.

The *emotional value* is associated with the hedonic motivation and is determined by the product's ability to arouse certain feelings and affective states (Vigneron and Johnson, 1999). It is the emotional merits of the product, rather than tangible cues (such as price or scarcity), contributing to its prestigious worth. Experiences, including tourism, lend themselves to enhancing prestige through emotional value. Therefore, perhaps not surprisingly, tourism boards and travel suppliers attempt to endow their products with emotional value (e.g., like magical, relaxing, thrilling). Yet, it is unknown how emotional value influences prestige.

The *quality value* is associated with the perfectionist motivation (Vigneron and Johnson, 1999). The quality effect refers to "when consumers value the perceived utility acquired from a prestige brand to suggest superior product characteristics and performance" (Vigneron and Johnson, 1999: 9). Traditionally, the quality value is related to the concept of luxury in that luxury products tend to feature excellence or leadership in quality (Mortelmans, 2005). While this association is likely to be valid in most types of tourism consumption, enhancement of prestige may result from "low-quality" value. Riley (1988) and Sørensen (2003) argued that prestige was associated with the extent to which the experience was "rough." It was the tourist's experience of living without the comforts of home available at most tourist destinations (e.g., comfortable room, good quality meals) that conferred prestige.

As far as the dynamics of the five values is concerned, Vigneron and Johnson (1999) hypothesized that the prestige worth of products should be made up of a combination of these values. However, they also stressed that the prestige worth of products should be regarded as a multidimensional construct and may be influenced more by some values than others. Therefore, caution should be taken when using measures relating to the antecedents as surrogates for prestige. For example, traveling to a remote village in Africa to experience the native lifestyle and staying in basic accommodation could be regarded as prestigious, but could hardly be due to the luxury (high quality) of this type of travel.

Prestige Motivation

The prestige tourist motivation model draws its foundation on the expectancy-value model of motivation. This model suggests that three factors—expectancy, instrumentality and valence—influence an individual's degree of prestige motivation. Expectancy refers to the person's perception that the effort to perform a certain type of vacation (tourism consumption) will result in prestige enhancement, while instrumentality is concerned with the perceived probability that a certain destination has the attributes (product values) needed to achieve the level of prestige sought by the tourist. The valence component of the model refers to the extent to which prestige consumption is valued by the tourist, that is, how desirable the prestige attribute is. When compared to Crompton's motivation model, instrumentality refers to the pull motivation, while the valence component refers to the push motivation.

Past research on prestige tourism indicates that tourists are not equally preoccupied with prestige when choosing tourism products (Sørensen, 2003). There is also anecdotal evidence that tourism products will comprise different degrees of prestige. Thus, the net benefit of using an expectancy-value approach to modeling prestige motivation lies in the fact that the investigation could focus on the expectancy, instrumentality, and valence. This permits the researcher to concentrate on the level of effort tourists intend to incur in order to achieve prestige, what types of value are more likely to enhance an individual's prestige (valence), and lastly the reasons why a certain tourism product is perceived as prestigious (instrumentality). Further, it is also possible to understand how the three components interact. In each case, research could also investigate whether there are particular consequences associated with different typologies of tourists and differential degrees of prestige.

The Consequences of Prestige

The consequences (goals) or responses refer to how a tourist behaves under different levels of motivation to travel for prestige purposes. One form of stipulating such consequences is through the cognitive-affective-conative trilogy (Rosenberg and Hovland, 1960). In other words, the consequences could take place in the realms of thoughts, feelings, or actions. A number of *cognitive consequences* may be associated to the consumption of prestigious tourism products. Two major cognitive outcomes are suggested: perceptions of greater acceptance, recognition, or reverence by others (O'Cass and Frost, 2002; Riley, 1995) and a perception of the extent to which the individual has moved higher on the status ladder (Pearce, 1988). The consumption of prestige could also impact on an individual's *feelings* (O'Cass and Frost, 2002), notably in the domain of self-esteem. This is because acceptance by others often influences self-esteem (Solomon, 2006).

Finally, the consumption of prestige tourism may also be associated with behavioral responses, whether overt actions or verbal statements concerning behavior (Rosenberg and Hovland, 1960). Behavioral consequences include greater levels of intention to (re)visit the destination, greater traveling propensity (Tiefenbacjer, Day, and Walton, 2000), engaging more in word-of-mouth communication (Correia and Pimpão, 2007; Dann, 1977; Fodness, 1994), and the display of mementos and artifacts (Riley, 1995). In other words, the greater the expectancy that traveling to the destination would result in prestige benefits, or the greater the importance of prestige for the traveler, the more intense such behavioral manifestations will be.

TESTING THE MODEL

As noted earlier, a number of studies addressing tourism motivation have researched the prestige/status motivations. Table 2.1 provides a summary of how the prestige/status concept has been operationalized in (quantitative) tourism-motivation studies. Several tentative conclusions can be drawn. First, the vast majority of the studies incorporating some sort of status/prestige motives focused on the valence (i.e., importance) of prestige, with little emphasis on the expectancy level. Second, antecedents and consequences have been used interchangeably as measures of prestige.

Third, the relationship of some of the items with prestige is not clear (e.g., homelike feel, safe-secure), raising questions about the validity of using the aggregated prestige factor value as a measure of prestige.

Fourth, many studies have inferred prestige motives from its antecedents or consequences (see Table 2.1). Yet, this is problematic and raises validity concerns. As the model demonstrates, there are multiple antecedents and consequences of prestige, and each consumption situation will involve a unique combination of antecedents and consequences. In other words, some of the antecedents and consequences may be of little or no relevance in a given context. Using antecedents or consequences as surrogate measures of prestige implies that not only the antecedent/consequence will be relevant to every individual, but also that there is a monotonic relationship between prestige and the antecedent/consequence. For example, Heung and Leong (2006) suggested that student travelers did not focus much on the prestige of traveling. Making such a claim based on one item pertaining to a behavioral consequence ("Talking about trip after return home") is supported by two questionable assumptions. First, that prestige will only be a motivator if a traveler talks about his trip once back home. Second, that the more intense the conversations, the more intense the prestige motive will be.

Finally, following factor analysis it is not uncommon to find low reliability values on the prestige/status factor. For example, Lau and McKercher (2004) "prestige and status" factor featured two items: "talk about my vacation when I get back home" and "visit a place that my friends and relatives have not been." The Cronbach's alpha for this factor was low (0.55) and this could perhaps be explained by the fact that the two items refer to different facets of prestige: an antecedent (snob motivation: need for differentiation) and a consequence (word of mouth) of prestige. The socialization factor, presented by Correia, Valle, and Moço (2007), in contrast, presented a high reliability Cronbach's alpha (0.8). The factor comprised two antecedents ("developing close friendships"; "talking with my friends about the trip") and one consequence ("going places my friends have not been").

While several authors assert that prestige is an important reason for traveling (e.g., Hanqin and Lam, 1999; O'Reilly, 2006; Sørensen, 2003), many others have questioned this assumption (e.g., Crompton, 1979; Heung and Leong, 2006; Pearce and Lee, 2005). However, assertions that prestige is not an important motivator may be routed in methodological difficulties and weaknesses, some of which are illustrated in Table 2.1. Respondents are often unaware of, or unwilling to admit, their real reasons for travel (Dann, 1981; Riley, 1988). Tiefenbacjer, Day, and Walton (2000: 308) noted that "many tourists are affected by the prestige that an area holds, even if they are not aware of it." In a similar vein, Riley (1988: 318) noted that "although no one admitted it, it seemed likely that in some cases, status or ego enhancement was also pursued in making a decision to travel."

Table 2.1 Operationalization of Prestige in Quantitative Tourism-motivation Studies

Study	Description of study	Label	Operationalization
Tiefenbacjer, Day, and Walton (2000)	Repeat visitors to small tourist-oriented communities (Texas)	Prestige	• Is it fashionable to visit this community?
Hanqin and Lam (1999)	Mainland Chinese visitors' motivations to visit Hong Kong	Prestige	• Fulfilling my dream of visiting a place • Visiting a destination which most people value and/or appreciate • Going to places my friends want to go • Visiting a destination that would impress my friends or family
Lau and McKercher (2004)	Motives for visiting of first-time and repeat pleasure tourists to Hong Kong (sample of visitors)	Status and prestige	• Talk about my vacation when I get back home • Visit a place that my friends and relatives have not been
Kim and Prideaux (2005)	Cross-cultural study	Social status	• To show up my social status • To show up your experience to others • To take pictures and show them to others • To visit where others did not visit

Study	Description	Category	Items
McGehee, Loker-Murphy, and Uysal (1996)	Pull motives of Australian International pleasure travelers	Prestige	• Safe/secure • Report on trip • Being entertained • Maximize experience • New places • Homelike feel
Kim and Lee (2000)	Comparative study of motivations to travel of Anglo-American and Japanese tourists	Prestige/ status	• To gain others' respect • To reveal my thoughts, feelings, or physical skills to others • To influence others • To demonstrate my ability to travel • To share what I have learned with others • To gain a feeling of belonging
Pearce and Lee (2005)	Examination of the relationship between patterns of travel motivation and travel experience	Recognition	• Sharing skill and knowledge with others • Showing others I can do it • Being recognized by other people • Leading others • Letting others know that I have been there

Unwillingness may exist when the recognition of a motive could result in some form of punishment. Engaging in activities that are perceived by prestige conferrents as driven by prestige objectives may create opposite reactions among the people who may confer this type of social honor (Chao and Schor, 1998; Mason, 1981; Sørensen, 2003; Vigneron and Johnson, 1999) because deliberately seeking prestige could negate honorable regard (Riley, 1995). In other words, "appearing not to care too much about status is often necessary to attain it" (Chao and Schor, 1998: 111), and therefore respondents may be reluctant to acknowledge prestige motives, in particular when they are answering face-to-face.

Despite the paucity of studies in the area, a review of the literature suggests that prestige motivation could be related to specific travelers' characteristics. Results show that sociodemographic variables do influence prestige travel motivation. This includes income (McGehee, Loker-Murphy, and Uysal, 1996; Hanqin and Lam, 1999), education (McGehee et al., 1996), age (Hanqin and Lam, 1999; Sirgy and Su, 2000), gender (McGehee et al., 1996), and nationality (Kim and Lee, 2000). In addition, research has also shown that prestige motivation is related to traveling propensity (Hanqin and Lam, 1999; Lau and McKercher, 2004) and travel experience (Pearce and Lee, 2005).

Finally, it has also been hypothesized that the prestige tourism motivation is influenced by the tourist's self-concept (Sirgy and Su, 2000). Notwithstanding these findings, much remains to be done before definite conclusions can be drawn. The relationship between these variables and prestige consumption may not be linear. For example, McGehee et al. (1996) found that the higher income travelers were less motivated by prestige, whereas Hanqin and Lam's (1999) results suggest the positive relationship between income and prestige motivation. Therefore, future research could focus on understanding how the traveler's characteristics relate to prestige motivation.

CONCLUSION AND IMPLICATIONS

Past research on the tourism motivation has provided sound evidence that tourists are motivated by both personal and interpersonal needs. Yet, while much is know about the variety of tourism motivations, the systematic study of specific motivations has received little attention. Due to its characteristics, travel has been recognized as one product category that could be consumed to satisfy prestige needs. Yet, despite evidence that prestige plays an important role in tourists' decision making, the area has been little researched and a model of prestige motivation in tourism was lacking.

To address this gap, an integrative model of prestige motivation in tourism was designed and explained. Grounded on the expectancy-value theory, the model isolates prestige as the central variable in the model and establishes a number of antecedents and consequences of prestige tourism motivation. The model's strengths rest on providing a framework for using and testing the expectancy-value model in the context of one specific travel motivation: prestige. While the focus was on the prestige motivation, the model's principles could be applied to other travel motivations. In summary, the usefulness of the expectancy-value model for studying motivation is extended beyond the broad analysis of what motivates tourists.

Moreover, the model also stresses the importance of separating antecedents and consequences of specific motivations. Therefore, tourism researchers considering studying the prestige motivation from an expectancy-value point of view could employ this model as the basis of their conceptual frameworks. From a conceptual point of view, the model also distinguishes prestige and status, which have been used interchangeably in motivation literature. It was advocated that they are related, though different concepts and that status are a consequence of prestige. Finally, the conceptualization adopted in this model also provides tourism managers with a better understanding of the factors contributing to the prestige of tourism brands.

An analysis of the model suggests a number of research opportunities in the field of prestige tourism motivation. First, scales need to be developed (or adapted) to measure each of the constructs. Second, the relationship between the three elements of the model—prestige, antecedents, and consequences— needs to be further investigated. For example, are prestige-seeking tourists driven by the same type of product value? Or are there different typologies of prestige-seeking tourists? To what extent specific are product values associated with certain travel experiences? Is there a relationship between antecedents (i.e., the travel product values) and specific consequences? These questions open up a range of research opportunities in the area of, for example, segmentation and structural equation modeling.

While the opportunities are immense, so too are the methodological challenges. Past research has shown the difficulties of researching a "hidden" motivation such as prestige. Respondents are usually reluctant to acknowledge that their purchasing decisions were also based on prestige considerations. And this difficulty is likely to be heightened when respondents are providing information in face of an interviewer or other individuals. Even when Correia et al. (2007) collected data based on a self-administration questionnaire that respondents filled in 'anonymously' during their flight to long-haul exotic destinations, this method resulted in a high Cronbach's alpha, but the prestige items still ranked among the lowest. While the difficulties are immense, this should not deter researchers from focusing on this area.

REFERENCES

Adams, J. S. (1963) Toward an understanding of inequity, *Journal of Abnormal & Social Psychology*, 67, 422–436.

Beard, J. G. & Ragheb, M. G. (1983). Measuring leisure motivation. *Journal of Leisure Research*, 15: 219–28.
Burn, S. M. (2004). *Groups: Theory and practice.* Belmont, CA: Thomson Wadsworth.
Chao, A. & Schor, J. B. (1998). Empirical tests of status consumption: Evidence from women's cosmetics. *Journal of Economic Psychology*, 19: 107–31.
Clark, R. A., Zboja, J. J. & Goldsmith, R. E. (2007). Status consumption and role-relaxed consumption: A tale of two retail consumers. *Journal of Retailing and Consumer Services*, 14: 45–59.
Cohen, J. B. (1972). *Behavioural science foundation of consumer behaviour.* NY: Free Press.
Correia, A. & Crouch, G. (2004). A study of tourist decision processes: Algarve, Portugal. In G. I. Crouch, R. R. Perdue, H. J. P. Timmermans, and M. Uysal (Eds.), *Consumer psychology of tourism, hospitality and leisure*, vol. 3. Oxon: CABI.
Correia, A. & Pimpão, A. (2007). Tourists behaviour in exotic places: A structural and categorical model for Portuguese tourist. In *Advances in culture, tourism and hospitality research*, vol. 2. W. A., R. Harrill, and J. Crotts (Eds.), forthcoming.
Correia, A., Valle, P. & Moço, C. (2007). Why people travel to exotic places? *International Journal of Culture, Tourism, and Hospitality Research*, 1(1): 45–61.
Crompton, J. L. (1979). Motivations of pleasure vacation. *Annals of Tourism Research*, 6(4): 408–24.
Dann, G. (1981). Tourist motivation—an appraisal. *Annals of Tourism Research*, 8(2): 187–219.
Dann, G. M. S. (1977). Anomie, ego-enhancement and tourism. *Annals of Tourism Research*, 4(4): 184–94.
Eastman, J., Goldsmith, R. G. & Flynn, L. R. (1999). Status consumption in consumer behavior: Scale development and validation. *Journal of Marketing Theory and Practice*, 7(2): 41–52.
Fodness, D. (1994). Measuring tourist motivation. *Annals of Tourism Research*, 21(3): 555–81.
Gnoth, J. (1997). Tourism motivation and expectation formation. *Annals of Tourism Research*, 24(2): 283–304.
Hanqin, Z. Q. & Lam, T. (1999). An analysis of mainland Chinese visitors motivations to visit Hong Kong. *Tourism Management*, 20(5): 587–94.
Harmer, J. (2001). *The practice of English language teaching.* Essex, UK: Longman Press.
Heung, V. C. S. & Leong, J. (2006). Travel demand and behavior of university students in Hong Kong. *Asia Pacific Journal of Tourism Research*, 11(1): 81–95.
Iso-Ahola, S. (1982). Towards a social psychology of tourism motivation—a rejoinder. *Annals of Tourism Research*, 9(3): 256–61.
Kay, M. (2003). *Motivation for achievement: Possibilities for teaching and learning*, 2nd ed. Mahwah, NJ: Lawrence Erlbaum Associates.
Kim, C. & Lee, S. (2000). Understanding the cultural differences in tourist motivation between Anglo-American and Japanese tourists. *Journal of Travel and Tourism Marketing*, 9(1/2): 153–70.
Kim, S. S. & Prideaux, B. (2005). Marketing implications arising from a comparative study of international pleasure tourist motivations and other travel-related characteristics of visitors to Korea. *Tourism Management*, 26: 347–35.
Kozak, M. (2002). Comparative analysis of tourist motivations by nationality and destinations. *Tourism Management*, 23: 221–32.
Krippendorf, J. (1987). *The holiday makers.* London: Heinemann.

Laing, J. H. & Crouch, G. I. (2005). Extraordinary journeys: An exploratory cross-cultural study of tourists on the frontier. *Journal of Vacation Marketing*, 11(3): 209–23.

Lau, L. S. & McKercher, B. (2004). Exploration versus acquisition: A comparison of first-time and repeat visitors. *Journal of Travel Research*, 42(3): 279–85.

Locke, E. A. (1968). Toward a theory of task motivation and incentives, *Organizational Behavior & Human Performance*, 3, 157–189.

Locke, E. A. & Latham, G. P. (1990). *A theory of goal setting and task performance*. Englewood Cliffs, NJ: Prentice Hall.

Maslow, A. (1943). A theory of human motivation. *Psychological Review*, 50: 370–96.

Mason, R. (1981). *Conspicuous consumption: A study of exceptional consumer behavior*. New York: St. Martin's Press.

McClelland, D. C (1988). *Human motivation*. Cambridge: Cambridge University Press.

McGehee, N. G., Loker-Murphy, L. & Uysal, M. (1996). The Australian international pleasure travel market: Motivations from a gendered perspective. *Journal of Tourism Studies*, 7(1): 45–57.

Mortelmans, D. (2005). Sign values in processes of distinction. The concept of luxury. *Semiotica*, 157(1/4): 497–520.

Neuman, Y., Pizam, A. & Reichel, A. (1980). Values as determinants of motivation: Tourism and other career choices. *Annals of Tourism Research*, 7(3): 428–42.

O'Cass, A. & Frost, H. (2002). Status brands: Examining the effects of non-product related brand associations on status and conspicuous consumption. *The Journal of Product and Brand Management*, 11(2): 67–88.

O'Reilly, C. C. (2006). From drifter to gap year: Mainstreaming backpacker travel. *Annals of Tourism Research*, 33(4): 998–1017.

Papatheodorou A. (2001). Why people travel to different places. *Annals of Tourism Research*, 28(1): 164–79.

Pearce, D. (1988). The spatial structure of coastal tourism: A behavioural approach. *Tourism Recreation Research*, 12(2): 11–14.

Pearce, P. L. & Caltabiano, M. L. (1983). Inferring travel motivation from travelers experiences. *Journal of Travel Research*, Fall: 16–20.

Pearce, P. & Lee, U. (2005). Developing the travel career approach to tourist motivation, *Journal of Travel Research*, 43: 226–37.

Riley, P. (1988). Road culture of international long-term budget travellers. *Annals of Tourism Research*, 15: 313–28.

Riley, R. W. (1995). Prestige worthy tourist behavior. *Annals of Tourism Research*, 22(3): 630–49.

Rogers, E. (1995). *The diffusion of innovations*, 4th ed. New York: Free Press.

Rosenberg, M. J. & Hovland, C. I. (1960). Cognitive, affective and behavioral components of attitudes. In C. I. Hovland & M. J. Rosenberg (Eds.), *Attitude organization and change*, pp. 1–14. New Haven, CT: Yale University Press.

Seaton, A. V. (1997). Unobtrusive observational measures as a qualitative extension of visitor surveys at festivals and events: Mass observation revisited. *Journal of Travel Research*, 35(1): 25–30.

Sirgy, M. & Su, C. (2000). The ethics of consumer sovereignty in an age of high tech. *Journal of Business Ethics*, 28: 1–14.

Solomon (2006). *Consumer behavior: Buying, having and being*, 7th ed. Upper Saddle River, NJ: Pearson.

Sørensen, A. (2003). Backpacker ethnography. *Annals of Tourism Research*, 30(4): 847–67.

Sparks, B. (2007). Planning a wine tourism vacation? Factors that help to predict tourist behavioural intentions. *Tourism Management*, 28(5): 1180–92.

Tiefenbacher, J. P., Day, F. A. & Walton, J. (2000). The attributes of repeat-visitors to small, tourism-oriented communities: A Texas case study. *The Social Science Journal*, 37(2): 299–308.

Vigneron, F. & Johnson, L. W. (1999). A review and a conceptual framework of prestige-seeking consumer behaviour. *Academy of Marketing Science Review*, 9(1): 1–14.

Vroom, V. (1964). *Work and motivation*. New York: Wiley.

Weiss, Y. & Fershtman, C. (1998). Social status and economic performance: A survey. *European Economic Review*, 42: 801–20.

Witt, C. A. & Wright, P. L. (1992). Tourist motivation: Life after Maslow. In P. Johnson and B. Thomas, (Eds.), *Choice and demand in tourism*. London: Mansell.

Woodside, A. G., Caldwell, M. & Spurr, R. (2006). Advancing ecological systems theory in lifestyle, leisure, and travel research. *Journal of Travel Research*, 44: 259–72.

Part II

Perception and Information Processing

3 Tourism Destination Image Formation

Robert Govers and Frank M. Go

INTRODUCTION

Over the years the body of literature on destination image has grown to a respectable size. However, as Baloglu and McCleary (1999: 869) suggest, "most studies have largely focused on its static structure by examining the relationship between image and behaviour," from a construct measurement perspective. "Little empirical research has focused on how image is actually formed, . . . analysing its dynamic nature by investigating the influences on its structure and formation . . . , especially in the absence of previous experience with a destination" (Baloglu and McCleary, 1999). However, in the networked information society and the experience economy, it is exactly this dynamic nature of destination image which is of key importance, and requires deconstruction of the destination image formation model (Govers and Go, 2003). Because like Toffler (1980: 301) argues: "in our modern world we cannot see the future in the same way we solve problems—by dismantling problems into their component parts. We must practice, instead, synthesis."

Figure 3.1 therefore tries to deconstruct destination image formation and identify those elements that have a dynamic influence on how destination image is formulated in the mind of the consumer. This model provides the basis for the detailed synthesis of the destination image paradigm, as addressed throughout this chapter. This is done from a "3-TDS" gap perspective, confronting host-guest (supply-and-demand) perspectives, based on the idea of the five-gap service quality analysis model by Parasuraman et al. (1985: 44) and with major contributions from Baloglu and McCleary (1999), Fesenmaier and MacKay (1996), and Gartner (1993). The emphasis in this paper will be on the bottom half of the model, as it is most relevant in the context of consumer behavior, focusing on the tourist demands specifications and tourism delivery and supply gaps.

TOURIST DEMANDS SPECIFICATIONS

The formation of image has been described by Reynolds (1965: 69), as one of the first commentators, as the development of a mental construct

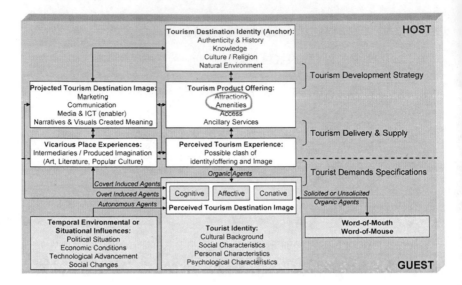

Figure 3.1   The three-gap tourism destination image formation model.

based upon a few impressions chosen from a flood of information. In the case of destination image, this "flood of information" has many sources including promotional sources (advertising and brochures), the opinions of others (family/friends, travel agents), media reporting (newspapers, magazines, television news reporting, and documentaries), and popular culture (motion pictures, literature). "Furthermore, by actually visiting the destination, the image will be affected and modified based upon first hand information and experience" (Echtner and Ritchie, 2003: 38).

As Reynolds (1965: 70) states: "often, of course, the word 'image' is used as equivalent to reputation . . . , what people believe about a person or an institution, *versus* character, what the person or institution actually is." The latter could also be referred to as identity, as discussed in the top half of the three-gap model. This section will focus on the image as the mental construct of the tourist. The following sections will expand on what Ryan (2000: 121) states the tourist to be, that is, "a voyeur whose very presence is a catalyst for action in both the meta and narrow narrative; an interpreter of experience within personal constructs of meaning, but able to discard those meanings in ludic moments . . . Within this framework of analysis the tourist place becomes a locus of selected meanings."

However, a challenge for hosts that attract culturally different groups of visitors is to exploit those few impressions in order to mould perceptions and thereby raise the right expectations. The further away and the more culturally different the visitor, the harder the task of influencing the perceived destination image will be. As explained by McCabe and Stokoe (2004: 604): "The changing nature and character of places, together with adapting modes of leisure consumption and commercialization of locales, have shifted the ways in which meanings are attached to places." The way in which consumers do this is the topic of the following section.

Perceived Tourism Destination Image

With regard to experiential products like travel and tourism, consumers are involved in an ongoing search for information (Leemans, 1994: 23). By collecting all this information, the consumer creates an image or "mental prototype" (Tapachai and Waryszak, 2000: 37) of what the travel experience might look like. As tourism services are intangible, images become more important than reality (Gallarza, Gil Saura, and Calderon-Garcia, 2002: 57) and the tourism destination images projected in information space will be of great influence on the destination images as perceived by consumers. The latter are generally accepted (Echtner and Ritchie, 1993: 4; Padgett and Allen, 1997: 50; Tapachai and Waryszak, 2000: 38) to be based on attributes, functional consequences (or expected benefits), and the symbolic meanings or psychological characteristics consumers associate with a specific destination (or service). As a consequence, projected images influence destination positioning and ultimately the tourist's buying behavior.

There seems to be a consensus among authors that the destination image research stream has emerged from Hunt's work of 1971 (Gallarza et al., 2002: 58; Hunt, 1975). "From this time onwards, there have been numerous and varied approaches to its study," totaling sixty-five works, between 1971 and 1999, as identified by the thorough synoptic work of Gallarza et al. (2002) as well as Pike (2002), who reviewed 142 papers. One influential study was published by Echtner and Ritchie (1993; 2003). Through their research, Echtner and Ritchie concluded that destination image should be envisioned as having two main components: those that are attribute based and those that are holistic. Each of these components contains functional (or more tangible) and psychological (or more abstract) characteristics. Images of destinations can also range from those based on "common" functional and psychological traits to those based on more distinctive or even unique features, events, feelings, or auras. This illustrates that there are many aspects involved in formulating the total destination image in the mind of the tourist.

Tourist Identity as Self-Focus

The interpretation of the many aspects involved in the formulation of destination image in the mind of the tourist will differ largely between destinations and the type of tourists visiting them (attributes differ according to object [type of destination] and subject [consumer] as Gallarza et al. [2002: 62] put it). The latter is also referred to in literature as "self-focus," where

Case Study 1. Different Dimensions of Destination Image in Nepal

The three-dimensional model envisaged by Echtner and Ritchie is depicted in Figure 3.2, together with some examples for four of the six components. The common versus unique dimension is missing in this example for Nepal, but normally identifies if image aspects are unique for the specific destination, or shared by others as well.

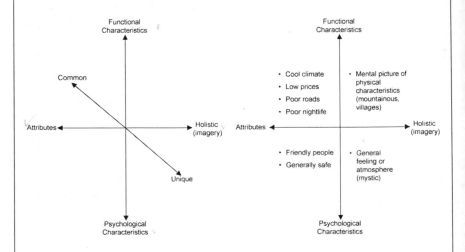

Figure 3.2   Components of destination image and an example of four of those (Nepal). Note: Reproduced from Echtner and Ritchie 2003: 37–48. Reprinted with permission.

the affective evaluations are not a description of the object, but of the relation between the consumer and the object (Leemans, 1994). Sirgy and Su (2000) emphasize the importance of "self-congruity" in this context, which "involves a process of matching a tourist's self-concept to a destination visitor image." A study by MacKay and Fesenmaier (2000) provides empirical evidence to support the notion that the manner in which people view images of a destination is mediated by cultural background, for one thing. Cultural background determines people's values, ideals, norms, beliefs, and folk wisdom. It would seem logical to assume that these will in turn have an impact on people's perceptions of places.

It is generally accepted in literature that in the mind of the consumer the perceived destination image is formed by two (Baloglu and Brinberg, 1997; Baloglu and McCleary, 1999; Embacher and Buttle, 1989) or three (Dann, 1996; Gartner, 1993) "distinctly different but hierarchically interrelated components: cognitive, affective and [according to some] conative"

(Gartner, 1993: 193). These are all processes of awareness according to Csikszentmihalyi (1995a: 19), who also identified attention and memory as the other two structural elements of human consciousness. "Cognitive evaluations refer to the beliefs or knowledge about a destination's attributes whereas affective evaluation refers to feelings toward, or attachment to it" (Baloglu and McCleary, 1999: 870). According to Gartner (1993: 196) "the affective component of image is related to the motives one has for destination selection." The conative component, on the other hand, "is the action component which builds on the cognitive and affective stages" (Dann, 1996: 49).

If self-congruity takes place, perceived destination image would surely also be mediated by sociodemographic characteristics, cultural background, personal identity, and psychological consumer characteristics, which is supported by Baloglu and McCleary (1999: 870). Beerli and Martín (2004a: 678; 2004b: 623) provide evidence for this as they have empirically established that: (1) tourist motivations (as affective psychological characteristics) influence the affective component of image; (2) the experience of vacation travel (as in learning as a psychological characteristic) has a significant relationship with cognitive and affective images, and (3) the sociodemographic and personal characteristics (gender, age, level of education, country of origin, and social class) influence the cognitive as well as the affective assessment of image. However, it has to be stated that these conclusions need to be treated with caution, as most hypotheses in Beerli and Martín's study were only partially maintained; a specific model of causality was not constructed and generalization of results was only permitted within the context of the case study of Lanzarote.

Temporal Environmental or Situational Influences

Temporal environmental or situational influences will also change people's perceptions in the short term (Gartner and Hunt, 1987). These are referred to as "autonomous agents" by Gartner (1993: 201–03). Beerli and Martín (2004a: 667), based on the work of Gartner, tried to measure the impact on destination image of autonomous agents. They distinguish: guidebooks, news, articles, reports, documentaries, and programs about the destination in the media. Obviously these components can take many different forms, and it would be impossible to try to list them exhaustively. The distinction between autonomous and induced agents might also not always be clear, as destinations can influence the impact of temporal environmental and situational factors through public relations, crisis management, and lobbying (Gartner, 1993: 202). This will be illustrated in the next section when covert induced agents are examined. The difference is that overt induced agents (such as destination marketing efforts) are initiated by the tourism destination (or one or more of its stakeholders) as proactive interventions, while responses to autonomous agents can only be reactive. Finally, covert induced agents are somewhere in the middle.

This can be quite relevant as Gartner (1993: 203) states that "news and popular culture forms of autonomous image formation, because of their high credibility and market penetration, may be the only image formation agents capable of changing an area's image dramatically in a short period of time." One of the reasons for this may be that news does not age well, and major events often receive massive attention in a relatively brief period of time. However, without reinforcement, in time, images are likely to revert back to what they were before. This can either be positive of negative, but whatever the case, one would expect that destination marketing organizations (DMOs) would want to influence this process. That's why covert induced agents are becoming increasingly important and the nature of many what-used-to-be autonomous agents is changed for them to become covert induced agents.

Shared Meaning through Narratives

Destination image is formed in what Go and Fenema (2003) refer to as mind or knowledge space. "We develop and express routines and experiences that are communicated . . . through stories and scripts . . . , processed and enhanced by other human beings." People interact and share meaning and subsequently shape each other's perceptions of objects and places. In Gartner's terminology these are called solicited or unsolicited organic agents (1993: 203–04).This is referred to in Figure 3.1 as word-of-mouth and word-of-mouse (Riedl, Konstan, and Vrooman, 2002), the latter being the contemporary reference to people communicating and willingly or unwillingly collaborating online, such as through the use of e-mail, newsgroups, collaborative filtering, personalized Web sites, chat rooms, or audio/video and pictures (digitalized, accompanied by people's comments, remarks, and critiques or not).

Because of the unique characteristics of services (i.e., intangibility and heterogeneity), consumer decision making in tourism is often associated with perceived financial and emotional risks. "In these high-risk situations, word-of-mouth or personal information sources are more influential than impersonal media sources" (Sirakaya and Woodside, 2005: 12). In relation to these organic agents, Beerli and Martín (2004a: 677) state that "the fact that word of mouth is considered to be the most believable and truthful communication channel, together with the fact that it also significantly influences the cognitive image, means that it is important that the messages transmitted in the markets of origin match the reality of the destination." In other words, the projected image must be realistic. If not, DMOs and the local tourism industry will struggle to satisfy tourists who will arrive at their destination with glorified expectations. This in turn will have a negative effect on the image that they will transmit by word of mouth on their

return home, causing clashes with other induced sources of image formation and a tourist demands specifications gap to occur.

TOURISM DELIVERY AND SUPPLY

Tourism is a service industry which creates experiences with a high dependency on human interaction. In particular, the quality of the experience is
derived from the interfacing between hosts (frontline employees) and guest,
the outcome of which can make or break such service encounters. Providing
a quality service encounter is an especially daunting challenge for tourism
destinations where the guest comes from a different cultural background.
Cultural differences are likely to result in miscommunication, which in
turn makes it harder for frontline staff to understand guests' expectations.
Of course, repeat interaction of these hosts and guests will alleviate this
problem through learning. Therefore, it is expected that familiarity with
a certain destination and the level of involvement of the tourist with the
destination will influence the perceived destination image.

The information acquired through personal experience or by visiting the
destination forms the primary image, which may differ from the secondary
image, which was examined in the last section. Indeed, some authors, such
as Gartner and Hunt (1987), point out that postvisit image tends to be more
realistic, complex, and different from the previsit images which is based on
secondary sources of information. Echtner and Ritchie (1993) believe that
the perceived destination image of travelers who are more familiar with a
destination is more holistic, psychological, and unique compared to first-
time visitors who's images are based more on attributes, functional aspects,
and common features.

Fakeye and Crompton (1991), however, emphasize the lack of agreement in literature about the impact of the actual experience on the image.
Nevertheless, several empirical works in academic literature (Chon, 1991;
Fakeye and Crompton, 1991; Milnam and Pizam, 1995) demonstrate that
perceived image is influenced by familiarity with, the number of visits to,
and the length of stay at a destination. Beerli and Martín (2004a: 663)
also explain that "one of the factors related to personal experience is the
intensity of the visit, or, in other words, the extent of an individual's interaction with the place." This would affect travelers' perceived image as:
"the primary source of information formed by personal experience or visits will influence the perceived image depending on the number of visits
and their duration, or on the degree of involvement with the place during
the stay" (measured by Beerli and Martín by number of different places
visited at the destination) (2004a: 663). Therefore, standards of delivery
and supply of the tourism product as an involved consumer experience
must be maintained everywhere, in every location visited by travelers, and
at all times.

Tourism Experience as Hedonic Consumption

The tourism experience, facilitated through tourism products and services, is typically an example of hedonic consumption. Leemans (1994: 210) argues that these "are emotion-laden goods and services for which the consumption experience is an end in itself." He discusses books as a hedonic product, but tourism also qualifies as such, due to its emotion-intensive properties (Vogt and Fesenmaier, 1998). Leemans later continues that "factual information on objective and often physical characteristics of single items are much less important than the (holistic, non-attribute based) image that is built around items." Urry (2002) clarifies and extends the argument that tourism experiences have a fundamental visual character, drawing an analogy with Foucault's concept of the gaze. He develops the notion that there are diverse tourist gazes. Others prefer the alternative metaphor of "performance," or the way Fairweather and Swaffield (2002: 294) describe it as "the graded experience of the Elizabethan theatre, . . . in which some of the audience become active participants, some choose to remain detached spectators, and others move between the two. Furthermore, watching others in the audience perform becomes part of the experience."

Experiences that are "*autotelic*, or rewarding in and of itself," have been termed by Csikszentmihalyi (1995b: 8) as states of *flow*. "Artists, athletes, composers, dancers, scientists, and people from all walks of life, when they describe how it feels when they are doing something that is worth doing for its own sake, use terms that are interchangeable in their minutest details. This unanimity suggests that order in consciousness produces a very specific experiential state, so desirable that one wishes to replicate it as often as possible" (Csikszentmihalyi, 1995a: 29). This is what has been termed "flow" or . . . optimal experience. The flow experience is characterized by several dimensions. "When a person's skill is just right to cope with the demands of a situation—and when compared to the entirety of everyday life the demands are above average—the quality of experience improves noticeably" (Csikszentmihalyi, 1995a: 32). When the demands are too high, it results in a feeling of anxiety. When the demands are too low, the person might get bored.

Other common characteristics of flow experiences include focused concentration and a distorted sense of time. People in flow commonly have no attention left to think of anything else. Also, "hours seem to pass by in minutes, and occasionally a few seconds stretch out into what seems to be an infinity" (Csikszentmihalyi, 1995a: 33). Although in flow experiences clear goals and quick and unambiguous feedback on performance are needed, the goals are often just an excuse to make the experience possible. "The mountaineer does not climb in order to reach the top of the mountain, but tries to reach the summit in order to climb" (Csikszentmihalyi, 1995a: 33).

Csikszentmihalyi (1995b: 14) argues that "whenever the quality of human experience is at issue, flow becomes relevant," hence its importance for tourism. This is also supported by Cary (2004: 68), who argues that "tourist motivation and experiences centre upon the demand for leisure and the subsequent escape from boredom and anxiety. As a sacred journey, tourism foments the optimum conditions for experiencing a heightened state of being; or, for experiencing flow." This illustrates why tourism is such an intricate business. The demands on people's skills while traveling, when compared to everyday life, will be above average in most cases. This most likely applies to any sort of tourism, from packaged tours to adventure travel, as demands are assessed relative to the person's everyday life, and different types of tourism experiences probably attract different markets with different domestic backgrounds. As Cary (2004) alludes to in "the tourist moment," many travelers report feelings of harmony with the environment, focused concentration, liminality, losing track of time, and the attractiveness of the act of traveling for its own sake. Obviously achieving an optimal experience while traveling improves the perceived image of place.

A Tourism Product Offering that Delivers the Tourism Experience

Human interactions are essential, as a large part of tourism experiences, including the tourism product delivery as a high customer contact service encounter refers to interactions with other people, hosts with guests, but also guests with other guests. Part of what is purchased in tourist-related services is a particular social composition of those serving in the front line as well as the social composition of other customers (Urry, 2003: 17). Tourism experiences take place in what Go and Fenema (2003) refer to as social space. People interact and create meaning in a joint process based on concurrent or similar past experiences. Therefore, interactions in social space do not necessarily have to take place in material space (at the physical destination) but can also take place remotely over the phone or online. Tourism experiences, although still primarily created in material space, are therefore also partly constructed pre- and postvisit, influencing perceived image.

It is not surprising that the service management and marketing literature repeatedly emphasizes the importance of frontline employees, also termed "emotional work" or "emotional labour" (Urry, 2002: 62; 2003: 17). Personalization in service encounters has therefore also received increased attention (Mittal and Lassar, 1996). Although the host-guest encounter is essential, relationships with other tourists with whom one shares the same experiences (either family and/or acquaintances in the same travel party, social encounters or friendships established during the visit) influence the tourism experience as well. This takes place during the trip, but is also instrumental to the process of creating multisensory, emotional, historic, or fantastic nostalgia prior to and after the visit. Due to the heterogeneity which characterizes tourism destinations and service performance in general, it is very difficult to set standards of service delivery and supply of the tourism product.

However, what needs to be emphasized here is that the personal experience of service delivery and the intensity of the host-guest encounter (or lack thereof) are clearly related to the guest' perceived image. The interesting consequence is that offering the tourists easy access and facilitating the co-opting of their competence may unlock the potential of a destination to take the necessary steps to enhancing service quality and influencing perceived destination image in a positive manner. What is often insufficiently appreciated by the industry is that most people, while traveling, are out to have fun, meet other people, new cultures, and share with others. Through dialog and the performance of genuine, what has been called "people-to-people" business, place experiences can be dramatically enhanced.

Experiencing Place in Alternative Ways

A tourism experience cannot be tested or sampled prior to visit, but there are other forms of hedonic consumption that can give a "reality-like" insight into living place identity. Just some examples are: movies, music, TV shows, exhibitions, events, literature, virtual communities, or any other forms of popular culture. The influence of movies on tourism destination image and choice behavior has received considerable attention in recent years. "Leisure products such as books and movies increasingly trigger consumers to travel to certain destinations (E.g.: Crocodile Dundee—Australia, The Beach—Thailand, Harry Potter—Great Britain, The Lord of the Rings—New Zealand)" (Klooster, Go, and Baalen, 2004, Introduction section, ¶ 1). However, DMOs should not make the mistake of thinking that these are autonomous agents that destinations cannot influence or take advantage of.

Case Study 2. Movie-induced Tourism

On July 14, 2004, eTurbuNews reported that "movies and television shows help boost tourism" (Alcantara, 2004). For instance, as a result of the success of the motion picture *Troy*, starring Brad Pitt, the western Turkish city of Çanakkale, the location of ancient Troy, had seen a 73 percent increase in visitor numbers. The number of tourists is expected to increase further when the Trojan horse used in the film is reused as a tourist attraction. Elsewhere, New Zealand is also benefiting from movie exposure. Tourism is said to have increased as a result of its exposure as the backdrop for the movie trilogy *The Lord of the Rings*. Over 7 percent of tourists visiting New Zealand were influenced by the movie. Hawaii's exposure in television shows (*North Shore, Hawaii, Lost, American Idol*) have helped boost tourism. In fact, Hawaii had to actively lobby and enter into a competition with other destinations in an effort to try to get producers to film on the island (Alcantara, 2004).

As mentioned earlier, current developments show that destinations increasingly try to turn what-used-to-be autonomous agents into covert induced agents. These days, even celebrities are often called to the rescue of destinations in crisis, such as in SARS-affected areas or destinations that have experienced the devastating effects of wars or terrorism (Alcantara, 2003). Also, museums can be useful providers of vicarious place experiences and a means to produce covert induced agents. The parallel between museum exhibitor and destination marketer has been identified by Fesenmaier and MacKay. "The roles of the museum exhibitor and destination marketer are paralleled by their efforts to control portrayal of culture and image. The planned exhibit and the constructed tourist destination image both represent a vision controlled by political ideologies" (Fesenmaier and MacKay, 1996: 38).

Lastly, with current-day technology, virtual communities become interesting instruments in providing vicarious experiences. "These communities may serve as extensions of the destination, and become colonies that revive destination-specific events (cultural, environmental etc.)" (Klooster et al., 2004: Destination Brand Communities section, ¶ 3). As such, the previous off-site destination consumption experiences are obviously interrelated. Relevant movies and books are discussed in destination virtual communities, and museum-like exhibitions of "the-making-of" will influence destination image in their own way. Even virtual destinations such as Second Life are becoming increasingly popular, with the Guardian's Observer Escape section announcing "this year's hottest destination: cyberspace" (Bowes, 2007). At the same time it is important though to distinguish them from overt induced agents and autonomous agents as discussed earlier. Nevertheless, recent research has focused on these phenomena, also as a way to influence place image (Choi, Lehto, and Morrison, 2007; Govers, Go, and Kumar, 2007a, b).

CONCLUSION AND IMPLICATIONS

What results, at the end of this chapter, is a perceived tourism destination image built up from an extensive set of customer expectations, be it functional or psychological, attribute based or holistic, or based on common traits or unique features. The extent to which the actual tourism experience meets or exceeds these expectations will determine the level of tourist satisfaction (Bigné, Sánchez, and Sánchez, 2001; Chon, 1990). As MacInnis and Price (1987: 481) put it: "Even if the actual outcome is favourable, it is likely to differ from the imagined outcome. Deviations of the actual outcome from the imagined outcome give rise to surprise." In other words, their expectations might be unrealistic. These deviations are an important cause of consumer dissatisfaction.

So one way in which tourists become dissatisfied is when a tourist demands-specifications gap occurs. This takes place when the perceived tourism destination image and the tourists' expectations are unrealistic and therefore clash with the actual identity of the place and its tourism product offering as experienced through consumption. This might occur if an unrealistic or incomplete destination image has been projected or the tourist's interpretation of the destination images is distorted because of temporal environmental or situational influences, interaction with others, or the person's own identity (selective attention and retention).

In contrast to the consumption of goods which customers acquire for utilitarian benefits, the tourism product is intangible and experiential in nature, involving emotions, feelings, drama, and fantasies and aims to satisfy primarily psychological benefits. Traditionally, researchers have viewed its labor-intensive character, the dependency on human interaction, and the involvement of a myriad of actors who participate in one way or another in the production, delivery, and consumption of a total experience as central issues. For example, consistency in service is often cited as being problematic, because any interruption in the delivery process will immediately affect service quality due to the simultaneous production and consumption.

But even when the DMO and local tourism businesses possess the "right" information about the visitor expectations and the perceived destination image in the mind of the visitor is realistic, the delivery of the tourism experience can still be disappointing, affecting service quality, if service personnel are not empowered to deliver a truly personalized yet consistent service that co-opts the customer. Not much is needed to negatively affect customer satisfaction whenever organizations fail to do this (see again, for effect of quality on satisfaction, Bigné et al., 2001), particularly in situations where host and guest come from different cultural backgrounds. When the value systems on which host and guest base their social expectations and behavior are different, it makes it more difficult for frontline service employees to anticipate guest expectations and to offer a rapid response accordingly. As a result, the second tourism delivery-and-supply gap appears.

The third and final gap to be presented in the three-gap model is concerned with the supply perspective and hence of less relevance within the context of this book. It argues that if the tourism product and the way it is communicated fails to be in line with the destination's true identity, it can create a tourism development strategy gap. The gap occurs as the fundamental prerequisites for a rewarding host-guest encounter are not present when the images generated within the tourism product offering and the way they are projected come to constitute a self-perpetuating system of illusions, which may appear as quaint to the local inhabitants as they do to the tourists themselves. Both hosts as well as guests will become alienated. It is therefore finally concluded that image-formation agents, including consumption experience and their effect on customer (dis)satisfaction, do not originate from a vacuum but should be linked to the way in which the tourism product offering is designed and linked to tourism promotion and the sense of place, as studied in recent research, particularly on destination branding as a area of future research.

REFERENCES

Alcantara, N. (2003). *Start to the rescue.* eTurbo News, 30 May. Retrieved from http://www.travelwirenews.com.

———. (2004). *Movies and television shows help boost tourism.* eTurboNews, 14 July. Retrieved from http://www.travelwirenews.com.

Baloglu, S. & Brinberg, D. (1997). Affective images of tourism destinations. *Journal of Travel Research,* 35(4): 11–15.

Baloglu, S. & McCleary, K. W. (1999). A model of destination image formation. *Annals of Tourism Research,* 26(4): 808–89.

Beerli, A. & Martín, J. D. (2004a). Factors influencing destination image. *Annals of Tourism Research,* 31(3): 657–81.

———. (2004b). Tourists' characteristics and the perceived image of tourist destinations: A quantitative analysis—a case study of Lanzarote, Spain. *Tourism Management,* 25(5): 623–36.

Bigné, J. E., Sánchez, M. I. & Sánchez, J. (2001). Tourism image, evaluation variables and after purchase behaviour: Inter-relationship. *Tourism Management,* 22(6): 607–16.

Bowes, G. (2007). *This year's hottest destination: Cyberspace.* Guardian (Observer Escape section), March 18. Retrieved on April 27, 2007 from http://travel.guardian.co.uk/article/2007/mar/18/travelwebsites.escape.

Cary, S. H. (2004). The tourist moment. *Annals of Tourism Research,* 31(1): 61–77.

Choi, S., Lehto, X. Y. & Morrison, A. M. (2007). Destination image representation on the web: Content analysis of Macau travel related websites. *Tourism Management,* 28: 118–29.

Chon, K.-S. (1990). The role of destination image in tourism: A review and discussion. *Revue de Tourisme,* 45(3): 2–9.

———. (1991). Tourism destination image modification process: Marketing implications. *Tourism Management,* 12(1): 68–75.

Csikszentmihalyi, M. (1995a). The flow experience and its significance for human psychology. In M. Csikszentmihalyi & I. S. Csikszentmihalyi (Eds.), *Optimal experience: Psychological studies of flow in consciousness,* pp. 15–35. Cambridge: Cambridge University Press.

———. (1995b). Introduction. In M. Csikszentmihalyi & I. S. Csikszentmihalyi (Eds.), *Optimal experience: Psychological studies of flow in consciousness,* pp. 3–14. Cambridge: Cambridge University Press.

Dann, G. M. S. (1996). Tourists images of a destination: An alternative analysis. *Journal of Travel and Tourism Marketing,* 5(1/2): 41–55.

Echtner, C. M. & Ritchie, J. R. B. (1993). The measurement of destination image: An empirical assessment. *Journal of Travel Research,* 31(4): 3–13.

———. (2003). The meaning and measurement of destination image. *Journal of Tourism Studies,* 14(1): 37–48.

Embacher, J. & Buttle, F. (1989). A repertory grid analysis of Austria's image as a summer vacation destination. *Journal of Travel Research,* 28(3): 3–23.

Fairweather, J. R. & Swaffield, S. R. (2002). Visitors' and locals' experiences of Rotorua, New Zealand: An interpretative study using photographs of landscapes and Q method. *International Journal of Tourism Research,* 4(4): 283–97.

Fakeye, P. C. & Crompton, J. L. (1991). Image differences between prospective, first-time, and repeat visitors to the lower Rio Grande Valley. *Journal of Travel Research,* 30(2): 10–16.

Fesenmaier, D. & MacKay, K. (1996). Deconstructing destination image construction. *Revue de Tourisme,* 51(2): 37–43.

Gallarza, M. G., Gil Saura, I. & Calderon-Garcia, H. (2002). Destination image: Towards a conceptual framework. *Annals of Tourism Research,* 29(1): 56–78.

Gartner, W. C. (1993). Image formation process. *Journal of Travel and Tourism Marketing,* 2(2/3): 191–215.

Gartner, W. C. & Hunt, J. D. (1987). An Analysis of state image change over a twelve-year period (1971–1983). *Journal of Travel Research,* 25(2): 15–19.

Go, F. M. & Fenema, P. C. V. (2003). Moving bodies and connecting minds in space: It is a matter of mind over matter. *Proceedings of the 19th European Group for Organizational Studies* (CD-ROM). *EGOS Colloquium 2003,* Copenhagen: http://home.hetnet.nl/~pcvf/Publications/EGOS%202003%20Mind%20and%20Matter%20Final%20Paper.pdf.

Govers, R. & Go, F. M. (2003). Deconstructing destination image in the information age. *Information Technology & Tourism,* 6(1): 13–29.

Govers, R., Go, F. M. & Kumar, K. (2007a). Promoting tourism destination image. *Journal of Travel Research,* 46(1): 15–23.

———. (2007b). Virtual destination image: A new measurement approach. *Annals of Tourism Research,* 34(4): 977–97.

Hunt, J. D. (1975). Image as a factor in tourism development. *Journal of Travel Research,* 13(3): 1–7.

Klooster, E. V. H., Go, F. M. & Baalen, P. V. (2004). Exploring destination brand communities: A business model for collaboration in the extremely fragmented tourism industry (CD-ROM). *17th Bled eCommerce Conference,* Bled, Slovenia: June 21–23, eCommerce Center, University of Maribor.

Leemans, H. (1994). *The multiform book: Using information in purchasing hedonic products.* Delft, Netherlands: Eburon.

MacInnes, D. J. & Price, L. L. (1987). The role of imagery in information processing: Review and extensions. *Journal of Consumer Research,* 13(4): 473–91.

MacKay, K. J. & Fesenmaier, D. R. (2000). An exploration of cross-cultural destination image assessment. *Journal of Travel Research,* 38(4): 417–23.

McCabe, S. & Stokoe, E. H. (2004). Place and identity in tourists' accounts. *Annals of Tourism Research,* 31(3): 601–22.

Milnam, A. & Pizam, A. (1995). The role of awareness and familiarity with a destination: The central Florida case. *Journal of Travel Research,* 33(3): 21–27.

Mittal, B. & Lassar, W. M. (1996). The role of personalization in service encounters. *Journal of Retailing,* 72(1): 95–109.

Padgett, D. & Allen, D. (1997). Communicating experiences: A narrative approach to creating service brand image. *Journal of Advertising,* 26(4) Winter: 49–62.

Parasuraman, A., Zeithaml, V. & Berry, L. L. (1985). A conceptual model of service quality and its implications for future research. *Journal of Marketing,* 49(4): 41–50.

Pike, S. (2002). Destination image analysis—a review of 142 papers from 1973 to 2000. *Tourism Management,* 23(5): 541–49.

Reynolds, W. H. (1965). The role of the consumer in image building. *California Management Review,* 7(3): 69–76.

Riedl, J., Konstan, J. & Vrooman, E. (2002). *Word of mouse: The marketing power of collaborative filtering.* New York: Warner Books.

Ryan, C. (2000). Tourist experiences: Phenomenographic analysis, post-positivism and neural network software. *International Journal of Tourism Research,* 2(2): 119–31.

Sirakaya, E. & Woodside, A. G. (2005). Building and testing theories of decision making by travellers. *Tourism Management,* 26(6): 815–32.

Sirgy, M. J. & Su, C. (2000). Destination image, self congruity, and travel behaviour: Toward an integrative model. *Journal of Travel Research,* 38(4): 340–52.

Tapachai, N. & Waryszak, R. (2000). An examination of the role of beneficial image in tourist destination selection. *Journal of Travel Research,* 39(1): 37–44.

Toffler, A. (1980). *The third wave.* New York: Bantam Books.

Urry, J. (2002). *The tourist gaze,* 2nd ed. London: Sage.

———. (2003). The sociology of tourism. In C. Cooper (Ed.), *Aspects of tourism,* pp. 9–21, *Classic reviews in tourism series,* vol. 8. Clevedon, UK: Channel View Publications.

Vogt, C. A. & Fesenmaier, D. R. (1998). Expanding the functional tourism information search model: Incorporating aesthetic, hedonic, innovation, and sign dimensions. *Annals of Tourism Research,* 25(3): 551–78.

4 Tourist Information Search

Kenneth F. Hyde

INTRODUCTION

Tourist information-search processes are one of the most widely studied areas in consumer research in tourism (Chen and Gursoy, 2000). Information on travel destinations forms the basis for tourists' travel planning, including their choices of destination, transportation, accommodation, attractions, and activities (Gursoy and Umbreit, 2004). An understanding of tourist information-search processes is invaluable to tourism service providers who seek to formulate effective marketing communications strategies that employ the best mix of media through which to reach target consumers.

This chapter commences by examining what motivates consumers to seek travel information. While it may be obvious that consumers have functional motives for information search—that is, to assist in selection of elements of the travel experience, such as choice of destination, transport, and accommodation—consumers may have other motives associated with the pleasures of learning about travel destinations. The chapter then presents a summary of the results of three decades of empirical research into functional information search and its determinants. The chapter places specific emphasis on empirical evidence from the last decade, during which period use of the Internet and other electronic media have come to play an integral part in a tourist's information-search behavior. The chapter presents research evidence regarding three questions: (1) Which sources of information does the tourist utilize? (2) How much information search does the tourist undertake? and (3) What are the demographic, psychological, and contextual factors that influence a tourist's choice of information sources and amount of information search?

The chapter introduces the concept of tourist information-search strategies—that is, the combinations of information sources utilized by tourists to plan their travel. The results of a recent study of the information-search strategies employed by first-time visitors to a vacation destination are explored (Hyde, 2006). The chapter introduces a contextual framework for understanding tourists' functional information search. The context for functional information search includes the purpose of travel, first-time versus repeat visits to a destination, and pretrip versus on-vacation information search. The chapter then considers a number of methodological shortcomings in past research on tourist information-search processes. The chapter concludes by suggesting a number of issues for future research into tourist information search.

MOTIVES FOR INFORMATION SEARCH

Research into tourist information search has largely taken the view that such search is purposeful. That is, tourists undertake search of travel information in order to plan their travel and make decisions about travel options such as choice of destination, transport, accommodation, and activities. Such a perspective emphasizes a *functional* motive for information search. This is the view of the consumer as goal-oriented and problem-solving. This chapter will focus on research findings regarding functional information search by tourists.

First, it is worth considering that consumers may have other motives for seeking travel information. To begin with, not everyone who searches for information on travel destinations intends to travel. Reading about exotic destinations, or leafing through glossy travel brochures or scanning travel Web sites online can be a pleasurable activity in itself, even when the tourist does not intend to travel in the immediate future. Travel information can enable the consumer to imagine what the experience of being at the destination may be like, and fantasize about the destination (Vogt, Fesenmaier, and MacKay, 1993). In the initial stages of travel planning, information on travel destinations might sensitize consumers favorably to the idea of having a vacation, and create fantasies about such a vacation; only in the latter stages of travel planning does information search become more functionally motivated (van Raaij and Francken, 1984).

Some consumers may gather information about travel destinations over a long period simply to store this information away in memory, in case it proves useful in the future. The consumer-behavior literature recognizes that information search not only occurs at the stage of prepurchase decision making. Consumer research also recognizes *ongoing search*, which is a term referring to those search activities that are independent of specific purchase decisions (Bloch, Sherrell, and Ridgway, 1986). Ongoing search may be driven by the recreational and pleasure gained from seeking information on a product or activity.

An alternative to the view of the consumer as goal-oriented and problem-solving is the view of the consumer as a hedonic being, motivated by the need to experience feelings and emotions (Holbrook and Hirschman, 1982). Consumers sometimes seek travel information for hedonic reasons, that is, in order to create feelings, experiences, and emotions rather than to solve problems. Five distinct motives have been identified underlying tourist-information search: functional, hedonic, innovation, aesthetic, and sign motives (Vogt and Fesenmaier, 1998). Hedonic motives include the need for excitement and entertainment, to imagine what an exotic location looks like, sounds like, and feels like. Innovation motives include the need for new and different information, the desire for newness and variety, the desire to be original in destination choices and to identify new places that few people have visited. Aesthetic motives refer to the enjoyment obtained from viewing visual images of beautiful places. Consumers may also on occasions be motivated by the status that can be gained from knowing about foreign places and talking about those places to other people—that is, sign motives (Cho and Kerstetter, 2004).

SOURCES OF INFORMATION

Though consumers may have many reasons for seeking travel information, research suggests that functional motives predominate (Vogt and Fesenmaier, 1998; Vogt et al., 1993). This section considers what empirical research has discovered about tourists' functional information-search activities, the sources of information used most often by tourists, and the amounts of information search undertaken by tourists. Information sources may be internal or external to the tourist, formal or informal, personal or impersonal, commercial or noncommercial (Quester et al., 2007). Gartner (1993) provides a useful taxonomy of eight alternative sources of travel information used by the tourist:

1. traditional forms of travel advertising
2. travel brochures and other promotional publications from tour operators and destination marketing organizations
3. endorsement of a travel destination by a celebrity spokesperson
4. articles and reports about a destination in the popular press
5. exposure of the destination in news reports, travel guidebooks, and the mass media
6. casual word of mouth from people who have been to the destination
7. asking advice from a person who has visited the destination, such as a travel agent or other consultant
8. information based on one's own previous experience of the destination

No complete model has yet been constructed which explains consumer choices in sources of travel information. From the earliest studies it appears that *personal* sources—particularly word of mouth from friends and relatives—are considered the most important sources of information for travel decision making (Gitelson and Crompton, 1983; Jenkins, 1978; Nolan, 1976). However, tourists' use of information sources varies by the purpose of travel, stage of travel planning, stage of the journey, characteristics of the journey, and characteristics of the traveler. The following discussion considers each of these contextual factors in turn.

If tourists have been to a destination before, they have past experience to call upon as a source of information (Lehto, Kim, and Morrison, 2006). If tourists are visiting friends and relatives, they have those friends and relatives as a source of information; and business tourists have different information needs from vacation tourists (Chen and Gursoy, 2000; Gursoy and McCleary, 2004; Lo, Cheung, and Law, 2002; Snepenger and Snepenger, 1993).

There may be greater use of nonpersonal information sources in the *early stages* of travel planning to learn about the availability and attributes of alternative destinations, and greater use of personal sources in the *latter stages* of travel planning to assist in evaluating those alternative destinations (van Raaij and Francken, 1984). Travelers en route to their destinations make use of travel information centers and other people to learn about attractions and activities; such information can influence an independent traveler's length of stay and choice of attractions and activities in the destination area (Fesenmaier, Vogt, and Stewart, 1993; Udd, Hulac, and Blazey, 1992). Travelers *at their destination* seek information from personal sources such as employees of accommodation houses and fellow travelers. Local brochures and commercial signage also influence travelers at their destination (Becken and Wilson, 2006; Hyde and Lawson, 2003; Ortega and Rodriguez, 2007).

The information sources employed by the traveler also vary by characteristics of the journey and characteristics of the traveler. Travelers taking routine trips to familiar destinations often utilize experience and advice from family and friends in their travel planning. In contrast, travelers traveling longer distances, taking longer vacations, or visiting new and unfamiliar destinations are more likely to use destination-specific literature, and less likely to use friends and family as a source of information (Gitelson and Crompton, 1983). Those travelers who want security and comfort are likely to utilize travel agents and tour operators; those motivated to explore new and unfamiliar destinations tend to utilize printed material such as guidebooks and brochures (Gitelson and Crompton, 1983; Snepenger, 1987).

Favored information sources also vary by nationality. Distinct groups exist amongst European nationalities, according to the information sources used most often (Gursoy and Umbreit, 2004). Tourists from France, Greece, the Netherlands, and Spain may use travel guides and travel brochures more often than other nationalities; tourists from Denmark and Finland may use the Internet more often; tourists from Belgium and Italy may use other written information more often; tourists from Austria, Germany, Ireland, Luxembourg, Sweden, and the United Kingdom may use television, radio, and travel agents more often (see Table 4.1). One comparison of Japanese and German tourists noted greater use of travel agents amongst Japanese and greater use of personal sources, destination marketing, and mass media sources amongst

Table 4.1   Differences in Favoured Sources of Travel Information Amongst European Tourists

Nations	Favored Sources of Information
France	Travel guides
Greece	Travel brochures
The Netherlands	
Spain	
Denmark	The Internet
Finland	
Belgium	Other written sources
Italy	
Austria	Television
Germany	Radio
Ireland	Travel Agent
Luxemborg	
Sweden	
United Kingdom	

Source: Gursoy and Umbreit (2004).

Germans; part of these national differences may reflect differences in cultural values such as uncertainty avoidance (Money and Crotts, 2003).

Internet as a Source of Information

The Internet is changing the way consumers search for travel information and purchase travel product (Bai, Jang, Cai, and O'Leary, 2001; Gursoy and McCleary, 2004). In 2002, some 30 percent of the worldwide Internet audience visited travel Web sites (Adlink, 2005). Twenty percent of all travel sold in the United States is currently sold online; within a decade more than 50 percent of U.S. travel bookings could be made online (*Economist*, 2004, 13 May). The Internet has thus become a key information source for the planning of vacation travel for some, but not all, demographic groups. The advantages of use of the Internet for consumer search of travel-related information are many. There is an enormous amount of information available online. Up-to-date information on inventories and pricings is available for ready comparison of suppliers. The Internet has the potential to reduce the total search time required to plan a vacation (Anckar, 2003).

Research conducted in the 1990s provided a relatively consistent profile of the consumer of that time who used the Internet to look for travel-related information. Such consumers tended to be younger, male, college-educated, Internet-experienced consumers (Bonn, Furr, and Susskind, 1999; Weber and Roehl, 1999). Even recent research suggests that males from high-income households may dominate in use of the Internet to seek travel information (Luo, Feng, and Cai, 2004). Yet, female travelers may have more favorable attitudes towards use of the Internet as an information source. Recent research observed that female Internet users visit local travel-information, restaurant, and entertainment Web sites more often than male Internet users do; male Internet users visit airline, accommodation, and rental-car Web sites more often than female users do (Kim, Lehto, and Morrison, 2007).

A number of surveys have identified the Internet as the preferred source of travel-related information for some, but not all, nationalities (European Travel Commission, 2006). According to survey research, more than 70 percent of Finnish citizens look for travel information online (Anckar, 2003). Amongst inbound business and leisure travelers to Hong Kong, the Internet was a more influential information source for business travelers than for leisure travelers (Lo et al., 2002). Amongst a national panel of Norwegians, nonpackage tourists ranked the Internet as the most useful information source, while package tourists ranked brochures and travel agents ahead of the Internet. Tourists seeking a city vacation ranked the Internet as the preferred information source, while those seeking a non-city vacation ranked brochures and travel agents the preferred information sources (Tjostheim, 2002; Tjostheim and Tranvoll, 2002).

There are differences in use of the Internet as a source of travel information, according to experience of the destination. Survey research has noted that first-time visitors to a destination may be more frequent users of Web sites, especially Web sites for airlines, destination-marketing organizations, local travel operators, visitor centers, maps, travel magazines, and travel guides (Lehto et al., 2006). Continued research is required to identify the demographic and national groups who make most use of the Internet in their travel-information search activities.

A new area of research has examined the development of expert systems to assist tourists with their travel planning. Such systems typically query the traveler on his or her travel preferences and requirements, and provide information and recommendations on appropriate destinations, transport, and accommodation (Fesenmaier, Wöber, and Werthner, 2006). This is a rapidly advancing area of research. Experimental research has examined consumer interaction with Internet sites during travel planning. Use of search engines appears a common search strategy amongst travel consumers (Ho and Liu, 2005). According to the results of experimental observations, online travel-information search may proceed through a series of *chapters* (e.g., look for a hotel, then look for attractions, then look for shopping malls), each chapter consisting of *episodes* of information search (e.g., evaluate the hotels on offer, or evaluate the attractions on offer) (Pan and Fesenmaier, 2006).

AMOUNT OF INFORMATION SEARCH

A number of demographic factors relate to the amount of information search undertaken by travel consumers. Jenkins's somewhat dated 1978 study on the respective roles of family members in the vacation decision process suggested that husbands dominate the search for information. In contrast, van Raaij and Francken (1984) suggested that females are more active information seekers. A number of researchers have found that the amount of information search—as measured by the number of different types of sources used—is positively associated with income and level of education (Gitelson and Crompton, 1983; Snepenger and Snepenger, 1993). Distinct *active search* and *passive search* groups have been identified (Schul and Crompton, 1983). Active searchers have longer planning horizons and consult more travel organizations; their vacations display a preference for activity, escape from the ordinary, variety in things to see and do, mixing with local cultures, and experiencing new ways of living (Gitelson and Crompton, 1983). Active searchers tend to be traveling greater distances, have limited prior experience with a destination, and have evaluated more vacation options (Crotts, 1992). The amount of information search undertaken also appears related to the purpose of the trip (i.e., vacation travel versus visiting friends and relatives versus business travel), stage of the family life cycle, and income (Fodness and Murray, 1997).

SEARCH STRATEGIES

The concept of an information-search strategy refers to the combination of information sources employed by a tourist. Use of this concept provides recognition that tourists rarely use a *single* source for all the information they require in planning their travel. Snepenger, Meged, Snelly, and Worrall (1990) used this term to describe the results for their study of first-time visitors to Alaska. They recognized three alternative search strategies amongst such travelers: use of just a travel agent, use of a travel agent plus other sources, or use of sources other than a travel agent. Those tourists on an organized tour or short visit were most likely to rely solely on a travel agent. Those tourists traveling independently or staying a long time were most likely to use sources other than a travel agent.

A number of studies have utilized multivariate cluster analysis to identify distinct groups of tourists utilizing alternative information-search strategies. A study of auto tourists to Florida identified three alternative search strategies amongst tourists: active search (i.e., use of a variety of information sources), passive search (i.e., consulting friends and relatives, and use of highway welcome centers), and possessive search (i.e., personal experience plus consultation with friends and relatives) (Fodness and Murray, 1997). An alternative set of search strategies is also reported for auto tourists to Florida: prepurchase use of a variety of sources; tourist bureau; personal experience; ongoing search of newspapers and magazines; on-site use of friends and relatives; automobile club; and travel agency (Fodness and Murray, 1998). Choice of search strategy varied with purpose of the trip, the length of the trip, mode of transport, travel party composition, family life cycle, and income (Fodness and Murray, 1999).

Amongst Swiss tourists, three search strategies have been identified as commonly used *prior* to a travel decision being made: the use of informal sources (such as word of mouth from friends and relatives), direct sources (being friends and relatives plus information from destination sources), or professional sources (such as tour operators and travel agents) (Bieger and Laesser, 2004). Likewise, three search strategies have been identified as commonly used *after* a travel decision has been made: no search, informal search (i.e., word of mouth from friends and relatives), or high search. Choice of search strategy has been shown to vary with distance to the destination, travel style (i.e., packaged versus independent travel), type of trip (i.e., simple local trip versus complex international trip), and type of accommodation (i.e., private versus commercial accommodation).

Contemporary Information-Search Strategies

The ready availability of travel information on the Internet is likely affecting the information-search strategies of today's traveler. The following section describes the results of a recent study of the information-search strategies used by first-time vacationers to an international destination (Hyde, 2006). The research involved interviews with 528 first-time vacation visitors to New Zealand. Interviewers approached survey respondents during the visitors' first twenty-four hours at the destination. The sample represented a group of tourists from a broad range of ages, nationalities, and travel styles who were undertaking an extended touring vacation for which extensive prior information search might be expected. Prior experience of the destination was lacking as a source of information for these tourists. The interviewer asked respondents *how many hours* they had spent consulting each of six information sources in the planning of their vacations—friends and relatives, travel guidebooks, travel agents, travel brochures, television and movies, and the Internet.

A record was made of respondents' ages and nationalities. In addition, each respondent was categorized into one of six travel style segments based on his or her choices in transportation and accommodation: coach tourist, auto tourist, backpacker, camper tourist, comfort tourist, and VFR (visiting friends and relatives) (Becken and Gnoth, 2004). Respondents could have employed any one of $^6C_{1-6} = 63$ alternative combinations of information sources. Multivariate cluster analysis identified six common search strategies, only some of which included use of the Internet:

> Low Search—The largest group of tourists (33 percent of travelers) utilized a low search strategy. On average, these tourists undertook just six hours' search in preparation for their international vacation. These tourists were more likely to be from Australia, more likely to be solo tourists, and more likely to be VFR or coach tourists.
> Guidebook-Brochure-Agent—11 percent of the travelers utilized a multiple-source search strategy involving use of travel guidebooks, travel brochures, and travel agents. On average, these tourists undertook twenty-seven hours' search in preparation for their international vacation. These tourists were more likely to be aged fifty years and over and more likely to be coach tourists.
> Guidebook-Friends—15 percent of the travelers utilized a search strategy characterized by reading of travel guidebooks and consulting with friends and relatives. This group of travelers undertook an average of thirty-two hours' search. These tourists were more likely to be from Europe and more likely to be camper tourists.
> Friends—11 percent of the tourists used a single-source search strategy. For this group most information search simply involved talking with friends and relatives. These tourists were more likely to be VFR tourists.
> Net-Guidebook—16 percent of tourists utilized a search strategy that combined use of the Internet and travel guidebooks. This group of tourists undertook an average of thirty-nine hours of search. These tourists were more likely to be from the United States, more likely to be traveling as couples, and more likely to be auto tourists or backpackers.
> Friends-Net—14 percent of the travelers adopted a high search strategy that emphasized use of the Internet and consultation with friends and relatives. These tourists were more likely to be from the United States.

Results of the study thus suggest that the Internet is not yet all things to all people. Use of the Internet to plan an international vacation varied with age, nationality, and travel style of the vacationer. Rather than replacing traditional sources of travel information, the Internet supplemented traditional sources, particularly for those tourists who sought the greatest amount of information when planning their vacations.

A CONCEPTUAL FRAMEWORK OF TOURIST INFORMATION SEARCH

Figure 4.1 presents a contextual framework for understanding tourists' functional information search. The framework specifies twelve distinct contexts (labeled a–l) in which tourist-information search occurs. These contexts vary according to the purpose of travel, first-time versus repeat visit to a destination, and pretrip versus on-vacation information search. The framework suggests that the *preferred sources* of travel information and *amount* of information search vary according to the travel context. Differences in preferred sources and amounts of search exist between vacation tourists, business tourists, and VFR tourists. Differences in preferred sources and amounts of search also exist between first-time tourists and repeat visitors to a destination.

A final contextual distinction is between information-search activities that occur prior to the journey versus information-search activities undertaken while on vacation (Hyde, 2004; Ortega and Rodriguez, 2007). Tourist-information search while on vacation is an important, though infrequently addressed, issue. Tourist-information search while on vacation includes information sought from visitor information centers, local residents, and mobile electronic devices (Becken and Wilson, 2006; Edwards, Blythe, Scott, and Weihong-Guo, 2006).

Research on tourist-information search over the past three decades has been somewhat hindered by the methods employed in data collection. Firstly, the use of overly heterogeneous samples has hindered research. Many of the studies conducted over the past thirty years have utilized samples that consist of a mix of vacationers, VFR tourists, and business travelers. Some samples

		First-time visit to DESTINATION		Repeat visit to DESTINATION	
		Pretrip	On vacation	Pretrip	On vacation
PURPOSE OF TRAVEL	Vacation	a	b	g	h
	Business	c	d	i	j
	VFR	e	f	k	l

Figure 4.1   A conceptual framework of tourist information search.

Case Study 1. Multiple Infomation Sources

Dave and Jan are businesspeople from Bristol in the UK. They are aged in their forties and have three children aged thirteen, eleven, and nine. They have booked online a four-day vacation at Disneyland Paris, staying at a Disney hotel. This will be their second trip to Disneyland Paris. The children have also checked out Disneyland Paris online, and between them have a list of fourteen attractions they must see. Dave and Jan are happy to go along with the kids' plans, but have already had to intervene in the occasional squabble between the kids. Dave and Jan are more interested in their evening meals than the park rides, so have asked friends about the best restaurants in Disney hotels. Based on this advice, they have chosen three restaurants they must visit on three of the evenings of the vacation. They have also looked at travel brochures for information on shopping at Disneyland Paris; they plan to buy some cute Disney memorabilia for the people at the office. Based on what they know and have researched about Disneyland Paris, there is little about their vacation that Dave and Jan are leaving to chance.

Case Study 2. *Lonely Planet* as an Information Source

Ulrika and Marianne are schoolteachers from Sweden, aged in their early twenties. They are commencing a six-month vacation away from home. They intend to visit Singapore, New Zealand, Indonesia, and Thailand. They have not visited any of these destinations before, nor do they have any close friends or relatives who have been to these countries before. They have booked their flight as far as Singapore, and have booked one night's accommodation in a backpacker hostel recommended in their *Lonely Planet* guidebook for Singapore. After a few days in Singapore, they will fly to New Zealand, where they will spend two or maybe three months. They have no specific itinerary for their New Zealand stay, but want to go to Queenstown, where they can go river surfing, and Kaikoura, where they can go whale watching. They had seen both of these activities featured in a travel documentary broadcast on Swedish television. While in Thailand, they hope to visit Chiang Mai and maybe Phuket. They have chosen these places as both are featured in their *Lonely Planet* guidebook to Thailand. For a vacation of 180 days' duration, Ulrika and Marianne have not undertaken much travel information search.

have consisted of a mix of first-time visitors and repeat visitors (Fodness and Murray, 1997, 1998, 1999; Gursoy and Chen, 2000; Vogt et al., 1993). Reference to the conceptual framework of tourist-information search presented earlier suggests that the use of heterogeneous samples is unlikely to result in unambiguous findings regarding information-search activities.

The use of unsophisticated measures has also limited the validity of some research findings. Many studies have used simple binary data on whether or not a tourist has utilized a particular information source (Fodness and Murray, 1997, 1998, 1999; Snepenger et al., 1990). Yet other studies have employed surrogate measures of the amount of information search, such as the length of time that the tourist has been planning the trip, or the cumulative number of categories of information source utilized (Fodness and Murray, 1987, 1998, 1999). The validity of some research findings can also be questioned based on inappropriate timing of data collection. In some studies, researchers have asked tourists to recall their information-search activities some months after the travel has been completed. Other studies have asked respondents to imagine what information search they might undertake if they were to take a hypothetical trip.

CONCLUSION AND IMPLICATIONS

There is little doubt that the Internet and mobile electronic devices are transforming tourist-information search, both prior to the time of travel and once the tourist reaches the destination. A wealth of research opportunities exists in investigating these areas. Researchers should adopt innovative methods of data gathering for such research, including the collection of weblogs and other behavioral data from the electronic sources used, observational studies, and experimental designs. Where traditional survey methods are used in future research on tourist-information search, researchers should take care to employ metric measures of information usage, with data gathering at appropriate times in the chronology of the travel experience, utilizing samples that are homogenous by purpose of travel and level of experience of the destination.

REFERENCES

Adlink. (2005). *Industry insights: The travel industry*. Retrieved 03/01/2005 from http://www.adlink.net/research/industry/travel.php.

Anckar, B. (2003). Consumer intentions in terms of electronic travel distribution. *e-Service Journal*, 2(2): 68–87.

Bai, B., Jang, S., Cai, L. & O'Leary, J. (2001). Determinants of travel mode choice of senior travelers to the United States. *Journal of Hospitality and Leisure Marketing*, 8(3/4): 147–68.

Becken, S. & Gnoth, J. (2004). Tourist consumption systems among overseas visitors: Reporting on American, German, and Australian visitors to New Zealand. *Tourism Management*, 25(3): 375–85.

Becken, S. & Wilson, J. (2006). Trip planning and decision making of self-drive tourists—A quasi-experimental approach. *Journal of Travel and Tourism Marketing,* 20(3/4): 47–62.

Bieger, T. & Laesser, C. (2004). Information sources for travel decisions: Toward a source process model. *Journal of Travel Research,* 42(4): 357–71.

Bloch, P. H., Sherrell, D. L. & Ridgway, N. M. (1986). Consumer search: An extended framework. *Journal of Consumer Research,* 13: 119–26.

Bonn, M., Furr, H. & Susskind, A. (1999). Predicting a behavioral profile for pleasure travelers on the basis of Internet use segmentation. *Journal of Travel Research,* 37(4): 333–41.

Chen, J. & Gursoy, D. (2000). Cross-cultural comparison of the information sources used by first-time and repeat travelers and its marketing implications. *International Journal of Hospitality Management,* 19(2): 191–203.

Cho, M. & Kerstetter, D. L. (2004). The influence of sign value on travel-related information search. *Leisure Sciences,* 26(1): 19–34.

Crotts, J. C. (1992). Information search behaviors of free and independent travelers. *Visions in Leisure and Business,* 15(1): 1–28.

Economist. (2004, 13 May). *Click to fly.* Retrieved 08/06/2004, from www.economist.com/surveys/displayStory.cfm?Story_id=2646182.

Edwards, S. J., Blythe, P. T., Scott, S. & Weihong-Guo, A. (2006). Tourist information delivered through mobile devices: Findings from the Image project. *Information Technology and Tourism,* 8(1): 31–46.

European Travel Commission. (2006). *Tourism trends for Europe* (September 2006). Retrieved 2 February 2007 from http://www.etc-corporate.org//DWL/ETC_Tourism_Trends_for_Europe_09–2006_ENG.pdf.

Fesenmaier, D. R., Vogt, C. A. & Stewart, W. P. (1993). Investigating the influence of welcome centre information on travel behavior. *Journal of Travel Research,* 31(3): 47–52.

Fesenmaier, D. R., Wöber, K. W. & Werthner, H. (2006). *Destination recommendation systems: Behavioral foundations and applications.* Oxon: CABI.

Fodness, D. & Murray, B. (1997). Tourist information search. *Annals of Tourism Research,* 24(3): 503–23.

———. (1998). A typology of tourist information search strategies. *Journal of Travel Research,* 37(2): 108–19.

———. (1999). A model of tourist information search behavior. *Journal of Travel Research,* 37(3): 220–30.

Gartner, W. (1993). Image formation process. *Journal of Travel and Tourism Marketing,* 2(2/3): 191–215.

Gitelson, R. & Crompton, J. (1983). The planning horizons and sources of information used by pleasure vacationers. *Journal of Travel Research,* 14(3): 2–7.

Gursoy, D. & Chen, J. (2000). Competitive analysis of cross cultural information search behavior. *Tourism Management,* 21: 538–90.

Gursoy, D. & McCleary, K. W. (2004). An integrative model of tourists' information search behavior. *Annals of Tourism Research,* 31(2): 353.

Gursoy, D. & Umbreit, W. T. (2004). Tourist information search behavior: Cross-cultural comparison of European Union member states. *International Journal of Hospitality Management,* 23(1): 55–70.

Ho, C. & Liu, Y. (2005). An exploratory investigation of Web-based tourist information search behavior. *Asia Pacific Journal of Tourism Research,* 10(4): 351–60.

Holbrook, M. B. & Hirschman, E. C. (1982). The experiential aspects of consumption: Consumer fantasies, feelings, and fun. *Journal of Consumer Research,* 9(September): 132–40.

Hyde, K. (2004). A duality in vacation decision making. *Tourism Analysis*, 8(2–4): 183–86.

———. (2006). Contemporary information search strategies of destination-naive international vacationers. *Journal of Travel and Tourism Marketing*, 21(2/3): 63–76.

Hyde, K. & Lawson, R. (2003). The nature of independent travel. *Journal of Travel Research*, 42(1): 13–23.

Jenkins, R. L. (1978). Family vacation decision-making. *Journal of Travel Research*, 16(4): 2–7.

Kim, D. Y., Lehto, X. Y. & Morrison, A. M. (2007). Gender differences in online travel information search: Implications for marketing communications on the Internet. *Tourism Management*, 28(2): 423–33.

Lehto, X. Y., Kim, D. Y. & Morrison, A. M. (2006). The effect of prior destination experience on online information search behavior. *Tourism and Hospitality Research*, 6(2): 160–78.

Lo, A., Cheung, C. & Law, R. (2002). Information search behavior of Hong Kong's inbound travelers—a comparison of business and leisure travelers. *Journal of Travel and Tourism Marketing*, 13(3): 61–80.

Luo, M., Feng, R. M. & Cai, L. A. (2004). Information search behavior and tourist characteristics: The internet vis-à-vis other information sources. *Journal of Travel and Tourism Marketing*, 17(2/3): 15–25.

Money, R. B., and Crotts, J. C. (2003). The effect of uncertainty avoidance on information search, planning, and purchases of international travel vacations. *Tourism Management*, 24(2): 191–202.

Nolan, S. (1976). Tourists' use and evaluation of travel information sources. *Journal of Travel Research*, 14(3): 6–8.

Ortega, E. & Rodriguez, B. (2007). Information at tourism destinations: Importance and cross-cultural differences between international and domestic tourists. *Journal of Business Research*, 60(2): 146–52.

Pan, B. & Fesenmaier, D. (2006). Online information search: Vacation planning process. *Annals of Tourism Research*, 33(3): 809–32.

Quester, P., Neal, C., Pettigrew, S., Grimmer, M., Davis, T., & Hawkins, D. (2007). *Consumer behaviour: Implications for marketing strategy*, 5th ed. North Ryde, NSW.

Schul, P. & Crompton, J. (1983). Search behavior of international vacationers: Travel-specific lifestyle and sociodemographic variables. *Journal of Travel Research*, 22(Fall): 24–30.

Snepenger, D. (1987). Segmenting the vacation market by novelty-seeking role. *Journal of Travel Research*, 26(2): 8–14.

Snepenger, D., Meged, K., Snelly, M. & Worrall, K. (1990). Information search strategies by destination-naive tourists. *Journal of Travel Research*, 29(1): 13–16.

Snepenger, D. & Snepenger, M. (1993). Information search by pleasure travelers. In M. Khan, M. Olsen, & T. Var (Eds.), *VNR's encyclopedia of hospitality and tourism*. New York: Van Nostrand Reinhold.

Tjostheim, I. (2002). *The Internet in competition with the traditional information sources: A study of vacation planning for package vs. non-package travel*. Paper presented at the Information and Communication Technologies in Tourism 2002, Vienna.

Tjostheim, I. & Tranvoll, B. (2002). *The Internet and city tourist: A study of preferences for information sources in travel planning*. Paper presented at the City Tourism 2002, Vienna.

Udd, E., Hulac, G. . & Blazey, M. A. (1992). Effect of Washington State visitor information centers on travel behavior. *Visions in Leisure and Business*, 11(2): 5–8.

van Raaij, W. & Francken, D. (1984). Vacation decisions, activities, and satisfactions. *Annals of Tourism Research*, 11: 101–12.

Vogt, C. & Fesenmaier, D. (1998). Expanding the functional information search model. *Annals of Tourism Research*, 25(3): 551–78.

Vogt, C., Fesenmaier, D. & MacKay, K. (1993). Functional and aesthetic information needs. *Journal of Travel and Tourism Marketing*, 2(2/3): 133–46.

Weber, K. & Roehl, W. S. (1999). Profiling people searching for and purchasing travel products on the World Wide Web. *Journal of Travel Research*, 37(3): 291–98.

Part III

Evaluation of Alternatives and Choice

5 Decision Strategies in Tourism Evaluation

Alain Decrop and Metin Kozak

INTRODUCTION

Evaluation of alternatives is a cornerstone of any decision-making process (DMP). Usual models of consumer decision making (DM) entail five main stages: need (problem) recognition, search for information, evaluation of alternatives and choice, purchasing, and postpurchase evaluation (e.g., Engel, Blackwell, and Miniard, 1986; Hawkins, Best, and Coney, 1995). The evaluation stage involves the selection of one option among a set of alternatives by using a specific decision strategy or a combination of multiple strategies. Vermeir, Van Kenhove, and Hendrickx (2002: 709) underline the major role of decision strategies in consumer DM: "another important factor of the DMP is the use of decision rules [strategies]. Each consumer uses certain decision rules to base their decisions on." Of course, evaluation becomes more difficult when there are more alternatives, multiple contingencies or events, and multiple conflicting preferences and values.

The issue of vacation DM has become a focal point in tourism research during the past three decades (Decrop, 2006; Moutinho, 1987; Um and Crompton, 1990; van Raaij and Francken, 1984; Woodside and Lysonski, 1989). The majority of DM studies in travel and tourism were devoted to exploring the factors influencing one's decision while choosing a destination (evaluation of alternatives and choice). Those prior studies have failed to investigate the DM process beyond the investigation of relative influence or the identification of factors during purchasing (e.g., risks, attitudes, family structure, economic structure, etc.). Moreover, the tourism literature has often reported both conceptual and empirical studies dealing with the DMP of consumers, particularly for destination choice. Few published studies have discussed the extent to which the vacation DMP is mediated by the elaboration of decision goals and strategies such as proposed in the consumer-behavior literature. The literature generally describes how vacationers go through different stages to make their decisions, that is, searching for information, evaluating considered alternatives, and finalizing the actual choice, but it fails to explain how they handle criteria and strategies in that process. This chapter tries to fill this gap to some extent by offering an overview of decision strategies that may be used in vacation DM.

EVALUATION OF VACATION ALTERNATIVES

The evaluation of product alternatives is a central stage of most tourism DMPs. Most models of vacation DM have included it, either in the form of choice sets in structural approaches of DM (Crompton, 1977; Um and Crompton, 1990; Woodside and Lysonski, 1989) or in the form of cognitive processes (Moutinho, 1987; van Raaij and Francken, 1984). In structural or input-output approaches (Svenson, 1979), evaluation focuses on the evolution of destinations (vacation plans) in consideration sets (CS). The CS (evoked set) comprises all the destinations the vacationer is contemplating for his/her current holiday. It is part of the perceived opportunity set (awareness set), which includes all the destinations known to the vacationer. As the latter is not omniscient, the awareness set is itself only a part of the total opportunity set that entails all possible destination alternatives (Woodside and Sherell, 1977).

Choice then consists in an evaluation and selection process where the different destinations in the CS are compared on an alternative or an attribute basis. In consideration set models, the focus is on structural relationships between inputs (traveler and marketing variables) and outputs (preferences, intentions, and choices). In the process approach to DM (Svenson, 1979), the focus is not on decision in itself but rather on psycho-behavioral variables that underlie DM and on the way consumers come to have cognitive and affective judgments, intentions, commitments prior to arriving at a final decision (Abelson and Levi, 1985). Most process models are sequential as they suggest an evolution of plans and decisions through different stages with prepurchase evaluation of alternatives as a central stage.

When evaluating alternatives, consumers may rely on preexisting product evaluations stored in their memory when they have direct experience (prior purchase or consumption experiences) or indirect experience (experiences or impressions gained secondhand) with the product. In contrast, when consumers lack product experience or are not able to retrieve previous evaluations in their memory, they will construct new evaluations "on the spot." Those new evaluations are based on information acquired through internal or external search (Figure 5.1).

As suggested by Figure 5.1, there are two major ways to construct new evaluations. In the categorical process, evaluation of a choice alternative is based on the evaluation of the category to which it is assigned. Categories may be either general (e.g., holiday destinations) or specific (e.g., cultural destinations). Following that principle, the evaluation of an existing category is transferred to a new product or brand assigned to that

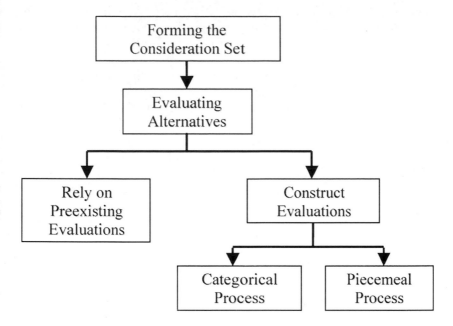

Figure 5.1 Prepurchase evaluation of alternatives.

category. Let's assume Uzbekistan is advertised as a new vacation destination; consumers could categorize it as a cultural destination based on the information they have gathered, and transfer to it positive evaluations they had before with other cultural destinations such as Egypt, Turkey, or Greece. In marketing practice, many firms use the categorization process to their advantage through such strategies as line or brand extensions. For example, Club Med has been successful in opening new resorts and developing new products such as sun cream or sunglasses much because positive evaluations of existing Club Med products have been transferred to those new offerings.

A second way to build new evaluations is the piecemeal process, which implies constructing an evaluation of a choice alternative using bits and pieces, that is, product attributes. In contrast with the categorical process, which suggests a holistic way to assess products, the piecemeal process is a more analytical approach to make decisions. It assumes that consumers do not evaluate the product as a whole but as a bundle of attributes such as price, performance, design, and so on. The piecemeal process entails two major steps. First, consumers determine particular criteria or product dimensions that will be used in evaluation. Second, they evaluate each considered alternative based on the identified criteria.

From a technical perspective, alternatives are compared on several attributes, the size of the difference between alternatives for an attribute is calculated, the value of each alternative is possibly weighted, alternatives are eliminated from the set, and the process ends when the preferred alternative is chosen (Payne, Bettman, and Johnson, 1997). For example, consider a group of people traveling to visit a destination. They may evaluate potential destinations in a piecemeal process, dealing with each specific attribute and comparing destinations on those attributes in order to find the best place to visit. We now present the range of decision strategies that may be used in such a piecemeal process.

DECISION STRATEGIES

A decision strategy is defined as "the sequence of mental and effector [actions on the decision environment] operations used to transform an initial state of knowledge into a final goal state of knowledge where the decision maker views the particular decision as solved" (Payne, Bettman, and Johnson, 1993: 9). There is substantial evidence of a strong relationship between decision goals and decision strategies. Based on the decision goal, the decision maker evaluates the costs and benefits of all these strategies and selects the strategy that represents the best accuracy-effort trade-off. This way of using decision strategies is referred to as the top-down method. But people sometimes adjust their strategies depending upon the changing task, which is an example of a bottom-up method of using decision strategies. The initial state of knowledge generally refers to general goal statements such as "to choose the best place for a family vacation" or "to choose the place with the best value for money" and so on. A set of elimination operators (i.e., editing information and using decision strategies) is applied to narrow down the range of considered alternatives (Payne et al., 1997). Through the application of additional operators and strategies, information is passed into the final goal state, where the final decision is made.

The consumer behavior and DM literature often present decision strategies from three broad perspectives: economic models, cognitive models, and simplistic models (Arnould, Price, and Zinkhan, 2004). Economic models follow the classical utilitarian approach in which consumers attempt to maximize the utility of their choices under some constraints. This principle is incorporated in a broad range of theories that are described following. Cognitive models describe consumers as combining pieces of information about alternatives and attributes to reach a decision. They emphasize beliefs rather than utilities, emotions, and behaviors. Consumers are assumed to make their decisions in a more or less systematic way by using alternative and/or attribute processing, and compensatory and/or noncompensatory rules. Simplistic models are applied by consumers to simplify their decisions mostly when they need to save time, energy, and/or money. The different strategies under those

Case Study 1. An Introduction to Decision Strategies

Imagine you were to choose a destination for your summer family holiday. Actually, you are considering three options: Turkey, Italy, or Greece. How will you evaluate those three alternatives in order to come to a final choice? This question is the focus of this paper, which deals with vacation evaluation. Of course, your choice is likely to be influenced by a substantial number of factors, including who you are as a vacationer (i.e., personal factors such as your knowledge/experience of those three destinations or your cognitive ability), with whom you are going to make your decision (i.e., social factors such as group membership or accountability to relevant others), and what the characteristics of the decision situation are (i.e., task and context factors such as available time or money). Goals that consumers pursue are another major factor influencing the evaluation process. For example, you may be driven by the goal of preserving family harmony, which will lead you to prefer Greece over the two other alternatives because both parents and children are satisfied with the solution. For achieving those goals, a broad range of decision *strategies*, also referred to as decision *rules* or *heuristics*, may be used.

three perspectives are presented next. Additional decision strategies are discussed as well, including affective rules, constraint-based heuristics, and opportunistic strategies.

Economic Decision Strategies

The maximizing rule is in line with the presentation of (bounded) rational decision makers and *expected utility theory*. The basic idea behind expected utility theory is that consumers make choices in order to maximize a utility function, subject to the constraints of time, income, information, and technology. Broadly speaking, utility refers to the amount of happiness a consumer derives from a product attribute. For example, the extent to which a vacationer may benefit from the sun and temperature in a summer destination may vary. In Figure 5.2, the utility level is plotted on the *y* axis and the amount of a particular attribute (e.g., temperature) is plotted on the *x* axis. Most utility functions have an inverted U shape, implying that consumer utility first increases when enjoying higher amounts of the attribute, comes to a peak (maximum or ideal point), and then decreases with still higher amounts of the attribute. For example, the vacationer may be happier with twenty than with ten degrees, still prefer levels up to twenty-six degrees but then start to suffer from heat and have decreasing utility amounts with higher temperature levels.

The second group of economic strategies pertains to *prospect theory*, which examines "how consumers value potential gains and losses that result from making choices" (Kahneman and Tversky, 1979). Prospect theory has put into light phenomena such as the endowment effect or decision framing. The *endowment effect* refers to the idea that consumers resist giving up something they already own. For example, when a stranger approaches John on the street and offers him 150 euros for a tourist souvenir (e.g., an antique statue) for which he has just paid 100 euros, John rejects the offer. Due to the endowment effect (and maybe to symbolic reasons as well), John values the souvenir more after he owns it. Giving up the souvenir would be viewed as a loss and losses are felt more strongly than equivalent gains (Plous, 1993).

Decision framing implies that the manner in which a decision task is (re) presented may affect preferences and final choices.Prospect theory assumes that consumers enter any decision process with an initial reference point: "if the reference point is defined in a way that the outcome appears to be a gain, decision makers will be risk averse. In contrast, if the same outcome appears to be a loss, decision makers will be risk seekers" (Arnould et al., 2004: 655). This difference in consumers' perceptions about gains and losses may be used by tourism managers. For instance, a tour operator has two ways of presenting a sales promotion. On the one hand, he could offer a 25 percent price reduction; on the other hand, he could offer a free trip with each order of three trips. These two promotions would offer the same gain to tourists, four trips for the price of three. However, according to prospect theory, tourists would value the free trip more than the discounted offer although the two promotions involve the same price savings.

Finally, the *satisficing strategy* assumes that consumers will try to make acceptable rather than optimal decisions. For example, a tourist may

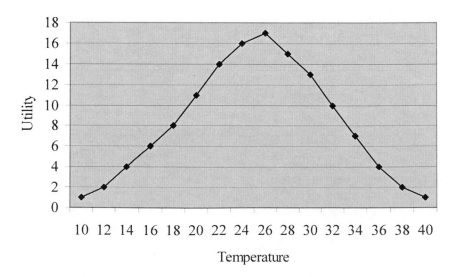

Figure 5.2 Vacationer utility function for a summer holiday destination.

choose a destination that satisfies goals of rest and relaxation while sacrificing other goals such as knowledge and discovery. Satisficing strategies imply that consumers set cutoff points on some important attributes for them and then only retain alternatives that meet those cutoff values when making their decisions. For example, Elisabeth considers distance and cost of living to be the prevailing criteria for her destination choice. She looks at three or four possible destinations but she certainly does not make an exhaustive search of every available destination. She finally chooses a destination that passes her cutoffs on distance and cost of living. This example shows that satisficing strategies are characterized by partial or abbreviated search behavior and a high level of adaptiveness (Bettman, Luce, and Payne, 1998).

Cognitive Decision Strategies

Bettman et al. (1998) propose four major dimensions to characterize cognitive decision strategies, that is, the total amount of information processed, the selectivity in information processing, whether processing is made alternative by alternative or attribute by attribute, and whether the strategy is compensatory or noncompensatory. We now shortly discuss those four dimensions. First, the amount of information that is used in evaluation can vary a great deal according to the product category and consumers' involvement with it and to the situation. For example, choosing a holiday destination may involve a detailed consideration of the available information (e.g., all cells in Table 5.1) or it may entail only a limited set of information bits (e.g., only info cells about climate). Second, information may be processed selectively, when different amounts of information are used for each alternative or attribute (e.g., all attribute information bits of Table 5.1 could be used for alternative A whereas only climate would be used for B, C, and D), or consistently when exactly the same amount of information is processed for each alternative/attribute.

The processing pattern is the third dimension that characterizes any decision strategy. The question is as to whether information will be processed line by line in Table 5.1, that is, attribute by attribute (*attribute-based process*) or column by column, that is, alternative by alternative (*alternative-based process*). In attribute-based strategies, "the values of several alternatives on a single attribute are processed before information about a second attribute is processed" (Payne et al., 1993: 31). Consumers first consider only one attribute and try to find the best alternative on that attribute although a second important attribute will be taken into account if the first one is not able to discriminate between alternatives (e.g., when there are ex-aequos). In contrast, in alternative-based strategies, "multiple attributes of a single alternative are considered before information about a second alternative is processed" (p. 31).

Finally, an important dimension of decision strategies is the extent to which they are *compensatory* or *noncompensatory*. Compensatory means that a perceived weakness of one attribute may be offset or compensated for by the perceived strength of another attribute. A positive value on one attribute can compensate for a negative value on another characteristic. For example, a poorer climate at the destination can be offset by nice shopping or relaxing nightlife perspectives. In contrast, noncompensatory strategies imply that a product's weakness on one attribute cannot be offset by strong performance on another attribute. A perceived negative value on one important/attractive attribute indicates that the alternative will never be chosen, regardless of its positive value on another attribute. For example, no matter how good a destination is on other attributes, a bad value on the most important or attractive attribute (e.g., climate) indicates that this destination would never be chosen. Thus, only one criterion can have a deciding influence on the decision process.

Attribute-based noncompensatory strategies

Bettman et al. (1998) report two strategies that rely on attribute-based noncompensatory evaluations, that is, the lexicographic and the elimination by aspect strategies. These two strategies are similar in the sense that product alternatives are compared on a single attribute before another attribute is possibly considered. According to the *lexicographic strategy*, consumers focus on a specific attribute (e.g., price, quality, etc.), which is usually the most important one, and evaluate all alternatives on that attribute. The alternative with the best value on that attribute is chosen. If more than one is evaluated similarly on that attribute, the second most important is considered, and so on, until a choice is made. Referring to the example of Table 5.1, the vacationer would first evaluate the four destinations that are part of his CS from the climate perspective.

Table 5.1 An Example of a Vacationer Decision Task

	Attribute importance ranking (weight)	Cutoff values	Performance ratings of destination alternatives			
			A	B	C	D
Climate	1 (0,4)	3	5	5	4	5
Scenery	2 (0,3)	3	4	3	5	2
Infrastructure	3 (0,2)	3	4	3	1	5
Cost	4 (0,1)	3	2	3	3	5

Rating scale: 1 = Poor, 2 = Fair, 3 = Good, 4 = Very Good, 5 = Excellent.

Case Study 2. An Example of Selected Decision Strategies

A family who is well-experienced in international tourism decides to take a summer vacation this year. The alternative destinations range from A to F. Discussions with family members result in making a choice in which they could all enjoy the activities both for children and parents. They keep three options in their set which meet their criterion at the end of the first round of elimination. But they need to introduce "climate" as the second attribute which is expected to assist them drop the two more options. In doing this, the destination "C" remains in the final set (attribute-based strategies). John is an unexperienced consumer in international tourism. His last vacation was almost five years ago. He wants to identify his favorable destination to vacation next year by checking pros and cons of five alternatives ranging from M to R. He evaluates each destination criterion by criterion that he develops by making use of the information obtained from various sources such as brochures and friends. He then compares the scores of the five alternatives and realizes that destination "P" is the best choice for him (alternative-based strategies).

As A, B, and D have the same highest score on climate (5), the second most important attribute, that is, scenery, is considered. There we see that A outperforms B and D. A is more likely to be chosen. The *elimination-by-aspect strategy* is similar to the lexicographic strategy, with the exception that an acceptable cutoff is set for each attribute. Options that do not meet the minimum cutoff value for the most important attribute are eliminated. This process continues until only one alternative remains in the choice set. In the example of Table 5.1, all cutoff values are set at three, meaning that the vacationer expects a minimum performance of "good" for each attribute. When going to climate, all four destinations pass the cutoff and are thus retained for further evaluation on the second most important attribute, that is, scenery. D is eliminated because it performs only "fairly" on scenery; A, B, and C remain in the set. When going to the third attribute, infrastructure, C is rejected because of its "poor" performance; A and B are kept for further evaluation. Finally, on cost, B passes the cutoff and not A; B is more likely to be the vacationer's final choice.

Alternative-based compensatory strategies

Beside attribute strategies, consumers may also process brands alternative by alternative using compensatory rules (Bettman et al., 1998). The *weighted-additive strategy* considers one alternative at a time and leads to the (mental) computation of a global score for each alternative resulting from the sum of the products of each attribute's subjective performance by its importance weight. The alternative with the highest overall value is chosen. Going back to the example of Table 5.1, the vacationer would compute a score for each of the four destinations that are part of his CS, leading to the following results:

- A: $(5 \times 0.4) + (4 \times 0.3) + (4 \times 0.2) + (2 \times 0.1) = 4.2$
- B: $(5 \times 0.4) + (3 \times 0.3) + (3 \times 0.2) + (3 \times 0.1) = 3.8$
- C: $(4 \times 0.4) + (5 \times 0.3) + (1 \times 0.2) + (3 \times 0.1) = 3.6$
- D: $(5 \times 0.4) + (2 \times 0.3) + (5 \times 0.2) + (5 \times 0.1) = 4.1$

Based on the weighted-additive strategy, destination A is the most likely to be chosen because it has the highest attitude score. Similarly, the *equal-weight strategy* consists in summing up an alternative's scores on all attributes considered in the evaluation process or by summing the number of times the alternative is judged favorably. However, attribute importance weights are not taken into account. From Table 5.1, this would lead to the following results:

- A: $5 + 4 + 4 + 2 = 15$
- B: $5 + 3 + 3 + 3 = 14$
- C: $4 + 5 + 1 + 3 = 13$
- D: $5 + 2 + 5 + 5 = 17$

In this case, alternative A is no longer the preferred destination but D appears to be the best option. These two strategies are similar in the sense that each alternative is given a global score and the larger this value for an alternative, the more likely it will be chosen at the end of the decision process. In the *frequency-of-good-and-bad-features strategy,* each alternative is evaluated on the basis of how good or bad it is as to the list of attributes included in the evaluation process (Alba and Marmorstein, 1987). For each attribute/feature, a cutoff level is set for specifying good and bad features. Depending on consumer's focus, s/he counts the number of good or bad features/attributes, or both, for each alternative. In Table 5.1, let's assume that the cutoff value for specifying a good feature is 3 (i.e., good) for all attributes. Destination B would be the winner because it has 4 good features whereas the three other alternatives only have 3.

Finally, the *majority-of-confirming-dimensions strategy* compares pairs of alternatives (Russo and Dosher, 1983). The values of two alternatives are compared on each attribute; the alternative with a majority of winning attribute values is retained and then compared to the next alternative from the choice set until all alternatives have been evaluated and only one option remains. For example, when first comparing A and B in Table 5.1, A outperforms B since it has two winning attributes (i.e., scenery and infrastructure) and one loosing attribute (i.e., cost). Then A is compared to C and we see that both destinations have two winning attributes. To solve this draw, we can take the score differences in absolute value for the winning attributes, resulting in a + 4 difference for A (+ 1 on climate and + 3 on infrastructure) and a + 2 difference for C (+ 1 on scenery and + 1 on cost). Again, A is considered as the winner and is finally compared to D. Here, we see that D has two winning attributes (infrastructure and cost) whereas A has only one (scenery). Following this strategy, D is considered as the best destination.

Alternative-based noncompensatory strategies

In satisficing strategies (see earlier), alternatives are considered sequentially in the choice set; the value of each attribute for the alternative at hand is considered to see whether it meets a predetermined cutoff level; if any attribute fails to meet the cutoff, that alternative is rejected and the next option is considered. The first alternative whose values meet the cutoff level for all attributes is chosen. This strategy is composed of two specific strategies: conjunctive and disjunctive (Arnould et al., 2004). In *conjunctive strategies*, consumers define minimum cutoff levels for each attribute and reject those alternatives whose values are lower than the cutoff level for any attribute. This means that in Table 5.1, A, C, and D are rejected whereas B is the winner because it passes all four cutoffs. A is eliminated because of its "fair" performance on cost, C because it is judged as "poor" on infrastructure, and D because its scenery is only "fair."

In cases where no alternative meets all cutoffs, the vacationer would have two options. The first one would be to consider destinations other than the four he initially considered. As a second option, he could lower cutoff levels for some attributes. In *disjunctive strategies*, consumers evaluate brands only on the most important attribute(s) and they only keep the alternative(s) that meet the cutoff on these attributes. In Table 5.1, A, B, and D would be considered on climate; A and B meet the cutoff on scenery and infrastructure; and only B has at least a "good" performance on cost. Again, B is the winner. These two strategies can be used as a filter to aid consumers to narrow down their choices by eliminating those out of the range.

Simple Decision Strategies

Consumers are more likely to choose *simple decision strategies* or heuristics either out of habit in routine decisions or to simplify the decision process in complex situations in which there is a large number of alternatives and attributes or a high intercorrelation among attributes, for example, between seaside and climate which complement each other for a summer vacation (Gregan-Paxton and John, 1997; Hammond, Keeney, and Raiffa, 1999; Swait and Adamowics, 2001). Those strategies are used to save time, energy, and money while simplifying consumers' decisions at the same time. For example, following a *brand-loyalty strategy*, the same alternative may always be chosen by consumers whose DMP is driven by routine and habit, due to a strong preference for a particular product/brand, or because a high level of risk aversion. Many vacationers are loyal to a destination or even to a particular hotel where they are going each year; they do not use complex decision strategies but just decide to live the same experience as before.

The *brand-familiarity strategy* consists in choosing well-established and well-known products/brands as a mere exposure effect or because reputation is used as a cue for inferring quality. Inexperienced consumers are more likely to select familiar products/brands to reassure themselves; they pay utmost attention to external factors such as packaging, appearance, and so on. For example, a French vacationer going to Egypt for the first time may prefer to stay in a hotel from chains he knows like Mercure or Novotel rather than choosing local brands he is not familiar with. Alternatively, in *price-related strategies*, consumers' final decisions are directed by sudden cuts in product prices resulting from sale promotions or coupons. For example, a vacationer could choose the cheapest travel package available or buy a last-minute offer.

Finally, the *avoiding-regret strategy* (or avoiding dissonance) consists in making a decision consumers are least likely to regret. Dissonance is a psychological state of feeling uncertain about the correct choice to make. It is most likely to occur when more than one alternative is attractive and the decision is important. Bettman et al. (1998) have shown that minimizing the experience of negative emotion may be a major goal when making choices. Therefore, some consumers will prefer to make a "safe" choice (i.e., a choice they are not likely to regret) rather than an optimal choice. For example, they will search for additional information from sources such as experts of magazines, in order to make the preferred/chosen alternative more attractive and the rejected ones less attractive, thereby reducing dissonance, regret, and other negative emotions.

Other Specific Decision Strategies

According to the rule of emotion-based strategies, sometimes tourists make their decisions in a more affective and embodied way than suggested by the cognitive strategies. Sometimes, the decision maker has a "gut feeling" about the right choice; s/he feels that the decision "fits like a glove" (FLAG). The central role of emotions and the embodied mind in fulfilling choices has been well documented in the literature (e.g., Lakoff and Johnson, 1999): "emotions may reflect deeply rooted cultural models about what's appropriate or moral, or may embody feelings we have for other people" (Arnould et al., 2004: 659). Embodied decision making refers to strategies based on a holistic perception and comprehension of a gestalt scenario. Woodside, Caldwell, and Spurr (2006) have explained how the FLAG model and ecological-systems theory are relevant and useful to account for leisure and tourism choices. For them, the decision to travel is not usually one that is rational and planned but one that is often automatic and unconscious: "the combination of an individual's lived experiences with their history, social environment and enabling factors make up a causal historical wave, which hits consumers when making a choice" (Woodside, 2006: xxi).

The discussion of decision strategies should be completed by a short description of adaptive strategies which include constraint-based and opportunistic strategies. In *constraint-based strategies*, the decision is ruled by elements external to the decision item itself, like constraints, motives, or other decision criteria (Decrop and Snelders, 2005). Three types of constraints can be considered as a barrier on decisions (McGuiggan, 2004): intrapersonal (attitudes, values, sociodemographics), interpersonal (group of friends, family structure), and structural (finance, time, climate, access problems). Some vacationers are weighted down by contextual inhibitors such as limited financial resources or the intervention of situational variables (e.g., house moving, health problems). Others are constrained by interpersonal differences or/and conflicts that arise within the decision-making unit. As a consequence, constrained vacationers are not really involved in a DMP; information search is very limited and passive, if existing at all; evaluation strategies are not elaborated but they just take the only decision that is possible according to the constraint(s).

Next, consumers may be characterized by *opportunistic-decision strategies* when they lack well-defined decision criteria and are open to many alternatives (Decrop, 2006). They do not use any well-defined strategy in making their vacation decisions. Decisions are not very planned nor reasoned but result from opportunities or special occasions. This may be an advertised commercial offer, or propositions or invitations by family and friends. Vacation choices are made haphazardly during discussions, meetings, walks, or phone calls. Both constraint-based and opportunistic strategies may be paralleled with the ideas of constructive choice processes (Bettman et al., 1998) and of "garbage-can" decision process (Cohen, March, and Olsen, 1972) in which almost any vacation solution can be associated with any problem, provided they are evoked at the same time. Decision strategies are developed as long as they are needed and are connected with the problem structure. With this in mind, several authors report that the opportunistic strategy represents a more bottom-up approach on product evaluation and involves editing (identical alternatives and attributes are eliminated) and problem restructuring (the information is reorganized to the changing task) during the decision process (Payne et al., 1993).

CONCLUSION AND IMPLICATIONS

In this conceptual chapter, there has been a particular attempt to investigate strategies that are used in vacation decision making. The strategies presented thus far have contained only those which are most commonly addressed in decision-making research. This chapter contributes to the literature in the sense that vacation decision making is classified on the basis of its timing, goals, and strategies. Although the literature illustrates the existence of a variety of strategies that individuals use in making their definite or indefinite choices, this study is limited to outline only those potential strategies that can be applied into vacation decision making. Some of these strategies have been identified and transformed into vacation decision-making settings; and also their descriptions and properties are given in this context. As understanding the factors that will determine the type of a strategy to be used while making a choice is of crucial importance for academics and practitioners alike, this study also poses theoretical implications.

One series of current research suggests that developing a model that fits all decision makers and every decision situation in a vacation evaluation may not be realistic as a vacation (leisure travel, tour, or trip) involves a lot of decisions and subdecisions (Decrop and Snelders, 2005; Sirakaya and Woodside, 2005). One useful approach is the segmentation of travel markets by taking into account their trip purposes (such as taking a pleasure vacation versus visiting family and friends, or leisure travel versus business travel). According to this line of argument, decision makers in different segments might have dissimilar approaches to solving their decision problems. For example, a potential traveler who is interested in visiting friends and relatives might lean towards applying a different decision-making strategy (i.e., low-involvement, less-risky conditions) than a person who is taking a pleasure vacation trip to an unfamiliar destination (i.e., high involvement, high perceived risk). This example points to the notion that decision strategies may be variant across those vacationers with different interests and reasons which needs further investigation of the vacation decision-making behavior.

Practically, the consideration of such strategies is expected to provide an insight into how and the extent to which they are useful in understanding vacation choices. Depending upon the type of strategies used by vacationers, tourism providers may have the opportunity to explore their most important attributes perceived by vacationers or their comparative weights with other alternative destinations, to which they should pay utmost consideration while designing their future marketing campaigns. Consequently, the ability of any vacation destination or tourism organization to increase its market share, the number of visitors, and thereby tourism revenues depend on a better assessment of the factors influencing consumer behavior on decision making, developing appropriate policies and strategies for this, and implementing them into the practice accordingly. For instance, compensatory strategies do not constitute any need about performance improvement; noncompensatory strategies are more likely to signal the need to develop effective managerial and marketing strategies to revisit those areas where service providers negatively perform.

REFERENCES

Abelson, R. P. & Levi, A. (1985). Decision making and decision theory. In G. Lindzey & E. Aronson (Eds.), *The handbook of social psychology,* pp. 231–309. New York: Random House.

Alba, J. W. & H. Marmorstein (1987). The effects of frequency knowledge on consumer decision making. *Journal of Consumer Research,* 14: 14–26.

Arnould, E., Price, L. & Zinkhan, G. (2004). *Consumers,* 2nd ed. New York: Irwin.

Bettman, J. R., Luce, M. F. & Payne, J. W. (1998). Constructive consumer choice processes. *Journal of Consumer Research,* 25: 187–217.

Cohen, M. D., March, J. G. & Olsen, J. (1972). A garbage can model of organizational choice. *Administrative Science Quarterly,* 17: 1–24.

Crompton, J. L. (1977). A systems model of the tourist's destination selection decision process with particular reference to the role of image and perceived constraints. Unpublished doctoral dissertation, Texas A&M University.

Decrop A. (2006). *Vacation decision making.* Oxon: CABI.

Decrop, A. & Snelders, D. (2005). A grounded typology of vacation decision making. *Tourism Management,* 26: 121–32.

Engel, J. F., Blackwell, R. D. & Miniard, P. (1986). *Consumer behavior,* 5th ed. Chicago: Dryden Press.

Gregan-Paxton, J. & John, D. R. (1997). Consumer learning by analogy: A model of internal knowledge transfer. *Journal of Consumer Research,* 24(3): 266–84.

Hammond, J. S., Keeney, R. L. & Raiffa, H. (1999). *Smart choices: A practical guide to making better decisions.* Boston: Harvard Business School Press.

Hawkins, D. I., Best, R. J. & Coney, K. A. (1995). *Consumer behaviour: Implications for marketing strategy,* 6th ed. Homewood, IL: Irwin Publishing.

Kahneman, D. & Tversky, A. (1979). Prospect theory: An analysis of decisions under risk. *Econometrica,* 47: 263–91.

Lakoff, G. & Johnson, M. (1999). *Philosophy in the flesh: The embodied mind and its challenge to Western thought.* New York: Basic Books.

McGuiggan, R. L. (2004). A model of vacation choice: An integration of personality and vacation choice with leisure constraints theory. In G. I. Crouch, R. R. Purdue, H. J. P. Timmermans, and M. Uysal (Eds.), *Consumer psychology of tourism, hospitality and leisure,* vol. 3, pp.169–80. Oxon: CABI.

Moutinho, L. (1987). Consumer behaviour in tourism. *European Journal of Marketing,* 21(10): 2–44.

Payne, J. W., Bettman, J. R. & Johnson, E. J. (1993). *The adaptive decision maker.* Cambridge: Cambridge University Press.

Payne, John W., Bettman, James R. & Johnson, Eric J. (1997). The adaptive decision maker: Effort and accuracy in choice. In W. M. Goldstein and R. M. Hogarth (Eds.), *Research on Judgment and Decision Making: Currents, Connections and Controversies,* pp. 181–204. Cambridge: Cambridge University Press.

Plous, S. (1993). *The psychology of judgment and decision making.* New York: McGraw-Hill.

Russo, J. E. & Dosher, B. A. (1983). Strategies for multi-attribute binary choice. *Journal of Experimental Psychology: Learning, Memory and Cognition,* 17: 759–69.

Sirakaya, E. & Woodside, A. G. (2005). Building and testing theories of decision making by travellers. *Tourism Management,* 26(6): 815–32.

Svenson, O. (1979). Process descriptions of decision making. *Organizational Behavior and Human Performance,* 23: 86–112.

Swait, J. & Adamowics, W. (2001). The Influence of task complexity on consumer choice: A latent model of decision strategy switching. *Journal of Consumer Research*, 28: 135–48.

Um, S. & Crompton, J. L. (1990). Attitude determinants in tourism destination choice. *Annals of Tourism Research*, 17: 432–48.

van Raaij, W. F. & Francken, D. A. (1984). Vacations decisions, activities and satisfaction. *Annals of Tourism Research*, 11: 101–12.

Vermeir, I., Van Kenhove, P. & Hendrickx, H. (2002). The influence of needs for closure on consumer's choice behavior. *Journal of Economic Psychology*, 23: 703–17.

Woodside, A. G. (2006). Vacation decision making: Bridging leisure, tourism and consumer behavior. In A. Decrop, *Vacation decision making*. Oxfordshire, UK: CABI.

Woodside, A. G., Caldwell, M. & Spurr, R. (2006). Advancing ecological systems theory in lifestyle, leisure, and travel research. *Journal of Travel Research*, 44(3): 259–72.

Woodside, A. G. & Lysonski, S. (1989). A general model of traveler destination choice. *Journal of Travel Research*, 27(1): 8–14.

Woodside, A. G. & Sherell, D. (1977). Traveler Evoked, Inept and Inert sets of Vacation Destinations. *Journal of Travel Research*. 16 (1): 14–18.

6 Planning and Exploratory Buying Behavior

Karin Teichmann and Andreas H. Zins

INTRODUCTION

Exploratory behavior has a long tradition in the psychology literature. The concept of the optimum stimulation level (OLS) was simultaneously introduced by two psychologist researchers: Donald Olding Hebb (1955) and Clarence Leuba (1955). OLS assumes that each individual has a certain need for stimulation. The optimum level is the stimulation level that is preferred and adjusted through increasing and decreasing the stimulation level, respectively, in order to balance the discrepancy to the optimum. This behavior of modifying the level of stimulation is termed as "exploratory behavior" (Raju, 1980). Basically, the concept of exploratory behavior supports the understanding of the effects of stimulus repetition, response to stimulus characteristics (e.g., novelty), individual differences in exploratory behavior, and information-search behavior of consumers. Raju (1980: 278–79) tried to classify the basic motivation underlying exploratory consumer behavior and differentiates seven types of exploratory behavior:

- *Innovativeness*: "the eagerness to buy or know about new products/ services";
- *Risk taking*: "a preference for taking risks or being adventurous";
- *Interpersonal communication*: "communicating with friends about purchases";
- *Information seeking*: "interest in knowing about various products and brands mainly out of curiosity";
- *Exploration through shopping*: "a preference for shopping and investigating brands";
- *Brand switching*: "switching brands primarily for change or variety";
- *Repetitive behavior proneness*: "the tendency to stick with the same response over time."

Basically, these types of behavior can be assigned to three motivations, namely, risk taking, curiosity-motivated behaviors, and variety seeking (see Table 6.1). Risk taking arouses from the desire to make "innovative

Table 6.1 Types of Exploratory Behavior

Risk Taking	Curiosity-Motivated Behaviors	Variety Seeking
• Innovativeness • Risk Taking	• Interpersonal Communication • Information Seeking • Recreational Shopping	• Brand Switching • Repetitive Behavior Proneness

Source: McAlister and Pessemier, 1982; Raju, 1980.

decisions" (Steenkamp and Baumgartner, 1992: 435), while curiosity-motivated behavior is defined as "the desire for knowledge for intrinsic reasons." In a consumer-behavior context, the tendency to risk taking implies that consumers are intrinsically motivated to experience novel products. Curiosity-motivated behaviors, on the other hand, express the wish to acquire information and knowledge. Variety-seeking behavior has been described as "those mechanisms which lead individuals to engage in varied behaviors" (McAlister and Pessemier, 1982: 311). In a consumption context this means that customers do not switch due to changed conditions or preferences, but because of the variation per se. In contrast to risk-taking tendency, variety seekers are thus motivated to experience and switch between products and brands they are already familiar with.

All these activities have in common that they are primarily intrinsically rewarding. These behaviors provide customers with stimulation and thus can be considered as having strong exploratory characteristics (Baumgartner and Steenkamp, 1996). As the list of behaviors is extensively accepted, their conceptualization meets with a square refusal. The trichotomy of exploratory behavior has also been criticized in literature. Steenkamp and Baumgartner (1995) argue that a strict distinction between the factors risk taking and variety seeking cannot be made. To better understand their reasoning, the authors give the example of trying a novel brand in a familiar product class that can satisfy both risk-taking and variety-seeking motives. On the other hand, a familiar brand that has not been used for some time might also entail risks.

TYPES OF EXPLORATORY BEHAVIOR

Innovativeness

The term "innovation" is coined predominantly from an entrepreneurial perspective and from the supply side in general. In this respect, production and logistic conditions, technologies, products, processes, and sometime target markets are qualified in terms of their newness in order to describe the degree of innovative attitude and behavior of companies. Even the investigation of consumers participating in the innovation development of firms is seen as a multistage process where ideas for innovations are generated through implicit or explicit feedback from the consumer side and not from the consumption experience itself. In contrast, Raju's concept of innovativeness refers to the degree of novelty a consumer is looking for. From this point of view many prominent publications can be referred to investigating the motivations behind traveling. Many of these studies stick to the concept of novelty seeking; some as the focal parameter, others as a component of an array of diverse driving forces.

Beard and Ragheb (1983) developed a four-dimensional Leisure Motivation Scale covering different domains and aspects of exploratory engagements. They distinguish an intellectual motive with mental activities involved allowing learning, exploring, discovering, or imagining; a social dimension offering interpersonal relationships and an esteem-of-others component; a competence-mastery factor offering the traveler achievement, challenge, or even competition; and finally, a stimulus-avoidance motive addressing the possibility to escape from routine environments into conditions and situations with lower stimulation levels. Ryan and Glendon (1998) replicated this instrument in a British context resulting in similar four motivational dimensions. All four major areas offer the traveler stimulating experiences: either by changing the activities in a well-known environment, by repeating familiar activities in new environments with maybe different social encounters, or by both.

Another conceptualization of leisure and tourism motivation was initiated by Iso-Ahola (1980). The basic assumption of his theory proposes two mutually nonexclusive factors: a seeking element (with intrinsic rewards) and an escape element (from routine environments). Later, this dual array was extended by a personal (psychological) and an interpersonal (social) component (Dunn Ross and Iso-Ahola, 1991) for both dimensions. Snepenger et al. (2006) tested this structure in tourism and recreation contexts concluding that personal seeking, personal escape, interpersonal seeking, and interpersonal escape seem to be an optimal approximation of the social psychological states related to tourism (as opposed to simpler models such as one- or two-dimensional or more complex higher-order configurations). The seeking dimensions come close to the concept of new experiences or Raju's innovative behavior: meeting new people, staying with people of similar interests, facing new things.

Lee and Crompton (1992) report on the development and validation of a novelty-seeking scale in tourism. They argue that a tourist's perception of the degree of novelty is associated with the perceived novelty of objects (e.g., historical landmarks), the environment (the cultural atmosphere), and other people (residents or visitors). The degree of novelty or familiarity (as the antithesis) is influenced by the degree of recency and intensity: With reference to the works of Berlyne (e.g., 1950), it is posited that novelty triggers exploratory behavior. However, this relationship was found to be U-shaped considering a discouraging effect by too extremely novel stimuli.

Based on literature review, Lee and Crompton (1992) proposed six dimensions for the novelty construct: change from routine, escape, thrill, adventure, surprise, and boredom alleviation. After having tested and validated the construct and the respective items on four independent samples, only four dimensions delivered a stable and meaningful configuration: thrill, change from routine, boredom alleviation, and surprise.

Another line of research into tourist motivations is based on Cohen's work differentiating tourist roles for international tourism (1972). His typology builds on the concept of novelty, which reflects a "desire for variety, novelty, and strangeness" (1972: 172). The familiarity-novelty continuum splits into three distinct dimensions: 1. Travel destination where people, places, and culture of a foreign country play the major role; 2. Institutionalized settings while on travel (the so-called environmental bubble), and 3. Social contact referring to the extent and variety of social contacts with local people. Mo, Howard, and Havitz (1993) developed, tested, and validated a measurement instrument which is based on this three-dimensional model. Jiang, Havitz, and O'Brien (2000) reanalyzed the twenty-items instrument. Gnoth and Zins (2008) again tested this International Tourist Role Scale (ITR) in Asian destination countries with travelers from a great variety of generating countries. In total, eighteen of the twenty original statements contribute to the meaningful measurement of travel-motivation dimensions anchored along a familiarity-novelty continuum (destination orientation, travel service or arrangement, and social contact).

Risk Taking

In almost all conceptualizations for exploratory intentions and activities, risk perceptions appear to play an elementary role. In most of the cases, risk is treated as an explanatory or intervening construct by which unplanned or undesirable effects are incorporated with a variable degree of uncertainty attached to it. However, concepts and meaning differ widely, while applications in the tourism domain are rather scarce. A limited number of dimensions have been developed in the perceived risk literature which is used to define the risk concept. Recent reviews are delivered by Mitchell (1998). In general, the following generic dimensions are widely accepted and used in various risk studies: financial, performance, physiological, psychological, social, and time risk (Cox, 1967; Peter and Ryan, 1976; to mention only the innovators with respect to particular facets). Two critical issues have to be made with respect to risk dimensions.

First, the psychometric properties of the risk construct do not seem to allow building unweighted indices or aggregated risk scores. Risk dimensions show different effects on overall perceived risk. The weights for the various risk dimensions vary according to the products and services and situations. Apart from this, they are mutually not independent (Chaudhuri,

1998; Jacoby and Kaplan, 1972; Stone and Gronhaug, 1993). Second, the outlined risk dimensions touch different aspects and stages of the consumption process. Functional or equipment risks (e.g., Roehl and Fesenmaier, 1992) address the compound quality expectation. Mitchell and Greatorex (1990) argue that before negative consequences could occur, the performance, function, or equipment would have to defect.

The latest supplement of risk dimensions refers to a category called satisfaction risk (Garner, 1986; Roehl and Fesenmaier, 1992). This facet can be seen as the emotional response to the purchase act or the product and service experience. It depends partly on the expected performance and partly on the psychological achievements associated with the product. While these facets cover different "get" components, time and financial risk address "give" components of the exchange process of consumption. The latter two describe more personal or personality-related characteristics than purchase, product, or situation-specific facets. They are suitable to define a consumer's wealth position, which puts the consumer in a more or less favorable situation to absorb losses (Dowling and Staelin, 1994).

Dowling (1986) gives a classification of risk measures according to different levels of abstraction. At the high level, we find the subjective desirability of risky situations as a general aspect of risk perception. At the intermediate level, risk measures are identified such as general risk handling with respect to new products (Schiffman, 1972) and constructs proposed by Bettman (1973) such as inherent and handled risk. At neither level can an explicit limitation to negatively shaped uncertainty be determined. Even at the low level, conceptual definitions of perceived risk have been proposed that comprise just the uncertainty aspect of purchase or consumption consequences. In contrast, the majority of low-level conceptualizations focus on adverse consequences. This inconsistency of conceptual boundaries has not been discussed so far. Nevertheless, it is conceivable that risk aversion is strongly related to efforts reducing the uncertainty associated with desired purchase outcomes.

Roehl (1988) worked on the development of a risk typology for holiday trips. He used the array of seven risk components (already known from Cheron and Ritchie, 1982), applying them to traveling in general and to the most recent trip. The fourteen risk measures were reduced to three risk dimensions: physical-equipment risk, vacation risk, and destination risk, with social risk not being strongly correlated to any of the three. Mitchell, Davies, Moutinho, and Vassos (1999) tried to advance the insights into the role of perceived risk in tourism behavior. They detailed the list of risk components into forty-three risk attributes which represent a part of all holiday attributes covering functional, financial, hotel dominated, tour operator related as well as destination specific aspects. Their study applied neural network analyses for associating different types of risks to a list of fifteen risk reduction strategies and finally to purchase intention using undergraduate students as study subjects.

Case Study 1. Taking Risks versus Avoiding Surprises

Elisabeth and Franz are working for the same company in Vienna. After both of them return from their summer holidays, they meet for lunch in the company's cafeteria and start talking about their vacation. Elisabeth spent her holidays as a backpacking tourist in Australia together with her friend Karl: "We had such wonderful six weeks . . . seeing and doing so much. It was awesome and extremely thrilling. We had only bought the flight tickets and we traveled cross-country. What a huge country! Sometimes the weather was not so nice and we had to change our plans. . . ." Franz says he is very happy his holiday was relaxing. He spent two weeks in Izmir, Turkey, with his wife and their two kids. "We've been there before and we are happy now that we have found a very nice place where we can spend our holidays. The food was as excellent as last year and we really enjoyed the sun and the beach. We knew from last year's trip which rooms had the best view. This was convenient when we made the reservation . . . no nasty surprises!"

McIntyre (2007) considers a totally different approach to the role and effect of risk in tourism consumption. From a series of different focus-group discussions, McIntyre develops his Survival Theory in contrast to the Risk Theory (Ewert, 1989) and the Insight Theory (Walle, 1997). He differentiates an everyday life state of mind from a holiday state of mind, describing the latter as being "generally a pleasure-seeking, although not necessarily purely hedonistic, one. . . . This affective state complements a proposed social and individual learning role of tourism/holidaymaking, partly operative at a subconscious or unconscious level, and based on the need for 'risk' consumption behaviors to stimulate a form of learning." (McIntyre, 2007: 125). This drive-based theory on tourist consumption motivation considers risk from a holistic perspective that is generally seen as a positive driving force. In this respect, McIntyre's Survival Theory comes much closer to the idea of exploratory behavior which is devised to adjust to the individual (optimum) stimulation level.

Interpersonal Communication

The exchange of product-related information between consumers—better known as "word of mouth (WOM)"—is an informal source of information since this type of communication is free from perceived commercial bias (Litvin, Goldsmith, and Pan, 2008). WOM comes close to Raju's "communicating with friends about purchases" but includes also people other than friends. Especially for tourists, sharing travel experiences can give pleasure to them when they return from their trip. Consumers are most likely to spread WOM when they associate affects and emotions with a product experience. When sharing these experiences with others, consumers can relieve tension which originates from positive or negative product experiences (Litvin et al., 2008). Some consumers are highly interactive and especially keen on sharing market-related information with others. Feick and Price (1987) refer to these consumers as "market mavens." Market mavens are attentive to market-related information and more involved in the marketplace.

Marketers have a special interest in consumers' information exchange since it has long been recognized that face-to-face communication is more effective in influencing consumers' purchase decisions than print media, broadcast media, or information from salespeople (Katz and Lazarfeld, 1955). The recent advancement of new communication technologies allows for word of mouth (WOM) communicated by electronic means such as instant messaging, e-mail, chat rooms, or blogs (Litvin et al., 2008). Consumers increasingly use reviews, as one form of electronic WOM, to support their decision making. Doing so, consumers are able to receive seller-independent information which helps them to make their own interpretation of products based on experiences of others. This development, however, facilitates companies adopting viral marketing practices and the characteristic of WOM as an informal source can thus be violated.

Information Seeking and Exploration through Shopping

In the travel-related context both concepts—information seeking and exploration through shopping—are very close to each other since the buying process mainly refers to the process of trip planning. Baumgartner and Steenkamp (1996) developed a two-dimensional framework of a consumer's tendency to engage in exploratory buying behavior. The authors distinguish exploratory acquisition of products (EAP) and exploratory information seeking (EIS). While EAP focuses on a "consumer's tendency to seek sensory stimulation in product purchase through risky and innovative product choices and varied and changing experiences" (Baumgartner and Steenkamp 1996: 124), EIS concentrates on the satisfaction of "cognitive stimulation needs through the acquisition of consumption relevant knowledge out of curiosity" (p. 123). Raju's definition of information seeking and recreational shopping comes very close to the definition of EIS. Baumgartner and Steenkamp (1996) argue that consumers who show a high tendency of exploratory information seeking enjoy going browsing and window shopping as well as like to communicate and inform themselves about consumption experiences.

While the focus of the role of information search was first on utility maximization and uncertainty minimization, the senses of tourism researchers have sharpened over the years. For many years, researchers mainly focused on the study of goal-oriented consumers' information search. However, there have been several research attempts showing that information search does not necessarily result in purchase. The concept of ongoing search or browsing raises this issue. Ongoing or continuous search encompasses search activities that are independent from the intention to purchase a product or make a decision. Prepurchase search, on the other hand, aims at improving purchase decisions. In a tourism and leisure context, magazine subscriptions or club membership may be examples of ongoing search activities. Also, browsing through travel catalogues, DMO Web sites, or travel agents' Web sites out of curiosity refers to ongoing search if the activities do not purpose decision making or purchasing.

Tourist information search is thus no longer considered a consequence of rational thinking or goal-oriented behavior. Tourists do not search information because they want to minimize the risk of their decision outcome. In fact, hedonic dimensions of information search have been added to the field of research interest and investigated more deeply. Tourists conduct information search because they want to satisfy their need for entertainment. In addition, being knowledgeable about traveling can even facilitate establishing a basis for communication with others—especially with regards to consumer reviews or blogging. Also, reading through tourist magazines, browsing on Web sites with travel-specific content, or watching tourism-related programs can give pleasure to travel-interested individuals (Gursoy and McCleary, 2004) or even encourage daydreaming. Processing tourism-related information, to a certain degree, is thus considered to be part of the travel experience.

Brand Switching

As McAlister (1982) argues, brand switching can occur for a number of reasons. For instance, external factors such as marketing or accessibility of a product can cause consumers' switching to another brand. However, only switching for the sake of variety refers to consumers' desire for stimulation. This refers to brand switching according to Raju's exploratory behavior of "switching brands primarily for change or variety." Van Trijp (1989) distinguishes three different conceptualizations of variety: variation-in-behavior or varied behavior, variety-seeking behavior, and variety-seeking tendency. Variation-in-behavior denotes the observable change of a consumer's behavior that is independent from the underlying motivation. For instance, variation in an individual's taste or changing conditions such as a new product launch or out-of-stock situations can prompt consumers to change their behavior. Also, if the product is to satisfy not only the individual but also other product users' needs, a variation in consumption behavior is likely. Varied behavior is thus only due to changing situations. It is not due to a change in individual's desire for variation.

The second classification of variety, variety-seeking behavior, is characterized by brand switching for the sake of variety. In this case, variety is independent from a change in an individual's preferences and the resulting change in utility is independent from the brand. In contrast to variation-in-behavior, variety-seeking behavior denotes the change in behavior which results from the individual motivation for variety. Thus, a consumer who switches from one product to another does so because s/he derives a utility from brand switching and not because s/he is dissatisfied or not loyal to a brand (Helmig, 1997). A strong connection has been found between variety-seeking behavior and optimum stimulation levels: the higher the stimulation needs are, the more likely people show variety-seeking behavior (Joachimsthaler and Lastovicka, 1984; McAlister and Pessemier, 1982; Raju, 1980; Steenkamp and Baumgartner, 1992).

Variety-seeking tendency, the third conceptualization of variety, denotes the fact that consumers vary in their tendency to seek variation. This tendency is considered as an "intervening variable which impacts consumer behavior together with other variables" such as personality (Helmig, 1997: 36). In the tourism context, variety seeking can be manifold: switching to a different tour operator, to another hotel, or even to another destination all refer to variety seeking in a tourism-related context (see Case Study 2). Typical variety seekers are tourists who want to experience something new and who are not afraid of taking chances in trying unfamiliar travel destinations. In addition to that, changing purposes of leisure travel (e.g., recreation, cultural events, sports, etc.) also refer to an individual's motivation to seek variety.

Repetitive Behavior Proneness

In the tourism literature, repeat visitation is often seen as an advantage for tourism marketers due to reduced marketing costs, positive word-of-mouth effects if previous visitors were satisfied with their experience, and stable tourist revenue. In an early study of repeat visitation, Gitelson and Crompton (1984) identified five factors which contributed to people returning to a familiar destination. Repeat visitation was perceived to (1) reduce the risk of an unsatisfactory experience, (2) assure that visitors would find their own kind of people there, (3) provide emotional childhood attachment, (4) give opportunities to experience previously omitted aspects of the destination, and finally (5) to expose others to an experience which had been satisfying. The authors found that travelers seeking relaxation were more likely to visit familiar destinations, whereas visiting new sites was ascribed to younger people seeking variety and novel experiences. Similarly, Bello and Etzel (1985) evidenced that individuals who seek arousal in their pleasure travel are more likely to travel to novel sites than individuals who have a stressful life and who, therefore, prefer familiar destinations.

While the concept of loyalty has a long tradition in the consumer-behavior literature, loyalty in tourism-related research is a much more recent phenomenon, dating back to the early 1990s. Repeat visitation is considered to be a vital factor in the broader field of loyalty and has been used to measure

---

Case Study 2. Seeking Variety versus Being Loyal to the Same Place

An excerpt from an in-depth interview with two individuals indicates that Interviewee A (male, fifty-three years, two children, widowed but now living with a partner) has vacationed in Croatia for more than twenty years. His family owns a sailboat in the harbor of Pula, Istria. "The reason why we always come here *(Croatia, A. N.)* is because we own this boat. It is scenic and this place offers lots of great opportunities. Still, I do not know all of them! We have some variation but basically the people are the same. There are a few places I like to call at every time . . . A little variation, however, is enjoyable." For Interviewee B (female, fifty-seven years, four children, living with a partner), it is important to have some variation in her holiday plans and in destinations visited. She enjoys getting to know different cultures and people and prefers adventure vacations. The only reason why she does not revisit a destination is for the sake of variety. "I've been to Ecuador three times and I won't go there anymore because I've seen it! There are so many other beautiful countries in South-America which I don't know."

---

tourists' destination loyalty (Chen and Gursoy, 2001; Kozak, Huan, and Beaman, 2002). However, according to Chen and Gursoy (2001: 80), repeat purchase of tourism products (i.e., repeat visitation) is not an appropriate measure for destination loyalty since "a touristic product, which is tied to total trip experience and novelty, differs from a manufactured product." This is obvious since for most people planning a summer vacation is an often long-prepared and high-involvement process with budgeted expenditure (Kozak et al., 2002). Chen and Gursoy (2001: 80) argue that for a product, all loyalty indicators are appropriate, whereas for a destination only one indicator, such as the intention to recommend the destination to others, is sufficient in order to measure destination loyalty. Other types of loyalty in the tourism context refer to loyalty with travel agencies, hotels, and tour operators.

CONCLUSION AND IMPLICATIONS

Exploratory travel behavior addresses consumption experiences which are defined to be essentially intrinsically rewarding. It covers a broad array of motivational settings that are directed towards regulating the traveler's individual stimulation level. This chapter linked the discussion about exploratory consumer behavior to Raju's classification (1980) of its underlying motivational drivers. Following his proposal of seven domains, it can be concluded that exploratory experiences may appear in all phases of a consumption episode. During the preparatory stage, the information-gathering process as well as the knowledge acquisition per se are potential sources for stimulating outcomes. The factors "innovativeness," "information seeking," and "exploration through shopping" can be attributed to this domain. "Brand-switching" behavior and "innovativeness" are characteristics of the outcome of the decision-making process.

During the travel experience, "risk taking" and "repetitive behavior proneness" are the most appropriate facets of regulating one's stimulation level. Depending on the preferred level, risk taking or repetitive behavior proneness can either increase or decrease the stimulation level in order to balance the discrepancy to the optimum. However, it was mentioned that the concept of risk can be split into different levels of abstractions. Only the subjective desirability of risky situations comes close to the motivational energy behind the need for exploratory experiences. In contrast, conceptualizations of perceived risk on low level focus on negative consequences and their uncertain occurrence, which does not imply any risk-prone or risk-adverse position of the consumer.

Finally, "interpersonal communication" may take place in all phases of the travel purchase and consumption. It acts as a means of information exchange activity beforehand and, hence, fulfills either curiosity-seeking needs or contributions to risk reduction. The notion of market mavens was briefly touched on in relation with word-of-mouth communication. The existence of this kind of consumers is not only interesting as a rich source of market-related information but also important for WOM communication after a particular travel experience. For the individual traveler, instances to share experiences and knowledge may act as stimulating as well. In addition, social contacts may be more or less existing during traveling. Sharing information about different cultures with hosts and/or other travelers can be seen as exploratory activities from both perspectives, as a process of interaction and as the outcome of a different knowledge level.

This chapter followed the framework of exploratory behavior outlined by Raju (1980) and investigated the existing tourism behavior literature along his seven different types of motivating deeds: innovativeness, risk taking, interpersonal communication, information seeking, exploration through shopping, brand switching, and repetitive-behavior proneness. Only a few publications can be found through the keyword "exploratory." Yet, many of the seven areas are touched by similar and closely related research topics. In general, one could expect to find most of the topics addressed in studies and publications about travel motivations. However, issues such as risk, brand switching, or communications are primarily focused on through other perspectives.

REFERENCES

Baumgartner, H. & Steenkamp, J.-B. E. M. (1996). Exploratory consumer buying behavior: Conceptualization and measurement. *International Journal of Research in Marketing*, 13: 121–37.

Beard, J. G. & Ragheb, M. G. (1983). Measuring leisure motivation. *Journal of Leisure Research*, 15: 219–28.

Bello, D. C. & Etzel, M. J. (1985). The role of novelty in the pleasure travel experience. *Journal of Travel Research*, 24(1): 20–26.

Berlyne, D. E. (1950). Novelty and curiosity as determinants of exploratory behavior. *British Journal of Psychology*, 41: 68–80.

Bettman, J. R. (1973). Perceived risk and its components: A model and empirical test. *Journal of Marketing Research*, 10: 184–90.

Chaudhuri, A. (1998). Product class effects on perceived risk: The role of emotion. *International Journal of Research in Marketing*, 15: 157–68.

Chen, J. S. & Gursoy, D. (2001). An investigation of tourists' destination loyalty and preferences. *International Journal of Contemporary Hospitality Management*, 13(2): 79–85.

Cheron, E. J. & Ritchie, J. R. B. (1982). Leisure activities and perceived risk. *Journal of Leisure Research*, 14: 139–54.

Cohen, E. (1972). Toward a sociology of international tourism. *Social Research*, 39: 164–82.

Cox, D. F. (1967). Risk handling in consumer behavior—an intensive study of two cases. In D. F. Cox (Ed.), *Risk taking and information handling in consumer behavior*, pp. 34–81. Boston: Division of Research, Graduate School of Business Administration, Harvard University.

Dowling, G. R. (1986). Perceived risks: The concept and its measurement. *Psychology and Marketing*, 3: 193–210.

Dowling, G. R. & Staelin, R. (1994). A model of perceived risk and intended risk-handling activity. *Journal of Consumer Research*, 21: 119–34.

Dunn Ross, E. L. & Iso-Ahola, S. E. (1991). Sightseeing tourists' motivation and satisfaction. *Annals of Tourism Research*, 18: 226–37.

Ewert, A. W. (1989). *Outdoor adventure pursuits: Foundations, models and theories*. Columbus, OH: Publishing Horizons.

Feick, L. F. & Price, L. L. (1987). The market maven: A diffuser of marketplace information. *Journal of Marketing*, 51(January): 83–97.

Garner, S. J. (1986). Perceived risk and information sources in services purchasing. *The Mid-Atlantic Journal of Business* (Winter): 5–15.

Gitelson, R. J. & Crompton, J. L. (1984). Insights into the repeat vacation phenomenon. *Annals of Tourism Research*, 11: 199–217.

Gnoth, J. & Zins, A. H. (2008). *Cultural dimensions and the international tourist role scale: Validation in Asian destinations*. Paper presented at the Biennial Conference on Tourism in Asia.

Gursoy, D. & McCleary, K. W. (2004). An integrative model of tourists' information search behavior. *Annals of Tourism Research*, 31(2): 353–73.

Hebb, D. O. (1955). Drives and the C.N.S. (Central Nervous System). *Psychological Review*, 62: 243–54.

Helmig, B. (1997). *Variety-seeking-behavior im Konsumgüterbereich: Beeinflussungsmöglichkeiten durch Marketinginstrumente*. Wiesbaden, Germany: Gabler.

Iso-Ahola, S. (1980). *The social psychology of leisure and tourism*. Dubuque, IA: Brown Company.

Jacoby, J. & Kaplan, L. B. (1972). *The components of perceived risk*. Paper presented at the Annual Conference of the Association for Consumer Research.

Jiang, J., Havitz, M. E. & O'Brien, R. M. (2000). Validating the international tourist role scale. *Annals of Tourism Research*, 27(4): 964–81.

Joachimsthaler, E. A. & Lastovicka, J. L. (1984). Optimum stimulation level: Exploratory behavior models. *Journal of Consumer Research*, 11(3): 830–35.

Katz, E. & Lazarfeld, P. F. (1955). *Personal influence*. Glencoe, IL: Free Press.

Kozak, M., Huan, T. C. & Beaman, J. (2002). A systematic approach to non-repeat and repeat travel: With measurement and destination loyalty concept implications. *Journal of Travel and Tourism Marketing*, 12(4): 19–38.

Lee, T. & Crompton, J. (1992). Measuring novelty seeking in tourism. *Annals of Tourism Research*, 19: 732–51.

Leuba, C. (1955). Toward some integration of learning theories: The concept of optimal stimulation. *Psychological Reports*, 1: 27–33.

Litvin, S. W., Goldsmith, R. E. & Pan, B. (2008). Electronic word-of-mouth in hospitality and tourism management. *Tourism Management*, 29: 458–68.

McAlister, L. (1982). A dynamic attribute satiation model of variety-seeking behavior. *Journal of Consumer Research*, 9(September): 141–50.

McAlister, L. & Pessemier, E. (1982). Variety seeking behavior: An interdisciplinary review. *Journal of Consumer Research*, 9(December): 311–22.

McIntyre, C. (2007). Survival theory: Tourist consumption as a beneficial experiential process in a limited risk setting. *International Journal of Tourism Research*, 9: 115–30.

Mitchell, V. W. (1998). *Defining and measuring perceived risk*. Paper presented at the Academy of Marketing Conference, Sheffield, UK.

Mitchell, V. W., Davies, F., Moutinho, L. & Vassos, V. (1999). Using neural networks to understand service risk in the holiday product. *Journal of Business Research*, 46: 167–80.

Mitchell, V. W. & Greatorex, M. (1990). Consumer purchasing in foreign countries: A perceived risk perspective. *International Journal of Advertising*, 9: 295–307.

Mo, C., Howard, D. R. & Havitz, M. E. (1993). Testing an international tourist role typology. *Annals of Tourism Research*, 20: 319–35.

Peter, J. P. & Ryan, M. J. (1976). An investigation of perceived risk at the brand level. *Journal of Marketing Research*, 13: 184–88.

Raju, P. S. (1980). Optimum stimulation level: Its relationship to personality, demographics, and exploratory behavior. *Journal of Consumer Research*, 7(December): 272–82.

Roehl, W. S. (1988). *A typology of risk in vacation travel*. College Station: Texas A&M University.

Roehl, W. S. & Fesenmaier, D. R. (1992). Risk perception and pleasure travel: An exploratory analysis. *Journal of Travel Research*, 30(4): 17–26.

Ryan, C. & Glendon, I. (1998). Application of leisure motivation scale to tourism. *Annals of Tourism Research*, 25(1): 169–84.

Schiffman, L. G. (1972). Perceived risk in new product trial by elderly consumers. *Journal of Marketing Research*, 9: 106–8.

Snepenger, D., King, J., Marshall, E. & Uysal, M. (2006). Modeling Iso-Ahola's motivation theory in the tourism context. *Journal of Travel Research*, 45(November): 140–49.

Steenkamp, J.-B. E. M. & Baumgartner, H. (1992). The role of optimum stimulation level in exploratory consumer behavior. *Journal of Consumer Research*, 19: 434–48.

———. (1995). Development and cross-cultural validation of a short form of CSI as a measure of optimum stimulation level. *International Journal of Research in Marketing*, 12: 97–104.

Stone, R. N. & Gronhaug, K. (1993). Perceived risk: Further considerations for the marketing discipline. *European Journal of Marketing*, 27(3): 39–50.

Trijp, J. C. M. V. (1989). Variety seeking in consumption behavior: A review. *Wageningen Economic Papers*, 3: 28.

Walle, A. H. (1997). Pursuing risk or insight: Marketing adventures. *Annals of Tourism Research*, 24(2): 265–82.

Part IV

The Tourism Experience

7 Understanding Tourist Experience through Mindfulness Theory

Gianna Moscardo

INTRODUCTION

Although Pine and Gilmore's 1999 book on the experience economy is often credited with introducing the importance of experience to understanding consumer behavior, experience has always been a central concept in tourism production and research (Uriely, 2005). Despite this long history and central role, the concept of experience has recently been given much more attention in tourism as consumers more explicitly focus on the experiential nature of the services for which they pay (Gretzel, Fesenmaier, and O'Leary, 2006). These trends suggest that attention to the development of theoretical models to explain, rather than simply describe, the nature of tourist experiences would be timely. It is in this context that the present chapter seeks to describe a psychological theory of tourist experience based on mindfulness theory from applied social psychology. The overall aim of the chapter is to present the mindfulness construct and to use this theory to set out a series of principles for the better design and management of tourist settings and activities, which in turn will enhance the sustainability of tourism in general.

THE CONCEPT OF EXPERIENCE IN TOURISM

In everyday use experience can be seen as having two related meanings—the process of observing or perceiving, sensing, encountering or undergoing some event, and the knowledge gained from the accumulation of these encounters or perceptions (Macquarie Library, 1987). These themes of sensation, cognition, affective response, and memory are also repeated in the more formal definitions of experience that can be found in the tourism and related literatures. Table 7.1 provides a selection of definitions of experience and allows us to identify a number of recurring elements in discussions of this concept. These recurring themes include the importance of experience being subjective, based on sensations, involving participation in activities, and resulting in learning or knowledge acquisition. The final definition in Table 7.1

Table 7.1   Selection of Definitions of Tourist and/or Leisure Experiences

Definition	Source
An experience is "any sensation or knowledge acquisition resulting from a person's participation in . . . activities"	Smith (2003: 233)
An experience is "the subjective mental state felt by participants during a service encounter"	Otto and Ritchie (1996: 166)
An experience can be seen as "events that engage individuals in a personal way"	Bigne and Andreu (2004: 692)
"Experience is the result of a process of assimilating the world into a structure of cognitive 'maps' or schemas"	Vitterso et al. (2000: 434)
"Tourism experience is a multi-functional leisure activity, involving either entertainment, or learning, or both, for an individual"	Li (2000: 865)
"An experience is a complex concept with many dimensions, influenced by situational and personal variables, and composed of many characteristics"	Den Breejen (2007: 1418)

highlights the multidimensional nature of experience and this is perhaps the most common theme in discussions of the nature of tourist experiences.

Building on these definitions, core features of tourist experience are:

- experiences are made up of a series of events or activities (Smith, 2003);
- a key element of experiences are tourists' constructions of meaning from the information available in the experience setting (Uriely, 2005) and experiences have symbolic value to participants (Kim, 2001);
- tourists express their memories of experiences through stories (Gretzel et al., 2006; Willson and McIntosh, 2007);
- experiences have multiple phases that emerge over time (den Breejen, 2007);
- experiences happen within physical places and the characteristics of these places and their management do influence experience (Uriely, 2005);
- social interactions are an important component of experiences (Trauer and Ryan, 2005);
- tourist experiences involve choice and have some expected benefit or value for the participants (Ateca-Amestoy, Serrano-del-Rosal, and Vera-Toscana, 2008), and this value is often related to desired lifestyle and/or personal interests (Gross and Brown, 2006); and
- tourist experiences depart in some way from everyday experiences (Uriely, 2005).

Based on these definitions and dimensions, a theory of tourist experience would need to recognize that these experiences are subjective psychological states and that tourists use the information available to them in a setting to make choices about activity participation and construct meaningful memories often presented as stories. Such a theory would also have to recognize the importance of different social roles and social interactions within the experience and explain how the processes and characteristics of the experience contribute to affective or emotional outcomes, cognitive outcomes, and evaluative outcomes. A final requirement is that a theory of tourist experience would have to take into account the impacts of the physical and symbolic characteristics of the places in which tourist experiences occur and the personal characteristics of the individuals who are involved in the experience. It is the major argument of this chapter that mindfulness theory can provide a strong foundation for the development of such a theory of tourist experience.

MINDFULNESS THEORY

The mindfulness construct to be explored in this paper is that developed by Ellen Langer, professor of psychology at Harvard University, to explain individuals' cognitive, affective, and behavioral responses in a range of social situations (see Langer, 1989 and 1997, for reviews of the concept). This is distinct from the Buddhist idea of mindfulness, which focuses on meditation and present awareness and has become a popular concept within clinical and counseling psychology (Carson and Langer, 2006). Langer's mindfulness theory builds upon one of the most basic concepts within psychology—dual processing (Evans and Curtis-Holmes, 2005). The dual processing argument proposes that there are two distinctive ways that people can respond to external stimuli and social situations. The first is a relatively automatic response style with limited information processing and reliance on existing behavioral routines to guide behavior (Evans and Curtis-Holmes, 2005). The alternative is to respond by focusing attention on the information and features of the situation, processing this information in detail, and creating new routines for behavior (Evans and Curtis-Holmes, 2005).

Langer (1989) took this dual processing concept from psychology and added findings from studies of curiosity, attention, and arousal to develop a theory that explains and predicts human responses in a range of everyday social situations. Langer refers to the two states as mindfulness and mindlessness. Mindfulness is defined as "a flexible cognitive state that results from drawing novel distinctions about the situation and environment. When one is mindful, one is actively engaged in the present and sensitive to both context and perspective" (Carson and Langer, 2006: 29–30). Key characteristics of a mindful state include awareness of multiple and/or alternative perspectives, being alert to new information, a sensitivity to

Case study 1. The Power of Mindlessness

Peter is a young businessman who drives the same route every day between home and his office. He and his wife Joan have a young baby, and in the last few months his wife has returned to part-time work, leaving the infant with Peter's mother. Usually Joan takes the baby to her mother-in-law on her way to work. On one occasion Joan has to attend an early meeting and asks Peter to take the baby to his mother's house on his way to work. But the power of a well-established routine is hard to break and Peter mindlessly drives all the way to work and only realizes when he parks outside the office that the baby is still in his seat in the back of the car. Peter's inability to step outside a routine meant that he wasted an hour of travel.

differences in situations, and a focus on the present situation rather than on previous experiences (Carson and Langer, 2006; Djikic and Langer, 2007). The alternative state is mindlessness, which can be defined as "a state of rigidity in which one adheres to a single perspective and acts automatically. When one is mindless, one is trapped in a rigid mindset and is oblivious to context or perspective" (Carson and Langer, 2006: 30).

Langer's work has concentrated on the outcomes of the two approaches and has sought to identify the conditions that predispose people to take either a mindful or mindless approach. The theory has been applied in a number of areas, and the evidence consistently shows that mindfulness is associated with a range of positive outcomes including better decision making, more effective learning, improved mental and physical health, better memory for the details of a situation, enhanced feelings of self-worth, more effective responses to crises, greater creativity, positive evaluations of experiences, and positive affective or emotional responses to situations (Carson and Langer, 2006). In mindfulness theory it is proposed that in any given situation the characteristics that individuals brings with them interact with the characteristics of the setting and the role of those individuals in that setting to create either a mindful or mindless state of cognitive functioning. It is important to note that even in new and unfamiliar situations, people are capable of learning behavioral routines or adopting routines from elsewhere very quickly (Moscardo, 1999).

There are a number of different pathways to mindfulness, but all result from different combinations of personal and situational attributes. More specifically, mindfulness is associated with:

- novel, unfamiliar, unexpected, or surprising situations or environments;
- situations that have high personal relevance to the individual;
- situations that are varied, dynamic, and changing;
- situations where there is ambiguity and multiple perspectives;
- multisensory stimulation;

- humor;
- personal cognitive style;
- situations where the individual is in control and responsible for decisions; and
- situations where other individuals act mindfully and communicate this (Carson and Langer, 2006; Houston and Turner, 2007; Kreiger, 2005; Ritchhart and Perkins, 2000; Sternberg, 2000; Thomas, 2006).

Relationship to other Concepts

Mindfulness can be linked to several other concepts relevant to understanding tourist experiences, including flow, authenticity, the construction of meaning through stories or narratives, and satisfaction. A number of authors have linked mindfulness to Csikszentmihalyi's (1990) concept of flow (Kee and Wang, 2008; Wright, Sadlo, and Stew, 2006). Mindfulness has also been linked to authenticity, which in turn has been identified as a key concept in understanding tourist experiences (Uriely, 2005). In this case there are two types of links. Firstly, Langer (1989) suggested that authenticity as a perceived feature of an object or experience could be a factor that encourages mindfulness. Secondly, a number of authors have suggested that mindfulness is a precondition for authentic experiences of self and interactions with others (Carson and Langer, 2006), which is similar to the concept of "existential authenticity" in discussions of tourist experiences (Kim and Jamal, 2007). Thus, mindfulness can be seen as a precursor to perceived authenticity in tourist experiences, but can also be encouraged by the perceived or subjective authenticity of the features of an experience.

The importance of meaning and the construction of stories and narratives to describe and remember experiences have both previously been identified as major themes in discussions of tourist experiences. There are also discussions in the mindfulness literature of the importance of mindfulness in the creation of meaning. According to Houston and Turner (2007: 139), for example, "mindfulness is a process through which meaning is given to outcomes." Finally, there is a clear link between mindfulness and satisfaction. While Langer recognizes that mindlessness can be associated in the short term with feelings of comfort and security as existing perspectives are unlikely to be challenged or changed, in the longer term mindlessness is more likely to be associated with feelings of helplessness, boredom, frustration, and incompetence (Carson and Langer, 2006).

MINDFULNESS AND TOURIST EXPERIENCES

It can be argued that mindful tourists are valuable to tourism management at several levels (Moscardo, 1996, 1998, 1999). Firstly, at the simplest level mindful visitors are more likely to pay attention to, and comprehend, management and safety requests while on-site. Mindfulness here is a necessary prerequisite for managing tourist behaviors that are potentially damaging to themselves, others, and the setting. Secondly, mindfulness is a necessary condition for tourists to learn, for increased awareness and for changes in attitudes and behaviors. Thus, in any heritage attraction or setting mindfulness is the first step to creating what McIntosh (1999) calls insightfulness, which refers to the personal meanings, sense of place, and appreciation that tourists can derive from their experiences in heritage environments. Finally, mindful visitors are more likely to be satisfied, to have better recall of the settings and features of their experiences, and therefore be more capable of recommending the experience to others.

APPLICATIONS IN TOURISM

The first application of mindfulness to tourism was in the context of understanding how visitors respond to the interpretation or informal education offered in cultural and heritage settings. In 1986 Moscardo and Pearce compared a number of environmental interpretation centers in the United Kingdom and found that centers with a greater number of the features predicted to support mindfulness were more likely to have higher reported learning and satisfaction amongst their visitors. Figure 7.1 presents an early model of mindfulness applications in tourism (Moscardo, 1996). This model and various predictions that can be derived from it have been subsequently explored, tested, and supported in a number of different tourism settings by Moscardo and colleagues (Moscardo, 1998, 1999). These settings have included heritage and natural environments (Moscardo, Ballantyne, and Hughes, 2007; Moscardo and Woods, 1998), wildlife-based tourism (Woods and Moscardo, 2003; Moscardo, Woods, and Saltzer, 2004; Moscardo, 2006), and built tourist attractions (Benckendorff, Moscardo, and Murphy, 2006). Support for the mindfulness model has also been reported in other research (see McIntosh, 1999; McIntosh and Prentice, 1999; Prentice, Guerin, and McGugan, 1998; Tubb, 2003).

Extensions to Mindfulness Derived from Tourism

The early application of mindfulness theory to the interpretation presented to tourists at heritage attractions added two elements to mindfulness that had not previously been discussed in other areas of application: the role of guides and the importance of orientation (Moscardo, 1996, 1998, 1999). These elements are both features that arose from reviews of the research evidence evaluating interpretation and visitor experiences in heritage settings, and from considering the defining or critical characteristics of tourist

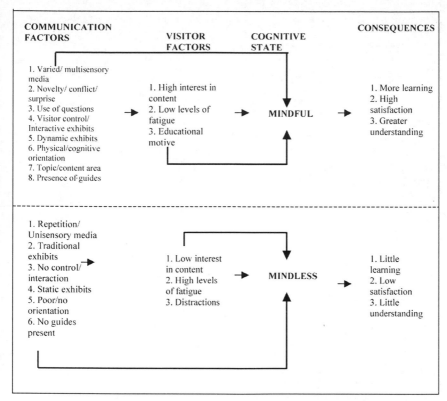

Figure 7.1   Mindfulness model of visitor behavior and cognition at built heritage sites (Moscardo, 1996: 383).

experiences. It has been previously noted that a particular defining feature of tourist experiences is that they are distinctive from everyday experiences (Uriely, 2005). Tourist experiences often take place in novel or unfamiliar settings and it could be argued that this would predispose tourists to be mindful. But it must be remembered that although the place in which the experience occurs may be novel, the type of activity may not be. For example, tourists may have well-established routines for guided tours in museums that can easily be used in mindlessness (Moscardo, 1991).

Novel tourism settings can also be challenging in terms of having to find one's way around both physically and mentally, and so it is possible that mindfulness is triggered by the novelty of the situation but becomes focused on safety, security, and orientation, leaving little capacity to pay attention to other features of the experience. Thus, the mindfulness model of interpretation presented by Moscardo in 1996 incorporated the need for good orientation systems as a factor supporting mindfulness in relation to the topic of the interpretation. In a related fashion, guides can provide the security and orientation that may be necessary in novel situations, and so

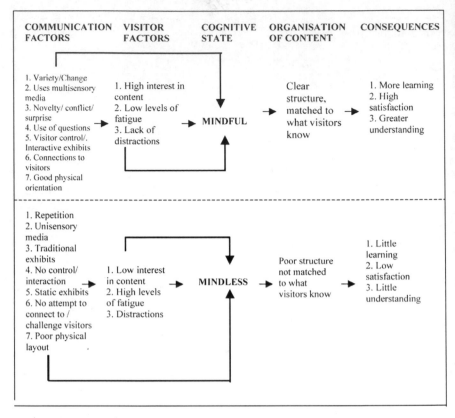

Figure 7.2   Woods and Moscardo's (2003) mindfulness model for communicating with visitors in wildlife-based tourism settings (p. 99).

the model incorporated the use of guides as a condition that would encourage or support mindful attention to the topic of the interpretation.

Three further extensions to the mindfulness model of interpretation were presented in Woods and Moscardo's (2003) discussion of wildlife-based tourism experiences. The first was the addition of a stage between cognitive state and outcomes, labeled Organization of Content, as displayed in Figure 7.2. This extension clarified the role of mindfulness as a core process underlying a tourist experience, not an outcome in its own right. This is consistent with McIntosh's (1999) discussion of mindfulness as a precursor to the desired outcome of insightfulness. It can be argued that mindfulness alone does not guarantee positive experience evaluations or changes in knowledge or awareness. Thus, the 2003 model of mindfulness presented in Figure 7.2 noted that a necessary condition for the desired outcomes of communication with tourists was that of providing well-organized or structured information that could be linked to what the tourists already knew. In this discussion it is important to note that the use of themes and stories has been consistently shown in interpretation research to be associated with more positive outcomes (Moscardo et al., 2007).

The second extension presented in Woods and Moscardo (2003) was a distinction between getting and keeping attention. This extension was based on research that indicated that some setting features were effective at getting tourists' attention, but on their own did not seem capable of holding that attention (see Moscardo and Woods, 1998). These precursors to mindfulness were listed as extreme stimuli (for example, large, loud, colorful), unexpected or surprising things, movement, and contrasts. Each of these setting features attract tourist attention but without further conditions mindfulness is unlikely. These further, or core, conditions included perceived authenticity, novelty, variety or diversity, interaction, control, personal interest or motivation, multisensory experiences, rare or unique features, and good physical orientation systems (Woods and Moscardo, 2003).

The third extension presented in Woods and Moscardo (2003) was the division of mindfulness inducing factors into four categories—features of the tourists or visitors, features of the interpretation or information provided to tourists, features of the topic or focus of the tourist experiences, and features of the experience itself. One final extension to the application of mindfulness to tourism settings is provided by Fraumann and Norman (2004). These researchers developed a scale to measure mindfulness as a cognitive style and applied it to visitors to a tourist destination examining the relationships between mindfulness as a cognitive style and tourist choices, behaviors, and evaluations. They were able to demonstrate that tourists came to a destination setting with differing predispositions towards a mindful style of cognitive processing, and these were related to differences in preferences, choices, behaviors, and evaluations of the actual experience (Fraumann and Norman, 2004).

A GENERAL MINDFULNESS MODEL OF TOURIST EXPERIENCE

Based on this review of the literature on the tourist experience, mindfulness theory, and the application of mindfulness to tourism to date, it is possible to propose a general mindfulness model of tourist experience. Figure 7.3 provides an overall framework for such a model identifying the main components that are involved in tourist experiences. These components are the tourist, the place, the management and communication systems, the focus of the experience, the cognitive state, the theme or narrative, and the outcomes. While it could be argued that there are both direct and indirect connections between all these components, the framework set out in Figure 7.3 includes the major connections that would be predicted from a mindfulness approach. The framework also distinguishes between the place and the focus of the experience.

It is important to note that in some tourism situations, such natural scenic areas and historic sites, the place is the focus of the experience, so for these specific applications these two elements could be combined. For other situations such as dining, shopping, sports activities, and wildlife-based attractions, there is a clear distinction between the place and the focus of the experience. Within each of the components set out in Figure 7.3 there are a set of specific factors, conditions, or variables that are predicted to either support mindfulness or encourage mindlessness. These are listed for each component in Table 7.2. There are also conditional variables listed for the components. Conditional variables are those that do not directly encourage either mindfulness or mindlessness, but that can interact with variables in other components to have an effect on cognitive state.

In the case of the tourist it is proposed that tourists are more likely to be mindful, regardless of other factors, if they have a predisposition to mindfulness as a cognitive style, high levels of interest in the place or experience focus, a social role in the situation that requires decision making, and low levels of fatigue. Within the tourist component, four variables were classified as conditional. Familiarity with a specific place or type of setting may support mindfulness if it is associated with management that offers variety of experience and choice allowing for change in the nature of the experience. Familiarity with a specific place may also encourage mindfulness in situations with poor orientation systems because tourists who are familiar with a place may find it easier to negotiate their way around. Alternatively,

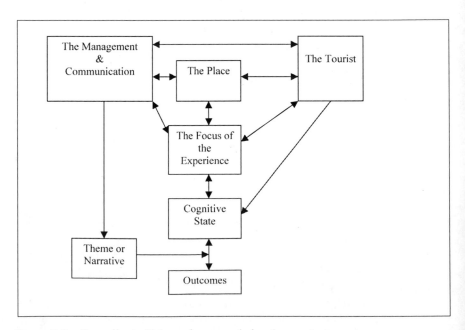

Figure 7.3   Overall mindfulness framework for the tourist experience.

familiarity with a place with little change or diversity or familiarity with a type of setting that is relatively homogenous across different places may encourage mindlessness because it will provide a readily available script or behavioral routines for use.

The other conditional factors listed for the tourist are visiting companions and nature of the existing representations of the experience. In the case of visiting companions, further research is needed to determine the relationship between social context and cognitive state, but it seems likely that different-sized groups and groups with different compositions and relationships will require different levels of attention paid to the social interaction and group management and thus could influence mindfulness in relation to the tourist experience. Finally, there are the existing representations that tourists hold of the place or focus of the experience. It has been argued that tourists are often given representations through tourism marketing that consist of very clear icons and images and that can generate expectations about what they will see and do in a tourism situation (Jenkins, 2003). It could be argued that strong, detailed representations that include behavioral routines and specific expectations could encourage mindlessness. But this is only likely if the actual experience meets or matches these expectations. Where there is a mismatch, a mindful response is more likely for the tourists. Alternatively, an existing representation may not provide detailed expectations or behavioral routines and so could encourage mindfulness.

In the case of the management and communication associated with an experience, the mindfulness approach proposes that the provision of good physical orientation systems, variety of activities, support for visitor comfort, multisensory stimulation and interactivity, choice, immersion, and multiple or new perspectives will all be associated directly with greater likelihood of mindful tourists. Conditional factors here include the provision of guides and safety and security issues. It is argued, for example, that guides may encourage mindfulness where they are effective communicators, but where they take on the role of decision maker they may encourage mindlessness. In a similar fashion to the argument made for the importance of physical orientation systems, in the case of safety and security and service encounters it could be argued that tourists who perceive that they are safe and that they have received quality service are more likely to focus their attention on the experience and thus be mindful about the experience. Tourists who have concerns over safety, security, and service may become mindful but that mindful attention will be focused on the safety or service issues.

The next two components in Table 7.2 are the place and the focus of the place. It is difficult to specify all the potential factors in these two components that could contribute to either mindfulness or mindlessness as these will depend partly on the nature of the place and the experience focus. The elements of authenticity, rarity, uniqueness, diversity, cultural significance, affective tone, and distinction can, however, be applied to most situations.

Table 7.2 Factors Associated with Mindfulness or Mindlessness

Component	Conditional Factors	Factors Associated with Mindfulness	Factors Associated with Mindlessness
The Tourist	Familiarity with the specific place	Predisposition to mindfulness as a cognitive style	Mindfulness is not a preferred cognitive style
	Familiarity with the type of setting	High levels of interest in the place or focus of the experience	Low levels of interest in the place or focus of the experience
	Visiting companions	Visitors motivated by learning and/or having memorable experiences	Social role without decision-making responsibility
	Existing representations of the experience	Social role with decision-making responsibility	High levels of fatigue
		Low levels of fatigue	
The Management & Communication	Provision of guides	Good physical orientation systems	Poor physical orientation systems
	Safety and security	Variety of activities provided	Homogeneity in activities provided
	Service encounters	Support for visitor comfort	No support for visitor comfort
		Information provided builds personal connections to the tourist	Information does not build any personal connections
		Multisensory stimulation and interactivity	Focus on passive participation and limited use of senses
		Provision of new or multiple perspectives on the focus of the experience	No choices available
			Distraction from external sources
			Single perspective offered only

		Distinguishing features	No distinguishing features
The Place	Heritage significance	Strong affective or emotional tone	Weak or no affective or emotional tone
		Surprise	Common
		Authenticity	Expected
		Rarity	Homogenous
		Uniqueness	
		Diversity	
The Focus of the Experience	Social interaction	Authenticity	Common
		Rarity	Expected
		Uniqueness	Homogenous
		Diversity	Limited cultural significance
		Cultural significance	

The final components of a general mindfulness model of tourist experience are the outcomes and the themes or narratives. It is proposed here that the nature and integrity of the theme and its accompanying narrative are variables that interact with the cognitive state to contribute to the outcomes. Those tourist settings which can be associated with a clear theme that creates personal value or connections are more likely to be able to create McIntosh's (1999) insightful tourists. Good themes are also those that can be used to build meaningful stories that have personal significance for the tourist (Moscardo et al., 2007).

CONCLUSION AND IMPLICATIONS

In the introduction to this chapter it was suggested that a theory of tourist experience would need to be based around the fundamental premises that experiences are a subjective mental state where tourists construct meaning. A tourist experience theory would also need to recognize the importance of features of the physical setting, social interactions, expectations, and information provision in determining the nature of the tourist experience. The concept of mindfulness offers all these features. A number of authors have used mindfulness in their analyses of tourist behavior and cognition. These studies have not only demonstrated the value of this theory for understanding tourist experiences; they have also extended the theory. These extensions have connected mindfulness to authenticity, tourism-specific interactions and the importance of marketing, and promotion of destinations.

Case Study 2. Applying Mindfulness to Tourism

The mindfulness model offers a number of ideas for enhancing tourist experiences. Brad runs a wildlife-spotting tour through a mangrove system in northern Australia. A number of such cruises exist and most follow a standard format where the passengers are spectators who sit and listen to a guided commentary as the boat cruises the waterways searching for wildlife to photograph. Brad thinks it may be possible to improve on this. Using the mindfulness principles, he decides to make the tourists on his cruise participants rather than spectators by assigning them tasks such as handling the boat, taking over the spotlighting on night tours, and helping identify birds using kits provided by the local parks service. He also decides to add variety by changing his commentary and route to suit different seasons, tides, and weather conditions. He adds multisensory components by collecting specimens of plants for visitors to touch and smell and always adds a session where he stops the boat so the tourists can focus on the sounds of the setting. Finally, he consults with local residents and builds up a set of stories about indigenous use of the area and local characters and their encounters with crocodiles on the river.

The mindfulness model set out in the previous section provides both specific predictions for testing in further research and a series of guidelines or principles for experience managers based on the theory. These principles include the provision of safe, secure, and comfortable settings with good physical orientation systems, the development of appropriate representations through marketing and previsit communication, provision of variety and diversity in activities with options for tourist choices, a focus on immersion, multisensory and participatory options, the presentation of multiple and/or new perspectives on a topic, and use of stories and clear and consistent themes.

It has been argued that the concept of experience is of growing importance to the consumption of many goods and services and increasing the practice of consumer management is focusing on the development of consumer experiences (Pine and Gilmore, 1999). In tourism, while experience has been a central element of what is being provided for consumers, there has been little attention paid to research that seeks to understand the interactions and processes that contribute to tourist experiences in a broad sense. This chapter has sought to address this by presenting mindfulness theory from social psychology as an integrating framework for understanding the nature of tourist experiences.

REFERENCES

Ateca-Amestoy, V., Serrano-del-Rosal, R. & Vera-Toscana, E. (2008). The leisure experience. *Journal of Socio-Economics*, 37(1): 64–78.

Benckendorff, P., Moscardo, G. & Murphy, L. (2006). Visitor perceptions of technology use in tourist attraction experiences. In G. Papageorgiou (Ed.), *Cutting Edge Research in Tourism* (available as pdf file on CD).

Bigne, J. E. & Andreu, L. (2004). Emotions in segmentation: An empirical study. *Annals of Tourism Research*, 31(3): 682–96.

Carson, S. H. & Langer, E. J. (2006). Mindfulness and self-acceptance. *Journal of Rational-Emotive and Cognitive-Behavior Therapy*, 24(1): 29–43.

Csikszentmihalyi, M. (1990). *Flow: The psychology of optimal experience*. New York: Harper Perennial.

den Breejen, L. (2007). The experiences of long distance walking: A case study of the west highland way in Scotland. *Tourism Management*, 28(6): 1417–27.

Djikic, M. & Langer, E. J. (2007). Toward mindful social comparison: When subjective and objective selves are mutually exclusive. *New Ideas in Psychology*, 25: 221–32.

Evans, J. B. T. & Curtis-Holmes, J. (2005). Rapid responding increases belief bias: Evidence for the dual-process theory of reasoning. *Thinking and Reasoning*, 11(4): 382–89.

Fraumann, E. & Norman, W. C. (2004). Mindfulness as a tool for managing visitors to tourism destinations. *Journal of Travel Research*, 42: 381–89.

Gretzel, U., Fesenmaier, D. R., & O'Leary, J. T. (2006). The transformation of consumer behaviour. In D. Buhalis & C. Costa (Eds.), *Tourism Business Frontiers: Consumers, Products and Industry*, pp. 9–18. Oxford: Elsevier.

114   *Gianna Moscardo*

Gross, M. J. & Brown, G. (2006). Tourism experiences in a lifestyle destination setting: The roles of involvement and place attachment. *Journal of Business Research*, 59(6): 696–700.

Houston, T. & Turner, P. K. (2007). Mindfulness and communicative language teaching. *Academic Exchange Quarterly*, 11(1): 138–42.

Jenkins, O. H. (2003). Photography and travel brochures: The circle of representation. *Tourism Geographies*, 5: 305–28.

Kee, Y. H. & Wang, C. K. J. (2008). Relationships between mindfulness, flow dispositions and mental skills adoption: A cluster analytic approach. *Psychology of Sport and Exercise*, 9(4): 393–411.

Kim, H. & Jamal, T. (2007). Touristic quest for existential authenticity. *Annals of Tourism Research*, 34(1): 181–201.

Kim, Y.-K. (2001). Experiential retailing: An interdisciplinary approach to success in domestic and international retailing. *Journal of Retailing and Consumer Services*, 8: 287–89.

Krieger, J. L. (2005). Shared mindfulness in cockpit crisis situations: An exploratory analysis. *Journal of Business Communication*, 45(2): 135–68.

Langer, E. J. (1989). *Mindfulness*. Reading, MA: Addison-Wesley.

———. (1997). *The power of mindful learning*. Reading, MA: Addison-Wesley.

Li, Y. (2000). Geographical consciousness and tourism experience. *Annals of Tourism Research*, 27(4): 863–83.

Macquarie Library (1987). *The Macquarie Dictionary*. Melbourne: Macquarie Library.

McIntosh, A. J. (1999). Into the tourist's mind: Understanding the value of the heritage experience. *Journal of Travel and Tourism Marketing*, 8(1): 41–64.

McIntosh, A. J. & Prentice, R. C. (1999). Affirming authenticity: Consuming cultural heritage. *Annals of Tourism Research*, 26(3): 589–612.

Moscardo, G. (1991). Museum scripts: An example of the application of social cognitive research to tourism. *Australian Psychologist*, 26(3): 158–65.

———. (1996). Mindful visitors: Creating sustainable links between heritage and tourism. *Annals of Tourism Research*, 23(2): 376–87.

———. (1998). Interpretation and sustainable tourism: Functions, examples and principles. *Journal of Tourism Studies*, 9(1): 2–13.

———. (1999). *Making visitors mindful: Principles for creating quality sustainable visitor experiences through effective communication*. Champaign, IL: Sagamore.

———. (2006). Is near enough good enough? Understanding and managing customer satisfaction with wildlife based tourism experiences. In E. Laws, B. Prideaux, & G. Moscardo (Eds.), *Tourism and hospitality services management*, pp. 38–53. Oxon: CABI.

Moscardo, G., Ballantyne, R. & Hughes, K. (2007). *Designing interpretive signs: Principles in practice*. Denver: Fulcrum.

Moscardo, G. & Pearce, P. L. (1986). Visitor centres and environmental interpretation: An exploration of the relationships among visitor enjoyment, understanding and mindfulness. *Journal of Environmental Psychology*, 6: 89–108.

Moscardo, G. & Woods, B. (1998). Managing tourism in the wet tropics world heritage area: Interpretation and the experience of visitors on Skyrail. In E. Laws, B. Faulkner, & G. Moscardo (Eds.), *Embracing and managing change in tourism: International case studies*, pp. 285–306. London: Routledge.

Moscardo, G., Woods, B. & Saltzer, R (2004). The role of interpretation in wildlife tourism. In K. Higginbottom (Ed.), *Wildlife tourism: Impacts, planning and management*, pp. 231–52. Altona, Victoria, Australia: Common Ground Publishing.

Otto, J. E. and Ritchie, J. R. B. (1996). The service experience in tourism. *Tourism Management*, 17(3): 165–74.

Pine, B. J. & Gilmore, J. H. (1999). *The experience economy*. Boston: Harvard Business School Press.

Prentice, R. C., Guerin, S. & McGugan, S. (1998). Visitor learning at a heritage attraction. *Tourism Management*, 19(1): 5–23.

Ritchhart, R. & Perkins, D. N. (2000). Life in the mindful classroom: Nurturing the disposition of mindfulness. *Journal of Social Issues*, 56(1): 27–47.

Smith, W. A. (2003). Does B & B management agree with the basic ideas behind experience management strategy? *Journal of Business and Management*, 9(3): 233–47.

Sternberg, R. J. (2000). Images of mindfulness. *Journal of Social Issues*, 56(1): 11–26.

Swanson, E. B. and Ramiller, N. C. (2004). Innovating mindfully with information technology 1. *MIS Quarterly*, 28(4): 553–84.

Thomas, D. C. (2006). Domain and development of cultural intelligence: The importance of mindfulness. *Group and Organization Management*, 31(1): 78–100.

Trauer, B. and Ryan, C. (2005). Destination image, romance and place experience—an application of intimacy theory in tourism. *Tourism Management*, 26(4): 481–91.

Tubb, K. N. (2003). An evaluation of the effectiveness of interpretation within Dartmoor National Park in reaching the goals of sustainable tourism development. *Journal of Sustainable Tourism*, 11(6): 476–98.

Uriely, N. (2005). The tourist experience: Conceptual developments. *Annals of Tourism Research*, 32(1): 199–216.

Vitterso, J., Vorkinn, M., Vistad, O. I. and Vaagland, J. (2000). Tourist experiences and attractions. *Annals of Tourism Research*, 27(2): 432–50.

Willson, G. B. and McIntosh, A. J. (2007). Heritage buildings and tourism: An experiential view. *Journal of Heritage Tourism*, 2(2): 75–93.

Woods, B. and Moscardo, G. (2003). Enhancing wildlife education through mindfulness. *Australian Journal of Environmental Education*, 19: 97–108.

Wright, J. J., Sadlo, G. and Stew, G. (2006). Challenge-skills and mindfulness: An exploration of the conundrum of flow process. *OTJR: Occupation, Participation and Health*, 26(1): 25–33.

8 Unlocking the Shared Experience
Challenges of Consumer Experience Research

Michael Morgan and Pamela Watson

INTRODUCTION

This chapter discusses the challenges of consumer-experience research. It outlines the growing importance in tourism marketing of experience management as a source of competitive advantage, and traces the parallel development in the consumer-behavior literature of a concern for the subjective hedonic and symbolic aspects of experience. This emphasis on the non-rational aspects of consumer decision making and behavior draws attention to the limits of the conventional forms of consumer research, which ask respondents to place a numerical value on the importance of a specific motivation or a discrete attribute of a destination.

The chapter reviews the advantages and disadvantages of a number of alternative approaches to understanding the consumer experience, based on research into consumer satisfaction, benefits, emotional flow, and derived meanings. It suggests that a full understanding of the dynamic process of experience requires a mix of largely qualitative methods. These too have disadvantages in terms of time, cost, and the risk of interview-induced bias. As a way of overcoming these difficulties, the chapter explores the potential of a newly emerging form of research known as netnography or Internet-based ethnography, which might offer a window into naturally occurring behaviors in a context which is not fabricated by the researcher.

HEDONIC CONSUMPTION IN THE EXPERIENCE ECONOMY

Understanding the complex and dynamic nature of tourism experiences is of great importance to all tourism and destination managers. One thing that all Tourism organizations have in common is that they all exist to provide consumers with something extraordinary, something which will stand out from everyday life and from all the competition for people's spare time and disposable income (Morgan and Watson, 2007). It is the growth of the tourism hospitality and leisure sectors, and the examples of high-profile companies like Disney and Starbucks, which have led to the concept of the experience economy and experience management. Pine and Gilmore (1999) propose this as an answer to the problems of how to remain competitive in markets where global competition and Internet technology have turned products and services into commodities, bought and sold on price alone.

Pine and Gilmore (ibid.), following Grove, Fisk, and Bitner (1992), say that sustainable competitive advantage can only be gained by stage-managing the service performance to give the customer a unique and memorable experience. Their approach has led to a growing number of management books on how to make the customer experience the center of the organization's strategic planning, marketing, and operations (Schmitt, 2003; Shaw, 2005; Smith and Wheeler, 2002). Later work (Holbrook, 2001; Prahalad and Ramaswamy, 2004) has criticized the emphasis on staging performances as superficial and product-centered. These writers call for a more strategic approach based on shared values, allowing customers to create their own experiences in a search for personal growth.

On the consumer side, a focus on experiences has arisen in response to the limitations of seeing consumer behavior purely in terms of cognitive information processing. As Holbrook and Hirschmann (1982) said, experiences are subjective, emotional states laden with symbolic meaning. Consumption is hedonic not utilitarian, particularly in leisure situations. A distinction is often made between everyday and extraordinary experiences (Abrahams, 1981). Many leisure-time experiences involve some kind of active involvement and participation, referred to as serious leisure (Stebbins, 1992), skilled consumption (Scitovsky, 1976), physical or intellectual challenge, and the sharing of experience with a community of like-minded people (Beard and Ragheb, 1983). The desired effect is the state of absorption in the activity Csikszentmihalyi (1990) calls flow. Motivation is a complex mixture of escapism, socialization, and self-actualization (Ryan, 1997).

Both strands of literature also come together in seeing the consumer as the product (Pine and Gilmore, 1999) but also as the cocreator of the product (Prahalad and Ramaswamy, 2004). The goal of extraordinary experiences is personal growth and fulfillment (Arnould and Price, 1993) leading to transformation (Pine and Gilmore). It is by providing a stage (Pine and Gilmore) or space (Prahalad) for this to happen that a company can attract and retain its customers. From the issues raised in the experience literature, a research agenda can be drawn up. More primary studies are needed to explore (a) what are the elements of the consumption experience? (b) how do consumers evaluate it? (c) how can managers enhance it to gain competitive advantage? and (d) what research methods best reveal this?

PROBLEMS OF EXPERIENCE RESEARCH

The need for new methods to research experience has been a theme of the literature since Hirschmann and Holbrook (1980) first drew attention to the emotional drives, subjective meanings, and dynamic evolving processes involved in a leisure experience such as watching a film or attending a rock concert. However, what they describe as the "sensorily complex, imaginative and emotion laden" nature of consumer behavior has prevented a consensus developing on how to research the noncognitive aspects of the experience. Borrie and Birzell (2001) say that the four most common approaches to studying visitor experiences are satisfaction, benefits-based, experience-based, and meanings-based, which can provide a useful framework for our review.

Satisfaction-based approaches commonly follow the expectancy disconfirmation approach to service quality. These approaches ask respondents to rate a selection of tangible and intangible elements of the service provided, including the reliability, responsiveness, assurance, and empathy shown by the service staff (Parasuraman, Zeithaml, and Berry, 1988). The perceived performance is compared to the expectations formed by previous experience and promotional messages. Such approaches are process-oriented, useful in evaluating the attribute-specific operations of the service, but they assume that satisfaction is derived from a cognitive evaluation of the process rather than an affective response to the overall outcome (Buttle, 1996).

Arnould and Price (1993) question whether consumers really evaluate extraordinary experiences against well-defined expectations through a summary index of service performance over several attributes. Instead, they suggest, people bring vague expectations of intense emotional outcomes (e.g., joy or absorption), and their satisfaction emerges over the time frame of the whole event. Fournier and Mick (1999) said that the satisfaction literature has ignored the culturally and individually constituted meanings which influence whether a customer feels satisfied.

Benefits-based approaches require individuals to indicate their level of agreement to the emotional or psychological benefits derived from the experience (Andereck et al., 2005). For example, Otto and Ritchie (1996) tested a methodology for measuring the customer-service experience through dimensions of hedonics (excitement, novelty, etc.), peace of mind (comfort, security, privacy), involvement (given information, choice, and control), and recognition (being treated seriously as an important customer). The importance of each dimension varied at different stages of the holiday experience (e.g., on airlines, in hotels, and on tours). However, as they acknowledge, this research is static in nature and does not lend insights into the dynamics of the service encounter or how consumers might trade off or weight their evaluations of different aspects of the service experience in arriving at overall satisfaction. In addition, Glaspell (2002) points out the limitation of such approaches for developing a deeper understanding of the nature of experiences, because the visitor is simply ticking the box rather than explaining what that box means to him.

As with satisfaction, quantitative measures of benefit can only capture what the respondent is feeling at the time of the survey, whereas experiences evolve over time. For example, Celsi, Rose, and Leigh (1993) found that, for skydivers, benefits such as flow, identity generation, mastery, feeling of catharsis, and attitudes toward risk changed and evolved within each event. Lee, Dattilo, and Howard (1994) found that although the retrospective views of outdoor leisure experiences were often expressed in terms of pleasure (i.e., "fun," "enjoyment," "relaxation"), the immediate recollections of the experience also described feelings of exhaustion, nervousness, disappointment, frustration, and guilt.

Experience-based approaches aim to capture this dynamic and evolving nature of experiences as they happened. Scherl (1989) used personal narratives in logbooks to study the day-to-day affective states, perceptions, and cognitions of adult participants on a nine-day Outward Bound program in the Australian wilderness. Arnould and Price's (1993) extended program of research into a white-water-rafting adventure holiday used diaries, pre- and postexperience interviews, and observation. Lee, Datillo, and Howard (1994) used in-depth interviews and self-initiated tape recordings to reveal the multidimensional nature of leisure experience. Experience sampling methods, as used by McIntyre and Roggenbuck (1998) and Borrie and Roggenbuck (2001), ask respondents to answer questions or complete diaries at random times during adventure holidays.

However, such experience sampling approaches still fail to uncover what the experience actually means to the participant. Borrie and Roggenbuck's wilderness adventurers' replies focused most on members of their group, followed by the environment and the task. Andereck et al. (2005) found that

---

Case Study 1. Grab Your Fork

Grab Your Fork is a blog that recounts the food and restaurant experiences of Sydney, Australia resident Helen Yee. In April 2005, she visited the famous *Tetsuya's* restaurant in Sydney. Her blog narrates the anticipation in the months leading up to the event, the joys experienced during the ten-course degustation menu, and even a glimpse of the famous chef himself. The style is based on that of a professional reviewer, but the language used borders on the hagiographic or religious in its intensity. Helen has built up a following over a period of more than four years. These community *insiders,* who share Helen's use of an *interpretative repertoire* of culinary terms, were still making comments about this meal in 2008. To this *foodie* community, or *tribe,* the discussion of a meal is a means of displaying skilled consumption by the use of the correct terms and values. Analysis of this discourse can reveal the importance of stage-managing the restaurant performance, but also the extent to which the experience is cocreated by the diner and the online community. As these foodie customers derive added value from their skilled consumption, restaurants should help them acquire the knowledge and vocabulary through informative menus, staff, and demonstrations. (Source: Watson, Morgan, and Hemmington, 2008.)

the diaries completed by visitors to the Arizona desert described what they had seen and done, the people and wildlife they had met, but said little about the meanings they derived from those experiences. Participant observation is another approach. Curtin (2005) accompanied wildlife tourist on bird- and whale-watching trips to observe and interview them throughout the experience. She also found that it was difficult to get people to talk about the significance of their experiences or place them in the broader context of their lives.

In the experience-management literature also, there is a similar concern to track the consumer through the course of the experience to uncover the critical moments of truth (Carlzon, 1987). A number of methodologies have been developed, such as service journey studies (Johns and Clark, 1993), experience mapping (Schmitt, 2003), or theatrical scripting (Harris, Harris, and Baron, 2003) to do so. Gyimóthy (2000) criticized most approaches to the analysis of the temporal flow of service processes (e.g., blueprinting, walk-through audits, and service-mapping) as based on an operational perspective, rather than that of the consumer. This, she said, is inappropriate, as tourists perceive the destination as an extraordinary holistic experience.

Gyimóthy's study is an example of the meanings-based approach. She interviewed tourists leaving the island of Bornholm and analyzed the narratives they gave of their holidays. Narrative analysis shows how people weave a complex stream of events into a coherent story revealing their interpretation of the meaning of the experience and the roles they ascribe to themselves and those they meet. These roles can reveal how the tourists see themselves—for example, Gyimóthy identified four types: Explorers, Vagabonds, Grand Tourists, and Colonists. Further analysis can then explore the inconsistencies between these "mythological" roles and the details of the narrative to uncover a deeper level of emotion and personal meaning. Later, Johns and Gyimóthy (2002) applied similar analyses to the theme park experience. This approach might be seen to support van Manen's (1990) view that experience only exists when it is reflected on in retrospect.

To understand the nature of the consumer or participant experience fully, it should be seen as a dynamic process, a blend of all four of Borrie's approaches, to explore, as Fournier and Mick (1999: 5) put it, "motivations, cognitions, emotions, and meanings, embedded in sociocultural settings, which transform during progressive and regressive consumer-product interactions." Their multimodal research approach involved lengthy and unstructured in-home interviews—some of which tracked new owners of technological products over time.

Several studies (e.g., Johns and Gyimóthy, 2002; Riley, 1995) used grounded theory as an alternative approach for representing the consumer experience. This starts with the phenomena (e.g., visitor behavior and comments) and seeks to explain it through an analysis of categories and relationships until a coherent theoretical understanding is reached. Daengbuppha, Hemmington, and Wilkes (2006) used this method to study the visitor experience at three world heritage sites in Thailand, beginning with participant observation and informal conversations before testing initial findings through in-depth interviews.

Participant observation as a method of ethnographic and anthropological research is well established but it has only recently been applied to consumer research (Arnould and Epps, 2006; Belk, 1995; Catteral and Maclaren, 2001). Ethnographers become part of a group for an extended period in order to gain insights into their culture and behavior. As consumers are "socially-connected beings" (Catteral and Maclaren, 2001), the ethnographic study of groups of consumers can provide useful insights for marketers. While being inside the group, the researcher can experience the dynamic process of consumption and gain a deep understanding of the roles, narratives, and meanings that are involved.

In summary, a growing number of authors feel that, as service experience is inherently interpretive, subjective, and affective (Arnould and Price, 1993), it requires qualitative approaches to understand and analyze it (Catteral and Maclaren, 2001). The implication is that only after in-depth interviews, continuous studies, or participant observation can the researcher gain access to the stories which reveal the true meaning and value of an experience (Andereck et al., 2005). This has three major drawbacks which limit its use in applied research.

The first problem is respondent inhibition, by which we mean that people are often reluctant to talk freely about their experiences (Elliott and Jankel-Elliott, 2003; Hill, 2003) and may not do what they said they would.

Second is the researcher influence as researchers may unintentionally influence the discussion by the kind of questions they use or simply by their presence (Curtin, 2005). In her participant observation of wildlife tours, Curtin found that revealing herself as a researcher led to the tourists being reluctant to talk to her and cautious about how they expressed themselves. Even in self-report methods like diaries, Arnould and Epp (2006) say that biases of acquiescence, self-censorship, and social desirability are inherent.

A more fundamental objection is that these kinds of qualitative research are time-consuming, and can be dismissed as unrepresentative. It does not meet Otto and Ritchie's (1995) criteria for research methods which are managerially relevant and applicable in a broad range of contexts.

ONLINE COMMUNITIES

In meeting these challenges, Internet-based methods can provide an attractive source of material for the study of consumer experiences. There are a rapidly growing number of sites where people with a common interest can go to share their news and reviews and to contribute to discussions on the topic of their enthusiasm. The interactive nature of the medium means that a loose community of people can quickly form, and as quickly dissolve. These communities are sometimes termed neo-tribes, interlinked and held together by a shared passion but otherwise heterogeneous in their demographic, economic, and geographic characteristics (Cova and Cova, 2001).

What unites them are a shared experience of reality, expressed through the values and interpretations they place on certain objects, events, and spaces. Such communities have always existed. In the past they communicated through special-interest magazines and gathered at particular places and events. Now the Internet has provided permanent spaces for asynchronous gatherings. In the past, the tribe could only be studied by prolonged participant observation. Now their communications and interactions are readily accessible online.

A typical site will have Web pages with news and features provided by an editor, plus a series of message boards for asynchronous discussion under different topic headings, a chat room for "live conversation," and a facility for private messages between members. Members use the site to exchange news, views, photographs, Web links, and music files. Some of these sites are provided by commercial Web hosts, but edited and moderated by amateurs, while others are linked to corporate Web sites. The community members may regularly visit other related sites, so that news and debate may quickly spread over a number of linked sites. They may also meet physically at events, festivals, or other gatherings.

Another type of virtual communication uses weblogs. More commonly referred to as *blogs,* these are Web pages that act as a publicly accessible, regularly updated personal journal. Those relating the writers' travel experiences are among the most popular forms of blogs. Again, the line between blogs and other virtual communities is blurred with some message-board sites offering 'blog space' for those who want to write longer reviews or diaries, while blog sites usually invite comments and discussion from readers. Some bloggers attract a regular readership which creates its own virtual community on the site.

Netnography or Virtual Ethnography

As these cyber communities characteristically have norms, rules, and shared value systems, several authors have argued that ethnographic-type research is appropriate to explore their common understandings and meanings of consumption experiences. According to Arnould and Epps (2006), ethnography systematically analyses the ways that a culture simultaneously constructs and is constructed by the behaviors and experiences of members. Virtual ethnography (also known as cyber-ethnography) is a research method which uses online cultures, communities, and Web sites as data sources for ethnographic analysis (Arnould and Epps, 2006; Elliott and Jankel-Elliott, 2003). When applied to online consumption communities, the term *netnography* is typically used (Catterall and Maclaren, 2001; Kozinets, 2002).

Netnography can be a way of gaining insights into the experiences of a group of participants without the problems of inhibition and influence that would result from the presence of a researcher, since the information is publicly available (Arnould and Epps, 2006). According to several authors (Arnould and Epps, 2006; Kozinets, 2002), the advantages of netnography are that it is not only less time consuming and costly than traditional techniques, but also it is less obtrusive and provides a window into naturally occurring behaviors in a context which is not fabricated by the researcher.

There are a number of limitations that need to be considered. Contributors to message boards can use pseudonyms and give no detail of their identity, age, or gender. However, this can be seen as an advantage. As Langer and Beckman (2005: 189) say, the opportunity to masquerade and to cover their identities allows contributors to express attitudes, opinions, and experiences freely. This enables researchers to study these messages in order to gain deeper insights into consumption motives, concerns, and experiences. While informants may be withholding their identity and presenting a controlled self-image, Kozinets (2002) argues that it is the "game" (the act, type, and content of the posting) that forms the relevant data.

Another problem is that the researcher has to rely on the written word alone rather than visual observation of the body language and spatial positioning of group members generally used by ethnographers. However, Kozinets considers that careful triangulation of information and long-term immersion in the community can help the researcher verify the trustworthiness of the contributors' views and observations. This is the equivalent of the member check carried out by traditional ethnographers to confirm their interpretation. Another problem shared with traditional ethnographers is that much of the conversation will be mundane socializing unrelated to the topic under discussion or to the shared interest linking the members.

Ethnography or Discourse Analysis?

A related debate is whether observing or participating in an online community is ethnography in the normal meaning of immersion in a community in "real life." Kozinets sees himself as part of the anthropological tradition where the researcher becomes an accepted member of a community for a considerable period of time in order to gain the kind of insights that only insiders can get from participant observation (see also Nelson and Otnes, 2003, study of intercultural wedding message boards). Others would argue that as the research involves mainly the study of written texts, it should be considered a form of content analysis (Langer and Beckman, 2005) or discourse analysis (Catteral and Maclaran, 2001) rather than ethnography.

As the online community is shifting and borderless, it is difficult to claim that it is representative of any underpinning reality. By concentrating on the text itself, however, valid insights can be gained as to how people interact with each other and with the object of their enthusiasm. As Langer and Beckman put it, "virtual communities of consumption unite and claim symbols and ways of life that are meaningful to them." Even if these interpretations may be only held by the group and not by the wider community, it is still useful for academics and marketers to study the way they are formed and modified.

Public or Private Communication?

The extent to which contributions to message boards and other Internet sites are in the public domain is an area of ethical concern. That message boards are public forums was first argued by Sudweeks and Rafaeli (1995), but it has continued to be a matter of debate. Catteral and Maclaren (2001) cite Waskul and Douglas (1996), who suggest that the distinctions between "public" and "private" online communities are blurred. Kozinets (2002) advocates a cautious approach to the ethical issues, with the researcher disclosing his presence and intentions to the

---

Case Study 2. Sidmouth Folk Festival

Sidmouth Folk Week is a music festival that has taken place for over fifty years in the Devon seaside resort. After uncertainty over finance and the withdrawal of the previous event-management company, the 2005 festival eventually went ahead under a different, collaborative, organization and on a reduced scale. The new format was vigorously debated by posters to an Internet message board, Mudcat Cafe, providing a wide-ranging and unprompted set of opinions on the criteria for a successful festival. These responses were first analyzed into discrete elements: design and programming, physical organization, social interaction, personal benefits, symbolic meanings, and cultural values. However, further analysis revealed that these are all evaluated through a subjective response to the whole event, interpreted within the broader narrative context of the consumer's life and their values. For example, ticketing problems, queues, and slow service in food outlets cause dissatisfaction mainly because they restrict the festival-goers ability to sample as much of the abundant choice on offer and to experience moments of discovery and amazement. The organizers should therefore aim to design a program which offers freedom to sample and choose a variety of performances and activities, consistent with the overall theme and values. (Source: Morgan, 2006.)

---

community members, ensuring anonymity and confidentiality, and incorporating feedback. Langer and Beckman (2005) say that this can endanger the unobtrusiveness of the study and inhibit responses. They argue that message boards are now accepted as public communications media, so similar ethical procedures should be followed as in the content analysis of readers' letters in newspapers.

Beaven and Laws (2006) also follow this interpretation in their research into online music fan communities, while stressing that care is needed if dealing with sensitive or personal matters. According to Langer and Beckman, the key is the access criteria for observation of and participation in such communication. If access is restricted (e.g., by use of passwords) and thus reserved for members only, then it is a private communication and Kozinets's guidelines apply. If anyone can participate without any restrictions, this can be defined as public communication. These criteria are still open to interpretation. For example, Yang and Fang (2004) use Internet review sites for a detailed content analysis of customer satisfaction and do not see any ethical issues in doing so.

EXPERIENCE RESEARCH ONLINE

Having outlined the potential of netnographic methods, let us examine in more detail how research into the outputs of online communities can be used to understand the elements of the consumer experience and reveal consumers' satisfactions, benefits, experiences, and meanings.

People who "post" messages on discussion boards (known as posters) or who write weblogs (bloggers) are examples of Stebbings's (1992) serious leisure and Scitovsky's (1976) skilled consumption. They become self-aware participants in their chosen activity and develop the ability to articulate their emotions and express their opinions. These are refined and sharpened through vigorous debate and criticism from other posters. As a result, the discussions can provide researchers with both positive and negative reviews of an experience in considerable depth and detail. Postings can be compared and similarities and dissimilarities noted and classified (Arnould and Epps, 2006).

In terms of understanding satisfaction, analysis of the discussion can identify the tangible and service attributes that consumers really consider significant, rather than those predetermined by a questionnaire such that used as in Perasuraman et al SERVQUAL System (1988). It can also reveal the affective responses and intense moments of emotion, which quantitative methods miss (Arnould and Price, 1993; Buttle, 1996). Similarly, a content analysis of blogs and discussions can be used to identify the emotional and psychological benefits that the bloggers and posters express and the language in which they do so. The methods are perhaps less useful in revealing the dynamic and evolving nature of the experience since the majority of blogs and posts are made in retrospect and so only reveal the high and low points that the blogger chooses in telling the story. However, it is now quite common to find postings taking place during a journey or even during sporting events, so it is possible to chart the immediate spontaneous first reactions as well as the considered reflections on the experience.

It is in the analysis of meaning, though, that netnographic approaches can make their most significant contribution to experience research. Blogs that describe a visit to a restaurant, a concert, or a festival are examples of narratives which weave a complex stream of events into a coherent story. The blogger plays a role—that of the discerning gourmet, the dedicated fan, or the intrepid adventurer. The audience is the community and the communication will be in the shared language of the tribe, full of nicknames, acronyms, and in-jokes. As Arnould and Epps (2006: 68) say, "The most useful interpretations of netnographic data take advantage of its contextual richness and result from penetrating metaphoric or symbolic interpretation rather than meticulous classification as in other analyses of qualitative data."

This shared language is even more evident in message-board debates. Here we can see the social construction of meaning taking place as posters argue and take up positions as they try to interpret and ascribe a value to what they have shared. This can provide data for discourse analysis (Muncie, 2006) to identify the interpretive repertoires with which the community expresses the shared understanding and values placed on objects and events (Potter, 1996; Wetherell, 2006). According to Hjørland (2006), such interpretative repertoires, or discourses, are "part of the symbolic capital of members of the relevant 'interpretative community' and constitute(s) the textual and interpretative codes available to them." To uncover the meanings and structures underlying these repertoires, researchers need to ask

1. What does the text reveal about the author's self-image and role?
2. What assumptions are being made about the audience? How does this influence the style and content of the message?
3. What values and behavior are viewed as normal or legitimate?
4. What are the social and cultural conditions from which the text emerges?

From this analysis, an insight can be gained into the complex ways in which an experience is interpreted and placed within the personal, social, and cultural narratives of the individual consumer.

CONCLUSION AND IMPLICATIONS

Tourism is part of the experience economy, and an understanding of the consumer experience in tourism is essential to the preparation of effective marketing strategies and programs. However, such research needs to go beyond conventional quantitative evaluation of the satisfactions and benefits consumers derive from participation in an activity, and in addition to uncover the emotions they experience during the process and the meanings they give it in retrospect. This challenges researchers to find the right blend of multimodal methods for the particular activity and market to be surveyed. Qualitative methods such as interviews, focus groups, and diaries can play a part but have limitations of respondent inhabitation and researcher influence.

We suggest that contributors to Internet message boards and blogs can provide a rich source of data from which to unlock the secrets of how experiences are socially, culturally, and personally constructed. This chapter has reviewed the advantages and the drawbacks of the emerging technique known as netnography. The main advantage is that the researcher is able to observe from his own computer the interactions of a community of likeminded consumers, without influencing these interactions by his presence as would be the case with field-based ethnography. This, however, makes it harder to verify the trustworthiness of the data, and also raises ethical questions about the extent to which postings on Internet sites are in the public domain rather than being private communications.

There is no doubt that discussions and reviews on Internet sites can provide insights into how consumer evaluate their experiences that conventional questionnaires cannot. Using techniques of content, discourse, and narrative analysis can reveal how feelings change over time, how one attribute reacts with others to create overall satisfaction or dissatisfaction, and how personal and social influences color the meaning given to these attributes and to the total experience. This can guide managers in enhancing the positive and removing the negative influences on the experience and aid marketers in communicating the appeal of the experience more effectively.

We predict that for these reasons netnographic methods will become of increasing interest to both academic and commercial researchers as the use of the Internet develops. Tourism is already seeing a rapid growth of sites which review hotels and destinations or share experiences with travelers with similar interests. These user-generated content sites can be sponsored by the travel industry, for example, Expedia's Tripadvisor, part of social networks like Facebook, WAYN, and MySpace, or independent blogs. The main limitation in the future may be the sheer volume of material posted on the Internet, which will make it harder for researchers to identify the best source for their target market and to select the sample of material to be analyzed.

REFERENCES

Abrahams, R. D. (1981). Ordinary and extraordinary experiences. In V. Turner (Ed.), *The anthropology of experience,* pp. 45–72. Chicago: University of Illinois Press.
Andereck, K., Bricker, K., Kerstetter, D. & Nickerson N. (2005). Connecting experiences to quality: Understanding the meanings behind visitor experiences. In

G. Jennings & N. Nickerson, Eds., *Quality tourism experiences*, pp. 81–96. London: Elsevier.

Arnould, E. J. & Epps, A. (2006). Deep engagement with consumer experience: Listening and learning with qualitative data. In R. Grover & M. Vriens (Eds.), *The handbook of marketing research: Uses, misuses, and future advances*, pp. 54–82. London: Sage.

Arnould, E. J. & Price, L. L (1993). River magic: Extraordinary experience and the extended service encounter. *Journal of Consumer Research*, 20(June): 24–35.

Beard, J. & Ragheb, M. G. (1983). Measuring leisure motivation. *Journal of Leisure Research*, 15(3): 219–28.

Beaven, Z. & Laws, C. (2006). *World in my eyes: An evaluation of netnography as a methodology for audience studies*. Paper presented at Leisure Studies Association Conference, Bristol, July 2006.

Belk, R. W. (1995). "Studies in the new consumer behaviour", *Acknowledging Consumption*, Routledge, London, pp. 58–95.

Borrie, W. T. & Roggenbuck J. W. (2001). The dynamic, emergent, and multiphasic nature of on-site wilderness experiences. *Journal of Leisure Research*, 33(2): 202–29.

Borrie W.T. & Birzell, R. (2001). Approaches to measuring quality of the wilderness experience. In W. A. Freimund & D.N. Cole (Eds.), *Visitor use density and wilderness experience: Proceedings*, pp. 29–38. Ogden, UT: U.S. Department of Agriculture, Forest Service, Rocky Mountain Research Station.

Buttle, F. (1996). SERVQUAL: Review, critique, research agenda. *European Journal of Marketing*, 30: 8–32.

Carlzon, J. (1987). *Moments of truth*. New York: HarperCollins.

Catteral, M. & Maclaren, P. (2001). Researching consumers in virtual worlds: A cyberspace odyssey. *Journal of Consumer Behaviour*, 1(3): 228–37.

Celsi, R. L., Rose, R. L. & Leigh, T. W. (1993). An exploration of high-risk leisure consumption through skydiving. *Journal of Consumer Research*, 20: 1–23.

Cova, B. & Cova, V. (2001). Tribal aspects of postmodern consumption research: The case of French in-line roller skaters. *Journal of Consumer Behaviour*, 1(1): 67–76.

Csikszentmihalyi, M. (1990). *Flow: The classic work on how to achieve happiness*. Rider Paperbacks.

Curtin, S. C. (2005). Nature, wild animals and tourism: An experiential view. *Journal of Ecotourism*, 1(4): 1–15.

Daengbuppha, J., Hemmington, N. & Wilkes, K. (2006). Using grounded theory to model heritage visitor experiences: Theoretical and practical issues. *Qualitative Market Research: An International Journal*, 9(4): 367–88.

Elliott, R. & Jankel-Elliott, N. (2003). Using ethnography in strategic consumer research. *Qualitative Market Research: An International Journal*, 6(4): 215–23.

Fournier, S. & Mick, D. G. (1999). Rediscovering satisfaction. *Journal of Marketing*, 63(October): 5–23.

Glaspell, B. S. (2002). *Minding the meaning of wilderness: Investigating the tensions and complexities inherent in wilderness visitors experience narratives*. Unpublished dissertation, University of Montana–Missoula, quoted by Andereck et al. (2006, op. cit).

Grove, S. J. Fisk, R. P. & Bitner, M. J. (1992). Dramatising the service experience: A managerial approach. In T. A. Swartz, S. Brown, & D. Bowen (Eds.), *Advances in services marketing and management*. Greenwich, CT. JAI Press.

Gyimóthy, S. (2000). Odysseys: Analysing service journeys from the customer's perspective. *Managing Service Quality*, 10(6): 389–96.

Harris, R., Harris, K. & Baron, S. (2003). Theatrical service experiences. *International Journal of Service Industry Management*, 14(2): 184–99.

Hill, D. (2003). Body of truth: Leveraging what consumers can't or won't say. Hoboken, NJ: John Wiley.

Hirschman, E. C. & Holbrook, M. B. (1982). Hedonic consumption: Concepts, methods and propositions. *Journal of Marketing*, 46(Summer): 92–101.

Hjørland, B. (2006). *Interpretative repertoire*. Online. Available at http://www.db.dk/bh/core%20concepts%20in%20lis/articles%20a-z/interpretative_repertoires.htm (accessed 12 September 2007).

Holbrook, M. B. (2001). Times Square, Disneyphobia, hegeMickey, the Ricky principle, and the downside of the entertainment economy. *Marketing Theory*, 1(2): 139–63.

Holbrook, M. B. & Hirschmann, E. C. (1982). The experiential aspects of consumption: Fantasies, feelings and fun. *Journal of Consumer Research*, 9(2): 132–9.

Jennings, G. (Ed.) (2005). *Quality tourism experiences*. London: Elsevier.

Johns, N. & Clark, S. (1993). Customer perception auditing: A means of monitoring the service provided by museums and galleries. *Museum Management and Curatorship*, 12: 360–6.

Johns, N. & Gyimóthy, S. (2002). Mythologies of a theme park: An icon of modern life. *Journal of Vacation Marketing*, 8(4): 320–31.

Kozinets, R. V (2002). The field behind the screen: Using netnography for marketing research in on-line communities. *Journal of Marketing Research*, 39(1): 61–73.

Langer, R. & Beckman, S. (2005). Sensitive research topics: Netnography revisited. *Qualitative Market Research*, 8(2): 189.

Lee, Y., Dattilo, J. & Howard, D. (1994). The complex and dynamic nature of leisure experience. *Journal of Leisure Research*, 26(3): 195.

McIntyre, N. & Roggenbuck, J. W. (1998). Nature/person transactions during an outdoor adventure experience: A multiphasic analysis. *Journal of Leisure Research*, 30: 401–22.

Morgan, M. (2006). Making space for experiences. *Journal of Retail & Leisure Property*, 5(4): 305–13.

Morgan, M. & Watson, P. (2007). *Resource guide to extraordinary experiences*. HLST Network of the UK Higher Education Academy Online. Available at http://www.hlst.heacademy.ac.uk/resources/guides/extraexperiences.html.

Muncie, J. (2006). Discourse analysis. In V. Jupp (Ed.), *The Sage dictionary of social research methods*. London: Sage.

Nelson, M. R. & Otnes, C. C. (2002). Exploring cross-cultural ambivalence: A netnography of intercultural wedding message boards., *Journal of Business Research*, 58: 89–95.

Otto, J. E. & Ritchie, J. B. (1996). The service experience in tourism. *Tourism Management*, 17(3): 165–74.

Parasuraman, A., Zeithaml, V. A. & Berry, I. L. (1988). SERVQUAL: A multiple item scale for measuring consumer perceptions of service quality. *Journal of Retailing* 64(1): 12–40.

Pine, B. J. & Gilmore, J. H. (1999). *The experience economy: Work is theatre and every business is a stage*. Boston: Harvard Business School Press.

Potter, J. (1996). Discourse analysis and constructionist approaches: Theoretical background. In J. T. E. Richardson (Ed.), *Handbook of qualitative research methods for psychology and the social sciences*. Leicester, UK: BPS Books.

Prahalad, C. K. & Ramaswamy, V. (2004). *The future of competition: Co-creating unique value with customers*. Boston: Harvard Business School Press.

Riley, R. (1995). Prestige-worth tourism behaviour. *Annals of Tourism Research*, 22(3): 630–49.

Ryan, C. (Ed.) (1997). *The tourist experience*. London: Thomson.

Scherl, L. M. (1989). Self in wilderness: Understanding the psychological benefits of individual-wilderness interaction through self-control. *Leisure Sciences*, 11: 123–35.

Schmitt, B. H. (2003). *Customer experience management: A revolutionary approach to connecting with your customers.* Hoboken, NJ: John Wiley.

Scitovsky, T. (1976). *The joyless economy.* Oxford: Oxford University Press.

Shaw, C. (2005). *Revolutionize your customer experience.* Basingstoke, UK: Palgrave Macmillan.

Smith, S. & Wheeler, J. (2002). *Managing the customer experience: Turning customers into advocates.* Harlow, UK: FT Prentice Hall.

Stebbins, R. A. (1992). *Amateurs, professionals and serious leisure.* Montreal: McGill-Queen's University Press.

Sudweeks, F. & Rafaeli, S. (1995). How do you get a hundred strangers to agree? Computer mediated communication and collaborative. In T. M. Harrison & T. Stephen (Eds.), *Computer networking and scholarship in the 21st century university*, pp. 115–36. New York: SUNY.

van Manen, M. (1990). *Researching lived experience: Human science for an action sensitive pedagogy.* London, Ontario, Canada: Althouse Press.

Watson, P., Morgan, M. & Hemmington, N. (2008). On-line communities and the sharing of extraordinary restaurant experiences. *Journal of Foodservice* (in press).

Waskul, D., Douglas, M. (1996), "Considering the electronic participant: some polemical observations on the ethics of on-line research", *The Information Society*, Vol. 12 pp. 129–39.

Wetherell, M. (2006). Interpretive repertoires. In V. Jupp (Ed.), *The Sage dictionary of social research methods.* London: Sage.

Yang, Z. & Fang, X. (2004). Online service quality dimensions and their relationships with satisfaction: A content analysis of customer reviews of securities brokerage services. *International Journal of Service Industry Management*, 15(3): 302–26.

Part V

Post-Choice Processes

9 Processes and Performances of Tourist (Dis)Satisfaction

Clare I. Foster

INTRODUCTION

Satisfactory travel experiences remain an important goal for both tourists and tourism organizations alike. Approaches to research in tourist (dis)satisfaction often stem originally from product-based industries and have been adapted for use in service industries. Yet as Pearce (2005: 163) notes, the mainstream literature on tourist (dis)satisfaction is replete with the challenge of operationalism, and measurement. However, whilst debate continues to flourish as to the most appropriate method to measure (dis)satisfaction, all share the assumption that (dis)satisfaction is a "postconsumption evaluative judgment" resulting from individual cognitive processing. Yet, in relation to tourism, and in the context of holidays (packaged leisure travel) particularly, which is the focus of this chapter, one of the consequences in adopting an approach which attempts to measure this outcome is one of timing; just "when" should (dis)satisfaction be measured. Whilst it may be easy to ascertain when this "postconsumption" period occurs in single service transactions, holidays are made up of numerous products and services, all of which are experienced over a longer period of time. Issues of timing to capture the postconsumption period are therefore open to some lengthy deliberation.

Furthermore, it is argued that within tourism, and in the context of package holidays in particular, approaches that prioritize the individual cognitive processing of evaluative judgments also fail to account for one major fundamental aspect. Holidays are not experienced in social isolation. As Urry (1990) notes, part of the enjoyment of the holiday is the social sharing of the experience with like-minded others. In fact, research conducted on the subject of tourist (dis)satisfaction (Foster, forthcoming PhD) suggests that the lack of other tourists with whom the experience can be shared can itself become an evaluative object against which complaints are made. Thus, if one is to accept that the success of a holiday is for many based on collective enjoyment, then it is argued that it is important to recognize that part of the holiday may also be the collective assessment of such enjoyment.

This theoretical chapter argues therefore for a respecification of tourist (dis)satisfaction research. It proposes that it is not only the performance of the product that is important, but also that the performance of the tourists whilst they experience the product should be of equal interest. Tourists are, after all, "holidaymakers" not "holidaytakers," in that they produce the holiday at the same time as they consume the product. The first part of the chapter thus introduces the notions of performance and discourse and argues for the incorporation of such notions in order to develop an understanding of processes of consumer evaluations of holiday experiences. The second part of the chapter then proposes how tourist (dis)satisfaction research can be approached from a discursive/performative perspective. It argues that by approaching tourist (dis)satisfaction from this perspective it is possible to overcome some of the difficulties with research in this field, and a deeper understanding of tourist evaluative processes and mechanisms can be gained.

RETHINKING TOURIST (DIS)SATISFACTION RESEARCH

Based on the idea that social life can be likened to drama, the performative approach predominately stems from the work of Goffman (1959), who used dramaturgical metaphors as a theoretical lens through which sociocultural practices of tourism can be captured, observed, and examined in terms of language, actions, and sociostrategic behavior (Doorne and Ateljevic, 2005). Within tourism it has been used to examine the notion of "staged authenticity" (Turner and Ash, 1975; MacCannell, 1999), institutionalized roles (Dann, 2000; Wickens, 2001), directed tourist roles (Edensor, 2001), tourism employment (Crang, 1997), as well as the production of "place" (MacDonald, 2002; Meltzer, 2002) and the formation of "identities" (Doorne and Ateljevic, 2005; Tucker, 2002). It is feasible, however, that the performative analogy can be extended to offer an alternative perspective in the understanding of the formation of evaluations and judgments of (dis)satisfaction.

In the mainstream approaches to tourist (dis)satisfaction, the context or setting in which evaluations occur tends to be factored out of consideration. However, from a performative perspective, special consideration is given to these matters. Holidays can be likened to performances in that performances often take place in special "places." Unlike office, home, or industrial places, special places are used on an occasional, rather than a steady, basis, and at specific times the places are used intensely (Schechner, 1988). These special places where holidays are experienced form the holiday "settings" and incorporate the furniture, décor, physical layout, and other background items. Goffman (1959) also notes that settings tend to stay put, geographically speaking, so that those who use a particular setting cannot begin the performance of their particular role until they have brought themselves to the appropriate place and they must terminate their performance when they leave it.

These places promote social solidarity and foster a sense of community, as essentially people are using them for the same reason (Schechner, 1988). People using these special places therefore share a commitment to the overall "drama." The drama depicts the theme of the experience, telling actors what they should do, and it remains the enduring crux of the activity regardless of the actors employed (Schechner, 1988).

Furthermore, from a performative perspective, these settings can often act as cues to the type of behavior appropriate within them. Therefore, as Edensor (2001: 60) argues, not only does behavior emerge out of identity-oriented dispositions such as gender, class, and ethnicity, but that "particular tourist contexts generate a shared set of conventions about what should be seen, what should be done, and which actions are inappropriate."

Along with the idea of the overall drama is the concept of "scripts," for, as Mangham and Overington (1987) note, all actors are aware of the direction of the performance and any performance is enacted with previous performances in mind. However, scripts are not rigid rules that limit behavior; rather, they are sets of guiding principles. A script is all that can be transmitted from time to time and place to place, and it is the basic code of events that preexists any given enactment (Schechner, 1988). Scripts denote, then, what "should" happen in the enactment of any performance: the form that the drama should take, what should be seen, what should be done, and what actions are inappropriate (Edensor, 2001). On a similar note. MacCannell (1999: 25) argues that *"each production* (of tourism) *is assembled from available cultural elements and it remains somewhat faithful to the other cultural models for the same experience."*

However, not only do contexts generate shared conventions in terms of behavior; they also generate shared conventions about the appropriate discourses to be used. Thus, just as we learn to adopt certain behavior within a specific social setting, we also develop shared vocabularies and other discursive patterns, and there are certain phrases or sayings that have a familiar or taken-for-granted quality in any culture at a time in history. These phrases and vocabularies are those that are appropriate to the situation and may thus be used with some stylistic coherence. Discourse can therefore be both constructed and constructive. It is constructed in the sense that discourse is put together from different culturally available linguistic elements. It is constructive in the sense that versions of the world are reproduced and stabilized in talk (Potter and Hepburn, 2007: 3).

Thus, people do not purchase a "product." as commonly assumed in most mainstream marketing theories; instead, they purchase a "setting" for a set period of time and, with it, an understanding of a culturally shared "role" to be adopted throughout that setting and time. Tourists are not therefore passive receptors of an experience as assumed in the mainstream approaches; rather, they are active agents "doing tourism" (Chaney, 2002).

They do not behave mechanically and deterministically in relation to external factors. Rather, they are viewed as actively constructing their experiences through their interactions with other people they encounter (Moore, 2002). "They are organisers of their social world and experiences, acting out roles, communicating their identities and purposefully structuring their time" (Pearce, 2005: 113).

Tourists as "active" agents, then, reassert the concept of "work" in the understanding of holiday experiences (Edensor, 2000). Tourists produce the experience through the practice of tourism. As such, there is a degree of "work" that needs to be undertaken in order for the experience to be realized. Tourism work is seen "not in terms of paid employment but in the form of the organised purposeful activities which are part of tourism" (Brown, 2007: 365). However, this chapter argues that not only is work undertaken by the tourists relating to activities, work is also undertaken by the tourists in how experiences and activities are evaluated. Furthermore, it is possible that evaluative work forms a crucial role in the overall work to accomplish the holiday experience as "evaluative talk" forms one of the most frequent topics of conversation amongst the tourists within the holiday (Foster, forthcoming PhD).

In relation to holiday postcards, Kennedy (2005) argues that there is a societal obligation to provide an assessment of the ongoing experience. However, it is also contended that this societal obligation should be extended to holidays in general, in that people appear to be socially obliged to provide an assessment of the holiday both during and upon returning home. Evaluative work thus forms part of the overall "work" of the enactment of "being a tourist." From this perspective, (dis)satisfaction is not simply realized; rather, (dis)satisfaction is "worked at" within the overall process and performance of being a tourist. (Dis)satisfaction is therefore not simply ascribed; rather, (dis)satisfaction is actively achieved.

Holidays, perhaps more than any other service product, are experienced in a social environment, and the social nature of the experience is often integral to the product. Holidays are interactive events where there is a strong sense of involvement with each other's actions. Holidays offer tourists the opportunity for social interaction and exchange with others, and it is with these others that tourists are able to share their experiences, offer advice, and establish social bonds (Brown, 2007). As Mangham (1978: xv) argues, the individuals of all societies move through life in terms of a continuous series of social interactions, and it is this collaborative approach (Brown, 2007) that needs to be more widely recognized, and for which narrative and performative approaches are ideally suited.

Evaluations then are expressed in interaction. They are expressed as part of the ongoing social interaction between tourists on holiday. Holidays are social experiences in respect that they are experienced in the company of others, but they only become social through the interactions between tourists. Evaluation of the holiday then can be seen in terms of its communicative aspects and in the way that it allows people to engage with others in this social experience. However, interaction is more than merely a communicative act; interaction "is a semantic activity, a process of making meaning" (Eggins and Slade, 1997: 6). Thus, it is through the interactions between tourists and others in the destination that the reality of the experience is constructed. Tourists continually make sense of their worlds and their experiences are literally "talked into meaningfulness" (Shore, 1996: 58), often by way of narrative accounts, as highlighted in the study by McCabe and Foster (2006).

Thus, (dis)satisfaction is a discursive concept constituted through language, the meanings of which are continuously constructed and reconstructed between social actors. As such, this can occur during real time, virtually as in the case of online exchanges or long after the experience has been completed (Jennings and Nickerson, 2006). Hence, the "evaluative work" undertaken in the holiday experience is viewed from this perspective as being a collaborative and socially negotiated undertaking. (Dis)satisfaction is therefore accomplished as an outcome of the evaluative work and not necessarily as a reflection of individual cognitive processing. Thus, it is contended that whilst survey-based research may well be able to measure resultant levels of (dis)satisfaction, any research that excludes the context in which the holiday takes place will fail to understand how that judgment has been achieved.

However, people do not simply communicate without first making an assessment of the context (people) with whom they are communicating. When people communicate with others they are also constructing a representation of themselves, and concern for this process of "impression management" (Goffman, 1959) is a feature that goes on in all communicative acts. Tourists therefore have to be accountable for their evaluations, and as such they need to express them in such a way that they will be acceptable to the receiving audience. When evaluations are performed to an audience, narrators have to guard against the "so what?" response (Elliot, 2005). Thus, narrators must provide an adequate evaluation of events, and one in which the meaning of the events is understood and accepted by the audience. "The evaluation should not therefore be understood as simply provided by the narrator; rather the achievement of agreement on the evaluation of a narrative is the product of a process of negotiation" (Elliott, 2005: 9).

However, although tourists are perceived as active agents purposefully working towards the production of an experience, and the evaluation of such, it has to be recognized that tourists are "members" of a specific culture and thus, as Edensor (2001: 71) notes, "when tourists enter particular stages, they are usually informed by pre-existing discursive, practical, embodied norms which help to guide their performative orientations and achieve a working consensus about what to do." Therefore, tourists as active agents are not free (Chaney, 2002); they are informed by the commonsense understandings of how to "do" tourism and. thus, how tourism experiences should be evaluated. As such, tourism experiences are neither totally fixed nor totally fluid. Rather, each experience is produced and reproduced in an ongoing interactive process, and the success of the performance is determined according to the skill of the actors (Edensor, 2001).

Tourists should be considered, therefore, as social subjects as well as socialized ones (Chaney, 2002). This dual perspective draws attention not only to the social contexts in which evaluations are constructed but also to the way evaluations may be socially constructed within these contexts. Thus, whilst the notions of drama and scripts can help to identify the socialized subject, the concept of "impression management" (Goffman, 1959) and discourse can help us understand the subject as social, interacting with others within their environment. Performative approaches thus share a commitment to a broadly social-constructionist perspective in that reality is socially constructed predominantly through language, but that the language used is context dependent and may alter according to the roles enacted within any particular social situation. Language is performed socially and thus it is used not only as a communication tool but also as a tool for action.

EVALUATIONS AND (DIS)SATISFACTION USING A PERFORMATIVE APPROACH

Holidays bring varying numbers of tourists together to a specific *setting*, and for a defined period, for the enactment of the holiday performance. These individual tourists form a company of players with whom the performance is enacted. Each individual tourist enters the setting with a prior understanding of what is required in order to perform his or her role. Participation in a holiday then can be a tangible sign that the individual holds certain ideals and that he or she shares them in common with a specific community. It is the shared ideals or beliefs that form the basis on which all holidays are performed. It is the dramatic form of the holiday, the script of the experience, telling actors what they should do.

Where the concepts and language required to express judgments are the products of sustained, intricate cultural learning (Woodward, 2006), then by paying attention to the script-like narratives produced can lend insight into the social structures and cultural practices of the tourist community. These common discursive practices that are used by tourists in the enactment of their roles can be analyzed to identify the bases on which the tourists evaluate their experiences. These bases are the ones which enable the role of the tourist to be successfully performed. Therefore, rather than assessing (dis)satisfaction using criteria imposed by the researcher, performative approaches reclaim the concept of (dis)satisfaction as defined by the tourists. Different holiday settings may produce different evaluative scripts, and thus analysis of these scripts can reveal different evaluative objects which are important to the dramatic theme of the holiday.

Identification of the dramatic form or script of the experience can lend insight into the socially constructed meaning of the experience. For example, as Krippendorf (1987) argues, holidays are supposed to be enjoyable experiences and failure to evaluate them positively is tantamount to social failure. Thus, part of the tourists' prior understanding may be that holidays should be enacted in this way. Identification of the dramatic form of the holiday can help to explain the tolerance of sometimes numerous failures and may also account for the negative assessment of specific elements whilst the holiday is still presented as being enjoyable. Analysis can therefore be aimed towards the ways in which individual activities and scripts may be modified to ensure the best performance, whilst remaining true to the drama's original meaning.

Similarly, rather than assuming that (dis)satisfaction is an outcome of a "postconsumption evaluative judgment" which occurs at a specific moment in time, a performative approach views (dis)satisfaction resulting from an ongoing evaluative process which occurs across time. From this perspective, performative approaches can be used to explore the evolution of (dis) satisfaction as it occurs throughout an extended service encounter such as a holiday. Through an analysis of how tourists negotiate evaluations of individual elements and encounters which occur throughout the holiday, the impact of each evaluation on the overall judgment of (dis)satisfaction can potentially be assessed.

The mainstream approaches tend to assume that expectations are only held in relation to the product. A performative approach does not dispute that people hold product-related expectations. On the contrary, it argues that just as people hold expectations of the product, then they may too hold expectations towards the dramatic theme of the holiday as well as that of the role they expect to enact. Goossens (2000: 308) identifies this

---

Case Study 1. Evaluating Backpacker Performative Expectations

A small group of backpackers set out on an organized tour of the Australian outback. However, following a minor accident, the tour van they were traveling in suffered damage, which meant that the group were unable to participate in some of the expected activities. In an attempt to recover from the service failure, the tour company arranged for the backpackers to stay in fully catered accommodation. Yet the backpackers were dissatisfied with this arrangement. Following discussions with the tour guide, arrangements were then made for the group to camp in the grounds surrounding the accommodation provided. Complaints in this situation were not made about the actual service failure, but about the inability of the group to perform the expected role of the backpacker. The tour company was thus evaluated not on the actual product, but on the ability of the company in providing a suitable product for the expected role enactment.

latter situation as "enactive imagery," which is described as "a kind of imagined action or role play." People commence the holiday experience carrying expectations that they will be able to enact a particular role within the holiday setting. Furthermore, different holidays may evoke different expectations in relation to the role individuals expect to be able to perform.

As demonstrated in the first case study, evaluation of (dis)satisfaction may therefore have as much to do with the degree to which the product enables a particular role enactment than (dis)satisfaction with the product itself, and similarly, evaluation of the tour organizer may be in terms of the ability of the company in providing this product. This situation may account for the ongoing success of companies such as 'Club 18–30' as they provide a suitable product and setting for the enactment of the role of young, single, and sociable tourists whilst it could be argued that the standards of the product in terms of quality (which is often used to assess tourist satisfaction) remain adequate. An analysis of how roles are enacted and defended in tourists' accounts can therefore lend valuable insight into the role expectations of different tourists and subsequently,

---

Case Study 2. Negotiating and Constructing Evaluations within Interaction

The conversational extract below stems from fieldwork data collected as part of a PhD study (Foster, forthcoming) and occurs between two tourists traveling on a package holiday in Greece.

1. Connie: what do you think of the apartments
2. Chloe: I think they are really nice, especially for Greek apartments
3. Connie: ↑really
4. Chloe: yeah, when my sister lived in Greece the only way they could get the
5.   bathroom light to work was to shove it with a broom so I'm really
6.   impressed with the Arlo for Greek apartments
7. Connie: oh, the light fitting that's hanging out is not that bad then, cause I
8.   had thought o:::h dear

The extract highlights that rather than proffering evaluations to one another, tourists often first seek the opinion of others. The positive evaluation that Connie receives is unexpected, heard in her surprised response "really." Furthermore, her later comment (line 7) suggests that her initial negative evaluation may have been revised in light of the positive evaluation from Chloe. This opinion seeking process in just one of the ways in which evaluations are negotiated between tourists party to the same experience. This simple extract demonstrates, therefore, the way in which (dis)satisfaction is constructed in a discursive process with other tourists through the negotiation of evaluations.

---

therefore, the degree to which a given product or company enables such an enactment.

Similarly, holidays require that co-performers enact their roles in accordance with the overall dramatic form. Analysis of the treatment of others, especially in relation to incorrect role performance, can lend insight into the socially shared understanding of the requirements of the role. For example, Edensor alludes to how social exclusion is commonplace to tourism enclaves because classificatory struggles produce discourses that rise to prominence and prescribe what is appropriate activity within their boundaries "undesirable elements and social practices are likely to be deterred" (2000: 328). Additionally, the way in which tourists offer dramatic guidance to others to ensure individual performers remain true to the script could also be a fruitful area of analysis.

A performative approach also views (dis)satisfaction as being constructed in a discursive process with other tourists, hosts, traveling companions, company personnel, and on some occasions, researchers. As demonstrated in the second case study, when viewed from this perspective, performative approaches are ideally placed to explore how evaluations are negotiated amongst those involved in the experience and hence also, therefore, the possible social influence that these others may have on the overall judgment of (dis)satisfaction. Similarly, the evaluative work in tourists' accounts may be analyzed in terms of how tourists negotiate the task of performing (dis) satisfaction and how evaluations are justified.

When evaluations are viewed as being constructed in interaction, then evaluations can also be analyzed for what "work" they achieve in the overall performance of the holiday. Analysis of tourists' accounts may, for example, be aimed at understanding how identities are performed or resisted through evaluative work, or how tourist communities, with whom the experience can be shared, are established (Foster, forthcoming PhD). Furthermore, where individuals are required to provide adequate accounts for the evaluations of their experiences as members of a specific community, then such accounts can be analyzed for not only what experiences contribute to (dis)satisfaction but also why (dis)satisfaction is experienced in this way.

(Dis)satisfaction as an attitude is not a fixed internal state and, thus performative approaches are sensitive to the different versions of an experience that a tourist might provide under diverse circumstances to various people. For example, tourists may evaluate experiences differently to company personnel than to fellow travelers, and similarly, the same holiday may be evaluated positively and negatively depending upon the context in which the evaluation occurs. The aim would not be to identify the "true" account of the evaluation but to understand the performative practices in which each account is constructed. By paying attention to how evaluations are performed in different contexts, an understanding of what actions evaluative work is being used to perform can be gained.

CONCLUSION AND IMPLICATIONS

At first glance it may appear incongruous to link the concept of 'performance' to the context of tourist (dis)satisfaction evaluations. However, this chapter has outlined various methodological approaches which, combined, allows a conceptualization of holiday evaluations as socially produced and sustained performative actions. It has argued that all social life can be likened to drama and a performative framework does appear particularly useful as a tool to understand such evaluations in the context of holiday experiences. Approaching the topic of evaluations from a performative perspective utilizes the skillful practices of the tourists involved in staging their own drama, rather than pre-imposing the drama from the researcher's perspective.

It has been argued that tourists may hold expectations in relation to not only the product but also to their own particular performance in the role of a tourist. A performative framework thus widens the relationships of interest and includes the evaluation of (dis)satisfaction not just of the product but also of the degree to which the company has provided a suitable product which enables a particular role enactment. Identification of the relative performative expectations of different types of tourists may therefore assist tour organizers to maintain and develop suitable performance-enabling products, and furthermore to offer packaged products within settings that are conducive to a successful performance.

Evaluative judgments of holidays are influenced by the social settings and the people with whom holidaymakers interact. Thus, when holidays are viewed as being special sites of social interaction, then the performative approach offers a general framework which can grasp both individual and group conduct whilst highlighting the situational constraints on individual and joint action (Mangham and Overington, 1987). Evaluations, then, are socially negotiated and constructed amongst the tourist community. This construction can be achieved in a variety of ways, but fundamentally, evaluations are neither immediate nor individual but are part of the ongoing socially negotiated work which is conducted by the tourists as part of their overall performance.

In survey-based approaches to measuring tourist (dis)satisfaction, individuals are asked to evaluate (dis)satisfaction with specific elements of the product. Whilst such methods may be useful to ascertain levels of (dis)satisfaction with these elements, they are less useful when trying to understand why such elements are evaluated in a particular way. It was noted, however, that from a communicative and collective performative perspective, tourists remain accountable for their evaluations within interaction, and as such they are required to provide adequate accounts for their evaluations as members of a specific community. Close attention to how evaluations are negotiated, performed, and justified in tourists' accounts can lend insight into not just "what" experiences contribute to (dis)satisfaction but also "why" (dis)satisfaction with a particular encounter or element was experienced in this way.

The chapter therefore argues that a performative framework permits a creative approach to holiday (dis)satisfaction and offers a resistance to heavy-handed models of systematic rationality that portray people as the victims of forces they cannot control. Furthermore, through adopting a performative framework, the researcher becomes reflexive in regards to his or her own performance in presenting the data. Where good performances are those which appear natural, bad performances are those where both the audience and performer are conscious of the contrived nature of what is being offered. A performative framework therefore goes someway in increasing the credibility, validity, and reliability of the research findings, which are criticisms often directed at qualitative studies (Mason, 2002).

REFERENCES

Brown, B. (2007). Working the problems of tourism. *Annals of Tourism Research*, 34(2): 364–83.

Chaney, D. (2002). The power of metaphors in tourism theory. In S. Coleman & M. Crang (Eds.), *Tourism: Between place and performance*. Oxford: Berghahn Books.

Crang, P. (1997). Performing the tourist product. In C. Rojek & J. Urry (Eds.), *Touring cultures. transformations of travel and theory*. London: Routledge.

Dann, G. (2000). Overseas holiday hotels for the elderly: Total bliss or total institution. In M. Robinson, P. Long, N. Evans, R. Sharpley, & J. Swarbrooke (Eds.), *Motivations, behaviour and tourist types*. Sunderland, UK: Business Education Publishers.

Doorne, S. & Ateljevic, I. (2005). Tourism performance as metaphor: Enacting backpacker travel in the Fiji Islands. In A. Jaworski & A. Pritchard (Eds.), *Discourse, communication and tourism*. Clevedon, UK: Channel View Publications.

Edensor, T. (2001). 'Staging Tourism, Tourists as Performers', *Annals of Tourism Research*, 27 (2), 322–44.

Eggins, S. & Slade, D. (1997). *Analysing casual conversation*. London: Cassell.

Elliott, J. (2005). *Using narrative in social research: Qualitative and quantitative approaches*. London: Sage.

Goffman, E. (1959). *The presentation of self in everyday life*. London: Penguin.

Goossens, C. (2000). Tourism information and pleasure motivation. *Annals of Tourism Research*, 27(2): 301–21.

Jennings, G. & Nickerson, N. (2006). (Eds.) *Quality tourism experiences*. Oxford: Butterworth-Heinemann.

Kennedy, C. (2005). Just perfect! The pragmatics of evaluation in holiday postcards. In A. Jaworski & A. Pritchard (Eds.), *Discourse, communication and tourism*, pp. 223–46. Clevedon, UK: Channel View Publications.

Krippendorf, J. (1987). *The holidaymakers: Understanding the impact of leisure and travel*. Oxford: Butterworth-Heinemann.

MacCannell, D. (1999). *The tourist: A New theory of the leisure class*, 3rd ed. Berkeley, CA: University of California Press.

MacDonald, F. (2002). *The Scottish Highlands as spectacle*. In S. Coleman & M. Crang (Eds.), *Tourism: Between place and performance*, pp. 54–74. Oxford: Berghahn Books.

Mangham, I. (1978). *Interactions and interventions in organizations.* Chichester, UK: John Wiley.

Mangham, I. & Overington, M. (1987). *Organisations as theatre: A social psychology of dramatic appearances.* Chichester, UK: John Wiley.

Mason, J. (2002). *Qualitative researching,* 2nd ed. London: Sage.

McCabe, S. & Foster, C. (2006). The role and function of narrative in tourist interaction. *Journal of Tourism and Cultural Change,* 4(3): 194–215.

Meltzer, E. (2002). Performing place: A hyperbolic drugstore in wall. In S. Coleman & M. Crang (Eds.), *Tourism: Between place and performance,* pp. 160–75. Oxford: Berghahn Books.

Moore, K. (2002). The discursive tourist. In G. M. S. Dann (Ed.), *The tourist as a metaphor of the social world.* Oxon: CABI.

Pearce, L. P. (2005). *Themes and conceptual schemes.* Clevedon, UK: Channel View Publications.

Potter, J. & Wetherall, M. (1987). *Discourse and social psychology: Beyond attitudes and behaviour.* London: Sage.

Schechner, R. (1988). *Performance theory.* London: Routledge.

Shore, B. (1996). *Culture in mind: Cognition, culture and the problem of meaning.* New York: Oxford University Press.

Tucker, H. (2002), Welcome to Flintstones-land: Contesting place and identity in Goreme, Central Turkey. In S. Coleman & M. Crang (Eds.), *Tourism: Between place and performance,* pp. 143–59. Oxford: Berghahn Books.

Turner, L. & Ash, J. (1975). *The golden hordes.* London: Constable & Company.

Urry, J. (1990). *The tourist gaze: Leisure and travel in contemporary societies.* London: Sage.

Wickens, E. (2001). The sacred and the profane: A tourist typology. *Annals of Tourism Research,* 29(3): 834–51.

Woodward, I. (2006). *Investigating consumption anxiety thesis: Aesthetic choice, narrativisation and social performance.* The Sociological Review. Oxford: Blackwell Publishing Ltd.

10 Service Failure, Tourist Complaints, and Service Recovery

Teoman Duman and Metin Kozak

INTRODUCTION

The most common consumer (buyer) behavior model consists of three stages: prepurchase, consumption, and postconsumption (Engel, Blackwell, and Miniard, 1995). In the first stage, potential tourists search for information about various destinations and choose one destination for their vacation (Um and Crompton, 1990). A variety of supply-and-demand-related factors influence the choice of destinations, and even whether or not to go on holidays, including psychological, economic, social, political, geographical, and demographic (Crompton and Ankomah, 1993). In the second stage, tourists experience the destination and its products or services. In the last stage, after having completed their holiday experiences, they evaluate their experiences by matching the outcome not only with information received from various sources such as media and relatives, but also with their own expectations (Pizam, Neumann, and Reichel, 1978).

Service failures are a part of our lives. The two prefatory customer complaints are examples of service failures in the hotel industry. In accommodation services where customers physically spend time, customers evaluate the service at every moment they experience it. Therefore, in most cases, service failures are inescapable in these kinds of services. Service failures and company responses to complaints influence the customers' future decision-making processes. Their evaluation of a service typically results in feelings of satisfaction or dissatisfaction, which has ramifications on their decisions whether or not to return, or to switch to other domestic or international destinations, and they will tell others about the favorable or unfavorable parts of their experiences (Baker and Crompton, 2000). In this sense, poor quality of products and services is accepted to be among the root causes of customer dissatisfaction.

Increasing competition in every area of business forces companies to provide better quality goods and services, and at lower costs. In fierce competitive environments, increasing value for customers means decreasing profitability for businesses. The business world and academics agree that customer trust, satisfaction, and loyalty are prerequisites for profitability in today's business environments. A successful management of the service recovery process and its related marketing, in which trust, value, satisfaction, and loyalty are established, is an integral part of customer-service missions (Reicheld and Sasser, 1990). Thus, the purpose of this chapter is to explain service failure and recovery with a focus on strategies for this in the hospitality and tourism industry. Following the introduction, service failure, customer complaints, and the factors which distinguish complaint behavior in these services are discussed. Later in the chapter, service recovery and its effects on tourist behavior will be considered.

SERVICE FAILURES

The subject of customer complaint has its roots in the literature of service failures. Services are composed of deeds, efforts, and performances (Hoffman and Bateson, 1997: 5). A service that is intangible, inseparable, perishable, and heterogeneous is always a prime candidate for customer complaint due to these inherent characteristics. It is usually hard for the service customers to develop an appropriate sense of what to expect and how to evaluate the product characteristics and the consequences of their choices. Since these services are mostly produced and consumed at the same time, employee attitudes and behaviors, delivery time, hygiene, capacity, and many other related issues create discomfort for those people regarded as service customers. These issues or breakdowns in the service-delivery process that create customer dissatisfaction comprise service failures (Hoffman and Bateson, 1997). Identifying service failures and their root causes will be invaluable information for service managers.

Bitner, Booms, and Tetreault (1990) classified service failures in three groups using critical incidents technique. These groups of service failures include (a) service delivery-system failures, (b) failures that result from responses to customer needs and requests, and (c) failures that result from unprompted and unsolicited employee actions (Hoffman and Bateson, 1997: 329–30). Service-delivery system failures pertain to core deficiencies in the service presentation process. These include the services being unavailable, slow, or of poor quality. Failures that result from responses to customer needs and requests include firms' or its employees' inadequate responses to customers' implicit or explicit needs and requests. Finally, failures that result from unprompted and unsolicited employee actions comprise employee behaviors that go against the cultural norms of society or are found unacceptable by customers.

CUSTOMER COMPLAINTS, INTENTIONS, AND OUTCOMES

The result of service failure is predicted to be customer complaint. However, research shows that the vast majority of service customers who are exposed to a service failure do not directly complain to the service firm

---

Case Study 1. An Example of an Unresolved Tourist Complaint (Service Failure)

Ozge booked a room for three nights in a 3-star hotel. The room rate was €70 per person including breakfast. After talking to the hotel manager she received a discount of €15 per night. She paid the bill the night before she was leaving the hotel. In the morning, she went down to Reception and asked if breakfast was ready. The receptionist replied "Yes, madam. But according to our records, you do not seem to have paid for it. If you require breakfast, then you must pay for it." Ozge complained and asked why she had to pay since breakfast was included in the price. The receptionist remained calm: "OK, here it is. I can show you the records on my computer." Ozge knew that there had been a mistake, she tried to sort the problem out, but the receptionist insisted on charging her for the breakfast. Ozge suddenly became angry, she demanded the name of the hotel manager, and said she would write a letter of complaint. She refused the breakfast. A few minutes later, the receptionist attempted to apologize and become friendlier: "Madam, I know this is my mistake. I should not be so rude. May I ask you to forgive me and offer you a cup of tea?" Ozge had been so happy with the hotel service and quality until this incident occurred in the last minutes before saying goodbye. She had to leave the hotel unhappy, and without having had her breakfast.

(Tax and Brown, 2000). Rather, they choose to share their negative experiences with friends and family members (Stephens, 2000). After a service failure, customers typically first decide whether to respond to the failure or not (Day and Landon, 1977). In the second phase, those who decide to respond make a second decision on whether to respond publicly or a privately (Day and Landon, 1977). Public responses could be seeking legal redress or approaching company officials, while private responses could be switching brand or using negative word of mouth.

McCole (2004) distinguishes between unavoidable and avoidable breakdowns. Unavoidable breakdowns are failures that the management has almost no control over while avoidable breakdowns are failures that the management can find recovery solutions to. A similar categorization includes complaints that are instrumental or noninstrumental (Hoffman and Bateson, 1997). Customers express instrumental complaints with the expectation that a desirable outcome can be achieved while they express noninstrumental complaints despite their having no expectation of a desirable outcome. A number of reasons are mentioned as the possible causes of customer complaint. Pricing-related failures, time inconveniences, core service failures, staff-related failures, ethical problems, and competition-related failures are some examples of causes of service complaint (Keaveney, 1995).

Stephens (2000) identifies three factors that can define customer complaints. These are market factors, seller and service factors, and consumer factors. Market factors are related to the dynamics of the market and competition level. Hirschman (1970) suggested that consumers complain less in competitive markets where consumers can find a number of alternative brands. Seller and service factors pertain to the commitment of service firms towards service excellence and the nature of service products these firms offer to the market. It is expected that service firms with a customer-oriented culture encourage their customers to express their feelings more. Furthermore, it is expected that customers of low-involvement service products complain much less than those of high involvement–high risk service products (Day and Landon, 1977; Blodgett and Granbois, 1992).

Consumer factors are related to demographics, beliefs, attitudes, personality characteristics, the affective aspects of consumer complaining behaviors. Those customers in a high-income bracket and with a high level of education were found to display more complaining behavior compared to customers who are in the lower levels of society (Day and Landon, 1977). Furthermore, those customers who attribute the failure to outside factors such as the firm itself were more complaining than those who attribute the failure to themselves (Godwin, Patterson, and Johnson, 1995). Customers who believe that complaining will make a difference (Blodgett and Granbois, 1992), who find marketing practices unjust (Zaltman, Srivastava, and Deshpande, 1978), and who think that the company itself is the reason for failure, though it could take measures to prevent it (Folkes, Koletsky, and Graham, 1987), choose to complain more to the company (Stephens, 2000). As to the customer personalities, those customers displaying assertive and defensive behaviors complain more than those with a conformist behavior (Fornell and Westbrook, 1979).

Recent research deals with the affective aspects of complaining behavior (Stephens, 2000). Anger, disgust, and contempt are the emotions that most commonly lead to the complaining behavior of customers who turn to the company as the cause of the failure (Stephens, 2000; Folkes, Koletsky, and Graham, 1987). Customers who blame themselves experience distress or fear and they avoid complaining (Stephens and Gwinner, 1998). Voice, exit, and retaliation are the three types of complaining outcomes (Hunt, 1991; Hoffman and Bateson, 1997). Customers may notify the firm about the failure (voice), choose to stop patronizing the store or the product (exit), or attempt to damage the physical operation of the firm (retaliation) (Hoffman and Bateson, 1997). In rare instances, these three outcomes may be experienced simultaneously.

SERVICE RECOVERY

Service recovery refers to firms' reactions to customer complaints (Hoffman and Bateson, 1997). A sincere apology, explaining the cause of the problem and offering refunds and exchanges, is an example of service-recovery action. Tax and Brown (2000: 272) define service recovery as a process "that identifies service failures, effectively resolves customer problems, classifies their root causes and yields data that can be integrated with other measures of performance to assess and improve the service system." Although service failures are unwanted situations for service firms, they are considered as opportunities to regain their customers (Hoffman, Kelley, and Rotalsky, 1995). Research shows that service recovery is related to customer trust, customer satisfaction, and loyalty (DeWitt, Nguyen, and Marshall, 2008; Karande, Magnini, and Tam, 2007). In many instances, effective service-recovery efforts are more important references for customers than their usual patronizing experiences (Tax, Brown, and Chandrashekaran, 1998).

Justice theory is used in services-marketing literature to explain customer expectations of a firm's recovery efforts (Karande, Magnini, and Tam, 2007). It has also been used to explain complaining behavior in different areas such as business management, law, and consumer studies (Tax and Brown, 2000). Justice theory categorizes service failure and the recovery process in three dimensions, distributive, procedural, and interactional justice. Following a service failure, customers expect compensation for their losses (Blodgett, Hill, and Tax, 1997). Refunds, credits, correction of charges, repairs, and replacements and apologies are the usual compensation forms (Kelley, Hoffman, and Davis, 1993; Tax and Brown, 2000). Distributive justice pertains to the perceived fairness of an actual outcome (i.e., compensation) or the results of the decisions made about the failure (Palmer, Beggs, and Keown-McMullan, 2000). Another aspect of justice as perceived by customers, procedural justice, includes procedures, policies, and criteria used by the firm to resolve the conflicts (McColl-Kennedy and Sparks, 2003). Finally, by interactional justice, customers evaluate the fairness of the way conflicts are resolved by the employees of the firm (McColl-Kennedy and Sparks, 2003). Sincere, polite, and trustworthy employee behaviors in complaint handling are important indicators of interactional justice perceptions (Tax, Brown, and Chandrashekaran, 1998).

Research shows that these three forms of justice are related to customer emotions (Dewitt, Nguyen, and Marshall, 2008), customer satisfaction, recommendation, and loyalty perceptions (Karande, Magnini, and Tam, 2007). The benefits of service recovery are countless for service companies. Solving the current customers' problems is considered an investment for the future of the businesses. It is known in today's business environment that companies have to spend five times more time, energy, and financial resources to replace a lost customer than gaining a new one (Odabasi, 2000). Proposed techniques of service-recovery management consist of encouraging complaints, anticipating needs for recovery, responding quickly after failure, training employees, empowering the frontline employees, and providing feedback to customers (Hoffman and Bateson, 1997). Similarly, according to Tax and Brown (2000), successful recovery strategies are possible with four managerial applications. These applications include human resources management practices (i.e., training, developing hiring criteria, empowerment), establishing guidelines and standards of services, providing easy access and effective responses (i.e., call centers, Internet use), and maintaining customer and product databases. As the developments in technology make everyone's life easier, they also provide numerous opportunities for firms to manage customer relationships in service firms.

Before starting a discussion about service failures and recovery in tourism, customer complaining and service-recovery process are summarized in a conceptual model pictured in Figure 10.1. As will be pointed out in the following sections, tourism services are consumed away from home, hence

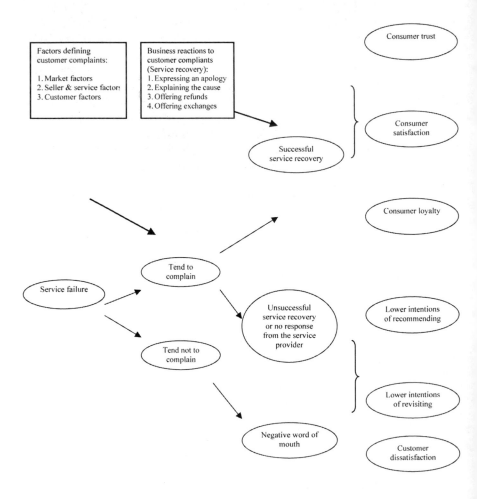

Figure 10.1   An interrelated model of customer complaining and service recovery process.

showing unique characteristics compared to most other service products. Therefore, causes of service failures, market, seller, and consumer factors that define tourist complaining behavior, service recovery tactics used by tourism firms and their effects on tourist behavior also have a number of different aspects.

SERVICE FAILURES AND RECOVERY IN TOURISM

As pointed out previously, service failures are more likely for certain services such as tourism and hospitality due to their inherent characteristics when compared with more tangible products. As a result, the management of the service-recovery process requires special attention. Moreover, customer services in high involvement–high risk service products such as tourism require a much more detailed service failure and recovery management because these services have a number of unique features. Tourism services typically involve travel; therefore, they are purchased and consumed away from home and they take a much longer time to consume (Sirakaya and Woodside, 2005). In addition, the tangible return of tourism services is very limited (e.g., souvenirs), making the product highly intangible. Furthermore, as tourists personally or with their accompanying partners (e.g., friends, family, relatives) engage in travel, they usually engage in preplanning and an information search. Also, high costs and longer consumption time make tourism services high-risk products (Sirakaya and Woodside, 2005). For these reasons, tourists rely heavily on personal recommendations.

The special characteristics of tourism services suggest some causes of dissatisfaction and complaint. Firstly, after an information search, the customer might make comparisons between the search findings and the actual experience. This might result in an unsatisfactory vacation experience. Expectations are important reference points for service quality and satisfaction evaluations in services (Zeithaml, Parasuraman, and Berry, 1990). Tourists who can't find what was promised in communication channels usually become upset. For example, throughout a package tour, a tourist has time to evaluate every stage of the vacation process including pretour briefing, travel to destination, accommodation, dining, excursions, shopping, and return (Wang, Hsieh, and Huan, 2000). The literature considers unsatisfactory experiences as a sacrifice tourists have to make (Duman, Koçak, and Tütüncü, 2006). During the vacation process tourists may complain about a number of issues such as disorganization, crowding, quality of goods and services received at the airports, accommodation units as well as about the destination in general. During the whole vacation process, tourists take various financial, physical, performance, social, and psychological risks.

Literature on service failures and recovery in tourism shows that consumer trust (DeWitt et. al., 2008) and consumer justice perceptions (Karande et. al., 2007) are important indicators of service-recovery and postfailure satisfaction. In some studies, hotel customers' nationality and demographics were found to play a role in their complaining behaviors (Yüksel, Kılınç and Yüksel, 2006). Kozak (2000) reported a list of destination attributes that were problematic for tourists, therefore in need of improvement. In his study, noticeable differences were observed between two study nationalities as well as between two study destinations in terms of the frequency of the attributes that are observed to be problematic. His findings demonstrated that some attributes in need improvement were the public's ability to speak German, the availability of facilities and services at resort airports, the availability of air-conditioning systems, and signposting for Mugla, Turkey. By contrast, there was a natural environment, quality accommodation facilities, and an availability of sports facilities and activities in Mallorca, Spain. The perception on problematic attributes differed between German and British tourists as well as between Turkish and Spanish destinations.

TOURIST COMPLAINTS, SATISFACTION, AND INTENTIONS

In recent years, measuring customer satisfaction has taken on a noticeable importance in academic marketing publications (e.g., Fornell, 1992; Oliver, 1980, 1981). But this interest is not exclusively academic, as many companies have begun to appreciate customer satisfaction as a key variable for gaining a competitive advantage. The importance of studying and

---

Case Study 2. An Example of a Resolved Tourist Complaint (Service Recovery)

During the Christmas period, irrespective of any intention to take a winter break, John's family suddenly found themselves taking a vacation to Italy. Their friends, the Johnson family, had already booked a villa at a ski resort for two weeks; they invited John's family to join them. John's family welcomed this invitation; it would be a good opportunity to take a vacation as a family, and to be with their close friends. The Johnson family had researched a number of options and decided to book this villa from a travel agency via the Internet. It looked to be the best option in terms of both capacity and price. However, upon their arrival at the resort, they at once felt their spirits dampened. There was no fireplace in the ground floor of the house even though it had been pictured on the Internet. The Johnson family went to Reception to complain. The receptionist said there was nothing she could do other than to inform the main office. After two days, the Administration accepted that they had made a mistake and offered the family an extra night free. The family considered this offer generous enough to compensate for their loss and decided to take no further action.

understanding customer satisfaction is based principally on the impact of this variable on brand loyalty and word-of-mouth communication (Cronin and Taylor, 1992; Oliver, 1999). Monitoring customer satisfaction in tourism can provide invaluable feedback for detecting problems that cause dissatisfaction with holidays and have a negative impact on future visitation (Baker and Crompton, 2000). The intangibility of the tourist industry renders the assessment of product quality through customer feedback to be a vital component for the effective management of tourism organizations.

As stated earlier, research on tourist complaints is of the utmost importance in leading managers to take effective actions to resolve the sources of complaints and improve products and services (Krishnan and Valle, 1978). The studies in marketing provide ample evidence to explicitly confirm the relationship between customer satisfaction and complaint behavior (Bearden and Teel, 1983; Day and Bodur, 1978). Customers with more complaints are found to be more likely to be dissatisfied and to report their complaints to suppliers more explicitly. That is, customer complaints are believed to directly relate to customer dissatisfaction; namely, complaints arise depending upon the level of dissatisfaction. Some researchers emphasized another type of relationship between complaint behavior and future behavior (Almanza, Jaffe, and Lin, 1994). In this context, customers whose complaints were resolved were more likely to come back to consume the products or services of the same organization than those whose complaints were not resolved. Unresolved complaints are postulated to bring negative word-of-mouth recommendation or force the customer to prefer shopping at other competing or substitute businesses or destinations (Richins, 1983).

Researchers seem to have reached a consensus about approaching customer complaint positively. Lewis (1983) underlines the significance of paying attention to customer complaints and encouraging customers to report their complaints, believing that dissatisfied customers may stop purchasing, while those who are encouraged to report their complaints and whose complaints are investigated may come back again. In a similar vein, Richins (1983) draws attention to the risk when complainants are discouraged about complaining. He reports that in a case where complaints are discouraged, there might be fewer complaints directly to the management, while more complaints will be delivered to the public about negative experiences and future purchasing is unlikely. Fornell and Wernerfelt (1987) postulate that complainants have stronger brand loyalty than noncomplainants; thus, complaining should be encouraged.

Linking back to the study findings in tourism research, Kozak and Tasci (2007) confirmed a significant relationship between the respondents' having complaints about their vacations in Turkey and their level of satisfaction, repeat visit, and recommendation intentions. Those who reported complaints were significantly more likely to be less satisfied, and have lower intentions of repeat visits or to recommend the destination to others. This finding is congruent with those of other previous studies on the harassment problem (Kozak, 2007). In Kozak's study (2007), those who experienced no problem of harassment were more likely to be satisfied with their holidays, and they intended to recommend their holidays and to return to Turkey in the future. The findings of both studies confirm that a positive holiday experience is influential over the level of overall satisfaction and future behavioral intentions in the context of tourist behavior.

The study by Kozak and Tasci (2007) measured the complaint intentions and potential consequences of complaint resolutions on tourist behavior by conducting an exit survey on a group of international tourists visiting Turkey, a popular summer vacation destination populated by mostly European markets. Among the twenty potential complaints about their vacation in Turkey, harassment, in the form of disturbances on the beach and in streets by vendors, topped the list. Among the potential reactions to problems with a vacation, the ones rated as the two most popular were "warning friends and relatives" and "changing the supplier (tour operator, hotel restaurant etc.)." The findings revealed that the most popular tactic for resolving tourist complaints was refunding their money and providing a free package holiday. The subjects of this study rated "travel agencies in their home country" as the first place where they would most likely report their dissatisfaction, while the least likely people they would report their complaints to was the "tourism information officers in Turkey."

The findings about the relationship between complaint resolution and tourist behavior variables such as satisfaction revisit and recommendation intentions revealed that those who believed that their complaints were resolved in an effective way were significantly more positive in two behavior variables. These findings are in line with Stauss and Schoeler's (2004) study. They proposed that resolving the consumer complaints results in different benefits: (1) the repurchase benefit, namely, customers remaining with the same company rather than switching to others, and (2) communication benefit in the form of word of mouth and recommendation. This study measured the attitude benefit (satisfaction) and the intentions rather than the actual behavior on repurchase and communication benefits. Future studies might investigate the actual behaviors in relation to the resolution complaints of consumers in the tourism and hospitality industry.

CONCLUSION AND IMPLICATIONS

This paper seeks to illustrate the interrelationship between service failures, tourist complaints, and service-recovery practices. As a result of the strong relationship between the first two subjects, the consumer-behavior literature underlines the significance of paying careful attention while handling customer complaints because any unresolved complaint could not only stop repeat visits but also bring negative word-of-mouth communication (Lewis, 1983; Richins, 1983). Feedback derived from customer complaints could therefore be a helpful baseline for marketing managers in monitoring the existing problems and defining the extent to which products and services are satisfactory for customers. In the tourism industry, as in all industries, tourist destinations face the problem of customer dissatisfaction with and complaints about particular products or services at one time or another (Kozak, 2004). Service providers are expected to improve their products or services as a result of dissatisfaction and complaints and take actions to recover such a failure, which may prevent other customers from experiencing similar dissatisfaction with those products or services (Richins, 1979).

Therefore, research on customer complaints is of the utmost importance in leading managers to take effective actions to resolve the sources of complaints and improve products and services. Although customer dissatisfaction and complaints might seem to be more relevant to the consumption of the goods and service products of hotel and restaurant establishments, its relevance to tourism destinations is also the center of discussion in this text. A plethora of studies have been undertaken concerning "destination image" (Chen and Hsu, 2000; Fakeye and Crompton, 1991; Sonmez and Sirakaya, 2002), "destination perception" (Driscoll, Lawson, and Niven, 1994; Vogt and Andereck, 2003), "tourist dis/satisfaction" (Kozak and Rimmington, 2000; Pizam, Neumann, and Reichel, 1978), which also reflect the manifestations of tourist complaints in the form of negative image, negative perception, and tourist dissatisfaction.

Complaint-handling and recovery strategies may differ according to the type of tourism service. In highly individualized tourism services such as luxury hotel stays, tourists may have high expectations and be highly selective in respect of their demands and requests. Customers who usually receive such services will have comparison referents (i.e., other hotels) where they may have received better quality services. It can also be expected that customers of high-quality tourism services will display strong loyalty behaviors. On the other hand, in nonindividualized tourism services such as in mass tourism activities (group tours, 3S vacations), it is possible to observe that tourists may be highly tolerant of service failures for a number of reasons. Customers of these services may firmly attribute the service problems to such factors as overcrowding, capacity problems, and the behavior of other customers. For example, in the context of product development for individual tourism facilities, through the introduction of all-inclusive holidays over the last few years, service failures have become a common problem.

REFERENCES

Almanza, J. & Lin, L. (1994). Use of the service attribute matrix to measure consumer satisfaction. *Hospitality Research Journal*, 17(2): 63–75.

Baker, D. A. & Crompton, J. L. (2000). Quality, satisfaction and behavioural intentions. *Annals of Tourism Research*, 27(3): 785–803.

Bearden, W. O. & Teel, T. E. (1983). Selected determinants of consumer satisfaction and complaint reports. *Journal of Marketing Research*, 20: 21–28.

Bitner, M. J., Booms, B. M. & Tetreault, M. S. (1990). The service encounter: Diagnosing favorable and unfavorable incidents. *Journal of Marketing*, 54(1): 71–84.

Blodgett, J. G. & Granbois, D. H. (1992). Toward an integrated conceptual model of consumer complaining behavior. *Journal of Consumer Satisfaction, Dissatisfaction and Complaining*, 5: 93–103.

Blodgett, J., Hill, D. J. & Tax, S. S. (1997). The effects of distributive, procedural and interactional justice on postcomplaint behavior. *Journal of Retailing*, 73(2): 185–210.

Chen, J. S., & Hsu, C. H. C. (2000). Measurement of Korean tourists' perceived images of overseas destinations. *Journal of Travel Research*, 38(May): 411–16.

Crompton, J. L. & Ankomah, P. K. (1993). Choice set propositions in destination decisions. *Annals of Tourism Research*, 20(1): 461–75.

Cronin, J. & Taylor, S. A. (1992). Measuring service quality: A re-examination and extension. *Journal of Marketing*, 56(3): 55–68.

Day, R. L. & Bodur, M. (1978). Consumer response to dissatisfaction with services and intangibles. *Advances in Consumer Research*, 5: 263–72.

Day, R. L. & Landon, E. L. (1977). Toward a theory of consumer complaining behavior. In A. G. Woodside, J. N. Sheth & P. D. Bennett (Eds.), *Consumer and industrial buying behavior*, pp. 425–37. New York: North Holland.

DeWitt, T. Nguyen, D. T. & Marshall, R. (2008). Exploring customer loyalty following service recovery. *Journal of Service Research*, 10(3): 269–81.

Driscoll, A., Lawson, R. & Niven, B. (1994). Measuring tourists' destination perception. *Annals of Tourism Research*, 21(3): 499–511.

Duman, T. Koçak, G. N. & Tütüncü, O. (2006). The role of non-monetary costs in a model of leisure travel value. In M. Kozak & L. Andreu (Eds.), *Progress in tourism marketing*. Kidlington, UK: Elsevier.

Engel, J. F., Blackwell, R. D. & Miniard, P. W. (1995). *Consumer Behavior*, 8th ed. Orlando, FL: The Dryden Press.

Fakeye, P. C. & Crompton, J. L. (1991). Image differences between prospective, first-time, and repeat visitors to the Lower Rio Grand Valley. *Journal of Travel Research*, 30(Fall): 10–16.

Folkes, V., Koletsky, S. & Graham, J. L. (1987). A field study of causal inferences and consumer reaction: The view from the airport. *Journal of Consumer Research*, 13(March): 534–39.

Fornell, C. (1992). A national customer satisfaction barometer: The Swedish experience. *Journal of Marketing*, 56(1): 6–21.

Fornell, C. & Westbrook, R. (1979). An exploratory study of assertiveness, aggressiveness consumer complaining behavior. In W. Wilkie (Ed.), *Advances in consumer research*, vol. 6, pp. 105–10. Ann Arbor, MI: Association for Consumer Research.

Fornell, C. & Wernerfelt, B. (1987). Defensive Marketing Strategy by Customer Complaint Management: A Theoretical Analysis. *Journal of Marketing Research*, 24 (November): 337–46.

Godwin, B., Patterson, P. G. & Johnson, L. W. (1995). Emotion, coping and complaining propensity following a dissatisfactory service encounter. *Journal of Consumer Satisfaction, Dissatisfaction and Complaining*, 8: 155–63.

Hirschman, A. O. (1970). *Exit, voice and loyalty: Responses to decline in firms, organizations and states*. Cambridge, MA: Harvard University Press.

Hoffman, K. D. & Bateson, J. E. G. (1997). *Essentials of services marketing*. Orlando, FL: The Dryden Press.

Hoffman, K. D., Kelley, S. W. & Rotalsky, H. M. (1995). Tracking service failures and employee recovery efforts. *Journal of Services Marketing*, 9(2): 49–61.

Hunt, H. K. (1991). Consumer satisfaction, dissatisfaction and complaining behavior. *Journal of Social Issues*, 47(1): 116.

Karande, K., Magnini, V. P. & Tam, L. (2007). Recovery voice and satisfaction after service failure. *Journal of Service Research*, 10(2): 187–203.

Keaveney, S. M. (1995). Customer switching behavior in service industries: An exploratory study. *Journal of Marketing*, 59(2): 71–82.

Kelley, S. W., Hoffman, K. D. & Davis, M. A. (1993). A typology of retail failures and recoveries. *Journal of Retailing*, 69(4): 429–52.

Kozak, M. (2000). Destination benchmarking: facilities, Customer satisfaction and levels of tourist expenditure. Unpublished PhD dissertation, Sheffield Hallam University.

———. (2004). *Destination benchmarking: Concepts, practices and operations.* Oxon: CABI.

———. (2007). Tourist harassment: A marketing perspective. *Annals of Tourism Research.* 34(2): 384–99.

Kozak, M. & Rimmington, M. (2000). Tourist satisfaction with Mallorca, Spain, as an off-season holiday destination. *Journal of Travel Research*, 39(3): 259–68.

Kozak, M. & Tasci, A. (2006). Intentions and consequences of tourist complaints. *Tourism Analysis*, 11(4): 231–39.

Krishnan, S. & Valle, V. A. (1978). Dissatisfaction attributions and consumer complaint behavior. In W. L. Wilkie (Ed.), *Advances in consumer research*, vol. 6, pp. 445–40. *Proceedings of the Association for Consumer Research Ninth Annual Conference*, Ann Arbor, MI, pp. 445–49.

Lewis, R. C. (1983). When guests complain. *Cornell Hotel and Restaurant Administration Quarterly*, August: 23–32.

McCole, P. (2004). Dealing with complaints in services. *International Journal of Contemporary Hospitality Management*, 16(6): 345–54.

McColl-Kennedy, J. R. & Sparks, B. A. (2003). Applications of fairness theory to service failures and service recovery. *Journal of Service Research*, 5(3): 251–66.

Odabasi, Y. (2000). *Satışta ve Pazarlamada Müşteri İlişkileri Yönetimi (CRM) (Customer Relationship Management in Sales and Marketing (CRM)).* İzmir, Turkey: Sistem Yayıncılık.

Oliver, R. L. (1980). A cognitive model for the antecedents and consequences of satisfaction decisions. *Journal of Marketing Research*, 27: 460–69.

———. (1981). Measurement and evaluation of satisfaction processes in retail settings. *Journal of Retailing*, 57(3): 25–48.

———. (1999). Whence consumer loyalty. *Journal of Marketing*, 63: 33–44.

Palmer, A., Beggs, R. & Keown-McMullan, C. (2000). Equity and repurchase intention following service failure. *Journal of Services Marketing* , 14(6): 513–26.

Pizam, A., Neumann, Y. & Reichel, A. (1978). Dimensions of tourist satisfaction area. *Annals of Tourism Research*, 5: 314–22.

Reicheld, F. F. & Sasser, W. E. (1990). Zero defections: Quality comes to services. *Harward Business Review*, 68(September–October): 105–11.

Richins, M. L. (1979). consumer perceptions of costs and benefits associated with complaining. In H. K. Hunt & R. L Day (Eds.), *Refining concepts and measures of consumer satisfaction and complaining behavior: Papers from the Fourth Annual Conference on Consumer Satisfaction, Dissatisfaction and Complaining Behavior*, Bloomington, Indiana, pp. 50–53.

———. (1983). Negative word-of-mouth by dissatisfied consumers: A pilot study. *Journal of Marketing*, 47(Winter): 68–78.

Sirakaya, E. & Woodside, A. G. (2005). Building and testing theories of decision making by travelers. *Tourism Management*, 26 815–32.
Sonmez, S. F. & Sirakaya, E. (2002). A distorted destination image? The case of Turkey. *Journal of Travel Research*, 41(2): 185–96.
Stauss, B. & Schoeler, A. (2004). Complaint management profitability: What do complaint managers know? *Managing Service Quality*, 14(2–3): 147–56.
Stephens, N. (2000). Complaining. In T. A. Swartz & D. Iacobucci (Eds.), *Handbook of services marketing and management*, pp. 287–98. Thousand Oaks, CA: Sage Publications.
Stephens, N. & Gwinner, K. P. (1998). Why don't some people complain? A cognitive-emotive process model of consumer complaint behavior. *Journal of the Academy of Marketing Science*, 26(3): 172–89.
Tax, S. S. & Brown, S. W. (2000). Service recovery: Research insights and practices. In T. A. Swartz & D. Iacobucci (Eds.), *Handbook of services marketing and management*, pp. 271–85. Thousand Oaks, CA: Sage Publications.
Tax, S. S., Brown, S. W. & Chandrashekaran, M. (1998). Customer evaluations of service complaint experiences: Implications for relationship marketing. *Journal of Marketing*, 62(April): 60–76.
Um, S. & Crompton, J. L. (1990). Attitude determinants in tourism destination choice. *Annals of Tourism Research*, 17: 432–48.
Vogt, C. A. & Andereck, K. L. (2003). Destination perceptions across a vacation. *Journal of Travel Research*, 41(4): 348–54.
Wang, K., Hsieh, A. & Huan, T. (2000). Critical service features in group package tour: An exploratory research. *Tourism Management*, 21(2): 177–89.
Yüksel, A., Kılınç, U. K. & Yüksel, F. (2006). Cross-national analysis of hotel customers' attitudes toward complaining and their complaining behaviors. *Tourism Management*, 27(1): 11–24.
Zaltman, G., Srivastava, R. K. & Deshpande, R. (1978). Perceptions of unfair marketing practices. In H. K. Hunt (Ed.), *Advances in consumer research*, vol. 5, pp. 263–68. Ann Arbor, MI: Association for Consumer Research.
Zeithaml, V., Parasuraman, A. & Berry, L. L. (1990). *Delivering quality service: Balancing customer perceptions and expectations*. New York: Free Press.

11 What Determines Tourist Loyalty?

In Search of a Theoretical Explanation

Xiang (Robert) Li and James F. Petrick

INTRODUCTION

Brand loyalty is considered one of the most valuable assets of firms (Shugan, 2005). Although leisure travel is generally considered to be motivated by "novelty seeking" (Lee and Crompton, 1992), a concept almost the opposite of loyalty, tourism marketers have also long focused on cultivating customer loyalty. This is evidenced by the wide employment of customer loyalty programs (Morais, Dorsch, and Backman, 2004) and increasing research attention on tourist loyalty (Alegre and Juaneda, 2006; Morais et al., 2004). Despite extensive research efforts, what determines customer loyalty development is not yet well understood (Agustin and Singh, 2005). Numerous variables have been suggested as plausible antecedents of loyalty. Nevertheless, the sometimes conflicting results imply that a whole picture of the loyalty-building process is yet to emerge. Fundamentally, this seems to result from a lack of theoretical support for the inherent social psychological mechanism of loyalty formation.

This chapter suggests that loyalty researchers should take advantage of the multidisciplinary research on interpersonal commitment, owing to (1) the conceptual proximity of loyalty and commitment and (2) the close resemblance of brand-person relationship and interpersonal relationship in a tourism/service context. The similarity of loyalty and commitment has been well documented (see Li and Petrick, 2007, for a review). In regards to the second reason, marketing theorists have argued that relational exchanges between customers and suppliers, characterized by "very close information, social, and process linkages, and mutual commitments made in expectation of long-run benefits" (Day, 2000: 24), are akin to interpersonal relationships, and interpersonal relationship theories could be useful in examining brand-person relationships (Fournier, 1998; Jones and Taylor, 2007). Thus, it can be argued that interpersonal relationship theory might be useful in explanation and examination of the brand loyalty phenomenon.

This chapter attempts to: conceptually compare several existing theoretical frameworks on commitment and identify the potential guiding theory for explaining loyalty development. These include Rusbult's Investment

Model (IM) (Rusbult, 1980a, b; 1983), Johnson's commitment framework (Johnson, 1991a, b), Pritchard et al.'s (1999) conceptualization of commitment formation, and the three-component model of organizational commitment in the organizational behavior literature (Allen and Meyer, 1990; Meyer and Allen, 1997) (Table 11.1). Among these, we propose that Rusbult's IM from the social psychology literature may be particularly relevant and helpful in identifying the determinants of loyalty. The rest of the chapter will introduce the premises of IM first, then review three alternative commitment models and finally draw conclusions.

Table 11.1   Multidisciplinary Theories on Commitment

Theories	*Antecedents*	*Commitment Types*
Rusbult (1980a, b; 1983)	(1) Satisfaction level (2) Quality of alternatives (3) Investment size	Commitment
Johnson (1991a, b)	(1) One's attitude toward the relationship (2) One's attitude toward the partner (3) One's relational identity	Personal commitment
	(1) A belief in the value of consistency (2) Values regarding the stability of particular types of relationships (3) A sense of obligation to the particular person	Moral commitment
	(1) Irretrievable investments (2) Social reaction (3) Difficulty of termination procedures (4) Availability of acceptable alternatives	Structural commitment
Pritchard et al. (1999)	(1) Informational processes (2) Volitional processes (3) Identification processes	Tendency to resist change
Allen and Meyer (1990); Meyer and Allen (1997)		Affective commitment Continuance commitment Normative commitment

THE INVESTMENT MODEL

IM is "a theory of the process by which individuals become committed to their relationships as well as the circumstances under which feelings of commitment erode and relationships end" (Rusbult, Drigotas, and Verette, 1994: 116). The model is theoretically grounded within interdependence theory (Kelley and Thibaut, 1978; Thibaut and Kelley, 1959), which is considered by many as a branch of social exchange theory (Anderson and Narus, 1984). According to interdependence theory, the behaviors one participant enacts in a dyadic relationship and the resultant outcomes of each behavior depend on the behavior of the other participant, which results in a condition of mutual dependence. Specifically, the interdependence theory proposes that one participant's dependence on a relationship is a function of (a) satisfaction with the relationship, and (b) a comparison of the best available alternatives to the relationship. To facilitate the following discussion, the participant in discussion is hereafter referred to as John, and his partner is referred to as Mary.

Thibaut and Kelley (1959) stressed the conceptual differences between satisfaction and dependence. To them, satisfaction level refers to the positive versus negative emotions John experiences in a relationship, while dependence refers to John's reliance on the relationship for need fulfillment (Le and Agnew, 2003; Rusbult, Drigotas, and Verette, 1994). Interdependence theory suggests that three things influence John's satisfaction: rewards (i.e., pleasure, gratification the person enjoys), costs (i.e., factors that operate to inhibit or deter the performance of a sequence of behavior), and comparison level (CL). Comparison level is "the standard against which a member evaluates the 'attractiveness' of the relationship or how satisfactory it is" (Thibaut and Kelley, 1959: 21). The outcomes obtained from the relationship, compared against this standard, determine the degree of satisfaction John experiences from the relationship.

However, satisfaction by itself may not explain more complex scenarios, in which individuals choose to stay in an obviously unsatisfying relationship (Rusbult et al., 1994). Interdependence theory further posits another comparison criterion, the comparison level for alternatives (CL_{alt}). Comparison level for alternatives is a standard that represents the average quality of outcomes available to the participant from the best alternative relationship. It represents the lowest level of outcomes John will accept and still remain in the relationship (Thibaut and Kelley, 1959). Thus, John compares the current relationship with anticipated outcomes in the best alternative option and decides whether to stay with or leave Mary.

IM extends interdependence theory in two aspects (Rusbult, Martz, and Agnew, 1998): First, while interdependence theory focuses on dependence (i.e., the degree to which one's needs are satisfied in a relationship), IM focuses on commitment, a consequence of increasing dependence.

Basically, commitment is a subjective, psychological experience of the state of dependence (Le and Agnew, 2003; Rusbult et al., 1994).

Second and more importantly, IM asserts that a third factor, investment size, is necessary when examining interpersonal relationship persistence (Rusbult, 1978). It argues that the explanation presented by interdependence theory does not capture the whole story. That is, there may exist another factor accounting for the survival of relationships in the face of tempting alternatives and fluctuating satisfaction. Rusbult suggested that this additional factor is the investment or any tangible or intangible resources attached to a relationship that may be lost or diminished once the relationship is dissolved. Thus, IM maintains that John's commitment to the relationship is strengthened by the level of satisfaction that John derives from the relationship, is fueled by his investments to the relationship, and is weakened by the quality of alternatives to the relationship (Figure 11.1).

Satisfaction Level

IM assumes that people are generally motivated to maximize rewards and minimize costs (Rusbult, 1980a). Following interdependence theory, the model proposes that John's satisfaction (SAT) with the relationship is a function of the subjective estimate of rewards (REW) John derives from Mary and the relationship, the amount of costs he suffers (CST) in the relationship, and John's expectations concerning the quality of relationships in general (CL). Thus, John will feel more satisfied to the degree that he derives rewards from the relationship, suffers few costs, or has a lower standard for evaluating relationships. Further, John's satisfaction with the relationship positively influences his commitment to Mary.

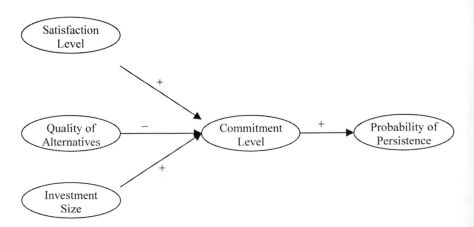

Figure 11.1   The investment model.
Source: Adapted from Rusbult et al., 1994; Rusbult, Martz and Agnew, 1998.

Case Study 1. Potential Application of IM in Understanding Destination Loyalty

Tim and Kate live in New York City, where Tim is a senior business manager and Kate is a stay-at-home mom. Both are in their early forties and have two children aged ten and eight. Every year, the family takes a two-week summer vacation together. Although there has been quite some discussion on "exploring new destinations," they keep coming back to Orlando and Disney in the past three years. Why it that? First of all, the two children really enjoyed their tour in Disney each time they went there (*high satisfaction*). Second, Tim and Kate found that, in comparison to other family vacation destinations, Orlando does provide very good value (*no competitive alternative options*). Finally, after several visits to the "Magic Kingdom," they do not need to go through any hassle of deciding what to do and where to go. Also, they can now enjoy some discounts only reserved for returning guests, which they will not get in other destinations (*investment*).

Moreover, the outcome value is a function of the subjective estimate of the value of the attributes associated with the relationship, each weighted by its subjective importance (Rusbult, 1991). Thus, John's satisfaction level can be defined as:

$$SAT = REWi \ (\Sigma[riii]) - CSTi(\Sigma[ciii]) - CL$$

where r_i represents John's subjective estimate of the reward of attribute i available in the relationship with Mary, c_i represents John's subjective estimate of the cost of attribute i available in the relationship, and i_i represents its subjective importance (Rusbult, 1980a, b; 1991).

Finally, as suggested by interdependence theory, John's generalized expectation (CL) results from two sources: John's past experiences and John's social comparison with friends and family. For instance, if John's parents have a happy marriage, he might expect something similar with his own relationship. On the other hand, if John's friends have been suffering from bad relationships lately, such comparison may change his own expectation.

Quality of Alternatives

At the same time John evaluates his own relationship, he may also contemplate what might be experienced outside the current relationship. That is, what the relationship experience would be if John were not with Mary, but in the best alternative situation (Rusbult et al., 1994). This "alternative" option could be an actual person or relationship, or it may be having no relationship at all (i.e., being independent is considered preferable to any relationship for some people). The quality of alternatives (ALT) is defined as:

$$ALT = REW_j(\Sigma[r_j i_j]) - CST_j(\Sigma[c_j i_j]) - CL$$

where $_j$ is the attribute available in the alternative situation (Rusbult, 1980b, 1991). The quality of alternatives is "individual-level forces" pulling one from sustaining the relationship. John's commitment to Mary is reduced to the degree that the quality of alternatives is high (e.g., there are other attractive females in John's life, or John finds that staying single is more enjoyable). Conversely, John may feel more committed to the relationship when the "pulling forces" are weak.

Investment Size

Finally, investment size is proposed to contribute to the stability of a partnership. A variety of things may be tied to John's current relationship, for which John becomes bound to his relationship with Mary. Investments (INV) refer to any tangible or intangible resources attached to a relationship that may be lost or diminished once the relationship is dissolved. This includes intrinsic/direct investments (DIR INV), such as time or self-disclosure. Also included are extrinsic/indirect investments (IND INV), such as mutual friends and social status that the relationship brings. In certain circumstances, "social norms and moral prescriptions may serve as compelling sources of investment" (Rusbult, 1991: 159). Therefore, John's subjective investment may be mathematically represented as:

$$INV = DIR\ INV\ (\Sigma[DI_k i_k]) + IND\ INV(\Sigma[II_k i_k])$$

where DI_k represents John's subjective direct investment in attribute k, II_k represents John's subjective indirect investment in attribute k, and i_k represents its subjective importance (Rusbult, 1991).

Commitment

IM conceptualizes commitment as a function of three basic forces. That is, John's commitment to the relationship is strengthened by the level of satisfaction that John derives from the relationship, is fueled by his investments to the relationship, and is weakened by the quality of alternatives to the relationship. The three forces may sometimes work in concert. For instance, poor satisfaction, attractive alternative option, and low investment size may work together and push John to leave Mary. Elsewhere, the three forces may strain against each other. For instance, substantial investment and poor alternatives may trap John in a less satisfactory relationship.

Case Study 2. Potential Application of IM in Understanding Passenger Loyalty to Airlines

As a sales manager living in Atlanta, GA, Jonathan flies at least 50,000 miles a year. He has been mainly flying with XXX Airline in the past five years. As a matter of fact, after the airline lost his luggage and rescheduled his flights without explanation or apology for several times, Jonathan does not like the service of XXX airline at all (*low satisfaction*). Another airline has been offering special discounts lately. Jonathan has flown with that airline a couple of times before, and did enjoy their service (*appealing alternative option*). However, whenever he can choose his own itinerary and flight, Jonathan will still fly with XXX Airline, simply because he has already saved more than 200,000 frequent mileage with the airline. With these many miles, Jonathan can occasionally enjoy free upgrades, priority boarding, and other privileges. His "investment size" to XXX is so large that he cannot easily switch to another airline.

This is why some individuals choose not to end their unhappy marriages for their children (i.e., huge investments).

It has been suggested that "not all of these factors must be present for commitment to be experienced," and "there can be a lack of commitment when only one component is promoting commitment" (Le and Agnew, 2003: 39). Represented mathematically, commitment (COM) is defined as:

$$COM = (SAT—ALT) + INV$$

Consequences of Commitment

IM suggests commitment directly mediates the effects of three determining forces on John's pro-relationship behaviors. Commitment is suggested as a "central macromotive in relationships" (Rusbult et al., 1994: 123). For John, feelings of commitment may serve to: (1) subjectively summarize the nature of John's dependence on a relationship; (2) direct John's reactions to both familiar and novel relational situations; and (3) shape tendencies to engage in relationship maintenance processes. Rusbult et al. (1994) summarized relationship maintenance behaviors as:

1. John's decision to remain in or end relationships;
2. John's tendencies to accommodate, including exit ("behaviors that are actively destructive to the future of relationship," p. 125), voice

("active attempts to improve conditions in a relationship," p. 125), loyalty ("optimistically waiting for positive change," p. 125), or neglect ("passively allow conditions in a relationship to deteriorate," p. 125);

3. Derogation of alternatives, to convince John that the alternative to Mary or their relationship is not that attractive;
4. Willingness to sacrifice self-interest for the good of a relationship; and
5. Perceived relationship superiority or relationship-enhancing illusion, to evaluate the current relationship through comparisons to similar ones.

Empirical Support of the Model

Since its introduction to the literature, the utility of IM has been extensively examined. Le and Agnew (2003) conducted a meta-analysis on fifty-two previous IM studies, including sixty independent samples, and 11,582 participants, and reported robust significant correlations between the three antecedents with commitment. Satisfaction was found to be the strongest predictor of commitment, whereas quality of alternatives and investments were of similar absolute magnitude. Collectively, these three factors accounted for an average of 61 percent of the variance in commitment.

Although IM was originally developed as a means of examining interpersonal relationships (e.g., romantic involvement and friendship) (Rusbult, 1980b), it has been tested in nonpersonal settings (Ping, 1997; Tuten, 2005), and so on. Support for the model has also been obtained in nonrelational domains, although the model has been shown to better predict interpersonal relations (Le and Agnew, 2003). Le and Agnew (2003: 54) concluded that IM "can be extended to such areas as commitment to jobs, persistence with hobbies or activities, loyalty to institutions, decision-making, and purchase behaviors."

COMPETING THEORIES ON COMMITMENT FORMATION

As indicated, commitment has attracted research attention from multiple disciplines over several decades. A number of commitment theories and classifications have been proposed. The following section briefly reviews three competing conceptualizations of commitment, which have all cast significant influences in the fields of marketing and leisure/tourism.

Johnson's Commitment Framework

Johnson's commitment framework evolved over time. Initially, Johnson (1973) classified commitment into personal commitment—defined as "the extent to which an actor is dedicated to the completion of a line of action" (p. 396), and behavioral commitment—"those consequences of the initial pursuit of a line of action which constrain the actor to continue that line of action" (p. 397), which can be further categorized into social commitment and cost commitment. Later, Johnson (1982) expanded the conceptual domain of behavioral commitment into structural commitment, which is defined as "external constraints which come into play as a consequence of the initiation of the line of action and which make it difficult to discontinue should one's sense of personal commitment decline" (p. 53).

In 1991, Johnson systematically amplified his original conceptualization, and added a third factor (moral commitment) to his "commitment framework" (Johnson, 1991a). He proposed that "the decision to continue a relationship is a function of three different experiences of commitment: (1) personal commitment, the feeling that one wants to continue the relationship; (2) moral commitment, the feeling that one ought to continue it; and (3) structural commitment, the feeling that one has to continue it" (pp. 118–19). The motivation and action of maintaining or dissolving a relationship is the joint effect of social structure, individual psychology, and dyadic negotiation (Johnson, 1991b).

Johnson (1991a) delineated the three forms of commitment based on two dimensions: (1) the extent to which a factor is experienced as internal or external to the individual, with personal commitment (stemming from one's attitude and self-concept) and moral commitment (stemming from one's own value system and sense of right and wrong) being internally experienced, while structural commitment (stemming from one's assessment of the costs of termination) is externally experienced; and (2) the extent to which the experience is voluntary or constrained in nature. Specifically, personal commitment is one's own choice, while moral and structural commitments both involve a sense of constraint.

Johnson (1991a) further specified the sources of these three commitments. According to the model, one's personal commitment flows from (1) his/her attitude toward the relationship, (2) attitude toward the partner, and (3) his/her relational identity (i.e., "the extent to which one's involvement in a relationship is incorporated into one's self-concept," p. 120). Our moral commitment also comes from three sources, which are (1) a belief in the value of consistency, (2) values regarding the stability of particular types of relationships, and (3) a sense of obligation to the particular person with whom one is involved in the relationship. Finally, there are at least four kinds of constraining factors resulting in structural commitment: (1) irretrievable investments, (2) social reaction, (3) difficulty of termination procedures, and (4) availability of acceptable alternatives.

Johnson's commitment framework is sociological in nature. His early conceptualization of commitment (as personal and behavioral commitment) is highly influential, particularly in leisure and recreation studies (Kim, Scott, and Crompton, 1997; Kyle et al., 2004). His 1991 work has not yet been widely tested, although data from his recent study (Johnson, Caughlin, and Huston, 1999) supported the major propositions of the framework. Further, Adams and Jones's (1997) review of the marriage commitment literature also seem to support Johnson's framework. Their analysis suggested that most conceptualizations of interpersonal commitment implicitly or explicitly contained three types: an attraction type, a moral type, and a constraint type.

Despite its merit, Rusbult (1991) argued that Johnson's personal commitments construct is conceptually similar to satisfaction level in the IM, while structural commitment is similar to the investment size and quality of alternative categories. What is unique about his commitment framework is the proposal that moral commitment, a construct that is captured in the investment size construct in the IM, should be considered as an independent force. However, the necessity of adding this dimension has been questioned (Levinger, 1991; Rusbult, 1991). Further, while moral commitment makes conceptual sense in an interpersonal context, its applicability in a nonpersonal setting (e.g., a customer is committed to a service provider because s/he feels that switching to other brand will be morally wrong) warrants further examination.

Pritchard et al.'s Conceptualization on Commitment Formation

Pritchard et al.'s (1999) conceptualization of commitment has recently gained popularity in leisure studies (Kyle et al., 2004). Their main premise is that "the strength of a consumer's commitment is determined by a complex causal structure in which their resistance to change is maximized by the extent to which they: (1) identify with important values and self-images associated with the preference, (2) are motivated to seek informational complexity and consistency in the cognitive schema behind their preference, and (3) are able to freely initiate choices that are meaningful" (p. 344).

Pritchard and his associates' (Pritchard, 1991; Pritchard et al., 1999; Pritchard, Howard, and Havitz, 1992) conceptualization is mainly based on the work of Crosby and Taylor (1983), who suggested that the "tendency to resist changing preference" provided the principle evidence of commitment, and commitment was best explained by two antecedent processes: informational processes and identification processes. In addition, they were inspired by Salancik's (1977) work, which suggested that commitment is strengthened when people sensed their decision was (1) not easily reversed (revocability, which is conceptually similar to Crosby and Taylor's "informational processes"), (2) known to significant others (publicness, which is conceptually similar to Crosby and Taylor's "identification processes"), and (3) undertaken as an exercise of free choice (volition).

Combining the two conceptualizations (Crosby and Taylor, 1983; Salancik, 1977), Pritchard et al. (1999) proposed that "psychological commitment is best defined by a tendency to resist change and that three formative processes activate this tendency" (p. 337). Resistance to change refers to individuals' unwillingness to change their preferences toward important associations with and/or beliefs about the commitment object. Consistent with Crosby and Taylor, Pritchard et al. argued "resistance to change, as the principal evidence of commitment, will act as a mediator between the construct's antecedent processes and loyalty" (p. 337).

The three formative processes activating the tendency to resist change are informational, identification, and volitional processes. After empirical testing and validation, Pritchard et al. (1999) found that (1) informational processes are represented by informational complexity, which refers to the degree of complexity of a person's cognitive structure; (2) volitional processes are represented by volitional choice, which is defined by the perception that a decision to perform an action has been taken out of one's free choice; and (3) identification processes are represented by position involvement, which is the degree to which self-image is linked to brand preference.

Some leisure scholars have started to accept Prichard et al.'s work in their conceptualization of commitment (Iwasaki and Havitz, 2004; Kyle et al., 2004). However, it remains debatable whether the model Pritchard et al. suggested should be considered as the formation process of commitment, or just an internal structure of commitment. For instance, Pritchard et al. themselves maintained that "psychological commitment is best defined by a tendency to resist change and that three formative processes activate this tendency" (p. 337). Thus, it may be argued that the model does not necessarily depict a whole picture of what determines commitment, as it does not include a description of the external driving forces of commitment.

Three-component Model of Organizational Commitment

The organizational behavior literature also has a rich history of commitment studies, which have been traditionally associated with employee turnover intention and efficiency (Bansal, Irving, and Taylor, 2004; Jones and Taylor, 2004). Similar to Johnson's commitment framework, Allen and Meyer (1990) integrated various organizational commitment conceptualizations, and proposed a three-component commitment model (affective commitment, continuance commitment, and normative commitment).

In their conceptualization (Allen and Meyer, 1990; Meyer and Allen, 1997), the affective component of organizational commitment refers to employees' emotional attachment to, identification with, and involvement in the organization. Affective commitment may be considered as a desire-based attachment to the organization (i.e., Ming remains with the hotel because he *wants to*) (Bansal et al., 2004).

The continuance component refers to commitment based on the sacrifice and costs that employees associate with leaving the organization. Continuance commitment may be considered as a cost-based attachment that binds employees in the organization (i.e., Ming remains with the hotel because he *needs to*). In marketing, this has been called "calculative commitment" (Gustafsson, Johnson, and Roos, 2005), which reflects a disposition to stay based on a rational, economic evaluation of the costs and benefits involved in maintaining a relationship.

Finally, the normative component refers to employees' feelings of obligation to stay with the organization. Normative commitment may be considered as an obligation-based attachment to the organization (i.e., Ming remains with the hotel because he *ought to*—it is the "right thing to do").

Measures of these three forms of commitment have been developed and refined (Allen and Meyer, 1990; Meyer, Allen, and Smith, 1993). The three-dimension conceptualization and their measures have been extensively employed and accepted by organizational behavior and management researchers (Jones and Taylor, 2004; Payne and Huffman, 2005). Marketing researchers have also started to adopt the three-component classification in their examination of business-to-business commitment (Gruen, Summers, and Acito, 2000) or business-to-customer commitment (Bansal et al., 2004; Jones and Taylor, 2004). In the leisure literature, Park (1996) borrowed Allen and Mayer's (1990) conceptualization and proposed a multidimensional model of attitudinal loyalty, consisting of: investment loyalty (accumulation of side bets); normative loyalty (awareness of expectations from social groups); and affective loyalty (identification with the activity).

Note that the three-component classification of commitment is by nature not an explanatory model of the commitment-formation process. Put differently, the classification provides a useful framework to catch the multiple dimensions of commitment, while not explicitly explaining why commitment occurs. Further, the three-component classification does not necessarily conflict with IM. One may argue that affective commitment can be captured by the satisfaction construct of IM, normative commitment is included within investment size, and continuance commitment is similar to investment size and quality of alternatives.

CONCLUSION AND IMPLICATIONS

The purpose of this chapter is to conceptually identify a useful theory to guide future research on loyalty development. The authors suggest that Rusbult's IM (Rusbult, 1980a, b; 1983) hold the most promise. IM proposes that one's commitment to a relationship is strengthened by the level of satisfaction that s/he derives from the relationship, is fueled by his/her investments to the relationship, and is weakened by the quality of alternatives to the relationship. Although originally developed and empirically supported as a theory about romantic involvement, IM has found its utility in examining nonrelational commitment.

The authors further compared IM to three competing frameworks on commitment: Johnson's commitment framework (Johnson, 1991a, b), Pritchard's

(Pritchard et al., 1999) conceptualization of commitment formation, and the three-component model of organizational commitment in the organizational behavior literature (Allen and Meyer, 1990; Meyer and Allen, 1997). Although there are other commitment theories (for instance, Levinger's (1979a, b) social exchange model of cohesiveness, the ones reviewed in this chapter are arguably the most influential ones to the fields of marketing and tourism. This review revealed that the three competing models focus more on the classification and internal structure of the commitment construct. As different typologies of commitment, they provide useful insights to the discussion of commitment formation, but may not be the best guiding theory to explaining loyalty development. In contrast, IM presents a parsimonious explanatory model of key driving forces of commitment.

To conclude from a conceptual perspective, this chapter suggests that IM on interpersonal commitment may lend a theoretical foundation to the discussion on loyalty formation. Interestingly, factors such as satisfaction (Anderson and Srinivasan, 2003) and investments (Dick and Basu, 1994; Morais et al., 2004) have been suggested by marketing researchers as determinants of customer loyalty. We believe this may not be coincidence. Future research is needed to empirically examine the utility of IM.

REFERENCES

Adams, J. M. & Jones, W. H. (1997). The conceptualization of marital commitment: An integrative analysis. *Journal of Personality and Social Psychology*, 72(5): 1177–96.

Agustin, C. & Singh, J. (2005). Curvilinear effects of consumer loyalty determinants in relational exchanges. *Journal of Marketing Research*, 42(1): 96–108.

Alegre, J. & Juaneda, C. (2006). Destination loyalty: Consumers' economic behavior. *Annals of Tourism Research*, 33(3): 684–706.

Allen, N. J. & Meyer, J. P. (1990). The measurement and antecedents of affective, continuance, and normative commitment to the organization. *Journal of Occupational Psychology*, 63: 1–8.

Anderson, J. C. & Narus, J. (1984). A model of the distributor's perspective of distributor-manufacturer working relationships. *Journal of Marketing*, 48(4): 62–74.

Anderson, R. E. & Srinivasan, S. S. (2003). E-satisfaction and e-loyalty: A contingency framework. *Psychology & Marketing*, 20(2): 123–38.

Bansal, H. S., Irving, P. G. & Taylor, S. F. (2004). A three-component model of customer commitment to service providers. *Journal of the Academy of Marketing Science*, 32(3): 234–50.

Crosby, L. A. & Taylor, J. R. (1983). Psychological commitment and its effects on post-decision evaluation and preference stability among voters. *Journal of Consumer Research*, 9(March): 413–31.

Day, G. S. (2000). Managing market relationships. *Journal of the Academy of Marketing Science*, 28(Winter), 24–30.

Dick, A. S. & Basu, K. (1994). Customer loyalty: Toward an integrated framework. *Journal of the Academy of Marketing Science*, 22(2): 99–113.

Fournier, S. (1998). Consumers and their brands: Developing relationship theory in consumer research. *Journal of Consumer Research*, 24(March): 343–73.

Gruen, T., Summers, J. O. & Acito, F. (2000). Relationship marketing activities, commitment, and membership behaviors in professional associations. *Journal of Marketing,* 64(July): 34–49.

Gustafsson, A., Johnson, M. & Roos, I. (2005). The effects of customer satisfaction, relationship commitment dimensions, and triggers on customer retention. *Journal of Marketing,* 69(4): 210–18.

Iwasaki, Y. & Havitz, M. (2004). Examining relationships between leisure involvement, psychological commitment and loyalty to a recreation agency. *Journal of Leisure Research,* 36(1): 45–72.

Johnson, M. P. (1973). Commitment: A conceptual structure and empirical application. *The Sociological Quarterly,* 14(Summer): 395–406.

———. (1982). Social and cognitive features of the dissolution of commitment to relationships. In S. Duck (Ed.), *Personal relationships 4: Discussing personal relations,* pp. 51–73) London: Academic Press.

———. (1991a). Commitment to personal relationships. *Advances in Personal Relationships,* 3: 117–43.

———. (1991b). Reply to Levinger and Rusbult. *Advances in Personal Relationships,* 3: 171–76.

Johnson, M. P., Caughlin, J. P. & Huston, T. L. (1999). The tripartite nature of marital commitment: Personal, model, and structural reasons to stay married. *Journal of Marriage and the Family,* 61(February): 160–77.

Jones, T. & Taylor, S. F. (2004). *The nature and dimensionality of the commitment construct: Does to whom or what we are committed matter?* Paper presented at the 2004 AMS Conference Services Track Vancouver, British Columbia.

———. (2007). The conceptual domain of service loyalty: How many dimensions? *Journal of Services Marketing,* 21(1): 36–51.

Kelley, H. H. & Thibaut, J. W. (1978). *Interpersonal relations: A theory of interdependence.* New York: John Wiley.

Kim, S. S., Scott, D. & Crompton, J. L. (1997). An exploration of the relationships among social psychological involvement, behavioral involvement, commitment, and future intentions in the context of birdwatching. *Journal of Leisure Research,* 29(3): 320–41.

Kyle, G., Graefe, A. R., Manning, R. & Bacon, J. (2004). Predictors of behavioral loyalty among hikers along the Appalachian Trail. *Leisure Sciences,* 26: 99–118.

Le, B. & Agnew, C. R. (2003). Commitment and its theorized determinants: A meta-analysis of the Investment Model. *Personal Relationships,* 10: 37–57.

Lee, T. H. & Crompton, J. (1992). Measuring novelty seeking in tourism. *Annals of Tourism Research,* 19(4): 732–51.

Levinger, G. (1979a). A social exchange view on the dissolution of pair relationships. In R. L. Burgess & T. L. Huston (Eds.), *Social Exchanges in Developing Relationships,* pp. 169–93). New York: Academic Press.

———. (1979b). A social psychological perspective on marital dissolution. In G. Levinger & O. C. Moles (Eds.), *Divorce and separation: Context, causes, and consequences,* pp. 37–60. New York: Basic Books.

———. (1991). Commitment vs. cohesiveness: Two complementary perspectives. *Advances in Personal Relationships,* 3:145–50.

Li, X. & Petrick, J. F. (2007). *Revisiting the commitment-loyalty link in a tourism context.* Paper presented at the 5th Bi-Annual Symposium of the International Society of Culture, Tourism, and Hospitality Research, Charleston, SC.

Meyer, J. P. & Allen, N. J. (1997). *Commitment in the workplace: Theory, research, and application.* . Thousand Oaks, CA: Sage.

Meyer, J. P., Allen, N. J. & Smith, C. A. (1993). Commitment to organizations and occupations: Extension and test of a three-component model. *Journal of Applied Psychology,* 78(4): 538–51.

Morais, D. B., Dorsch, M. J. & Backman, S. J. (2004). Can tourism providers buy their customers' loyalty? Examining the influence of customer-provider investments on loyalty. *Journal of Travel Research*, 42(3): 235–43.

Park, S. H. (1996). Relationships between involvement and attitudinal loyalty constructs in adult fitness programs. *Journal of Leisure Research*, 28: 233–50.

Payne, S. C. & Huffman, A. H. (2005). A longitudinal examination of the influence of mentoring on organizational commitment and turnover. *Academy of Management Journal*, 48: 158–68.

Ping, R. (1997). Voice in business-to-business relationships: Cost-of-exit and demographic antecedents. *Journal of Retailing*, 73: 261–81.

Pritchard, M. P. (1991). *Development of the psychological commitment instrument (PCI) for measuring travel service loyalty*. Unpublished PhD dissertation, University of Oregon. Eugene, Oregon.

Pritchard, M. P., Havitz, M. E. & Howard, D. (1999). Analyzing the commitment-loyalty link in service contexts. *Journal of the Academy of Marketing Science*, 27(3): 333–48.

Pritchard, M. P., Howard, D. & Havitz, M. E. (1992). Loyal measurement: A critical examination and theoretical extension. *Leisure Sciences*, 14: 155–64.

Rusbult, C. E. (1978) *The development of Commitment in Interpersonal Relationships: An Investment Model*. Unpublished Ph.D. Dissertation, University of North Carolina at Chapel Hill.

———. (1980a). Commitment and satisfaction in romantic associations: A test of the investment model. *Journal of Experimental Social Psychology*, 16: 172–86.

———. (1980b). Satisfaction and commitment in friendships. *Representative Research in Social Psychology*, 11: 96–105.

———. (1983). A longitudinal test of the investment model: The development (and deterioration) of satisfaction and commitment in heterosexual involvements. *Journal of Personality and Social Psychology*, 45: 101–17.

———. (1991). Commentary on Johnson's "Commitment to personal relationships": What's interesting, and what's new? *Advances in Personal Relationships*, 3: 151–69.

Rusbult, C. E., Drigotas, S. M. & Verette, J. (1994). The investment model: An interdependence analysis of commitment processes and relationship maintenance phenomena. In D. J. Canary & L. Stafford (Eds.), *Communication and relational maintenance*, pp. 115–39. San Diego: Academic Press.

Rusbult, C. E., Martz, J. M. & Agnew, C. R. (1998). The investment model scale: Measuring commitment level, satisfaction level, quality of alternatives, and investment size. *Personal Relationships*, 5, 357–91.

Salancik, G. R. (1977). Commitment and the control of organizational behavior and belief. In B. M. Staw & G. R. Salancik (Eds.), *New directions in organizational behavior*, pp. 1–54. Chicago: St. Clair.

Shugan, S. (2005). Brand loyalty programs: Are they shams? *Marketing Science*, 24(2): 185–93.

Thibaut, J. W. & Kelley, H. H. (1959). *The social psychology of groups*. New York:

Tuten, T. L. (2005). The effect of gay-friendly and non-gay-friendly cues on brand attitudes: A comparison of heterosexual and gay/lesbian reactions. *Journal of Marketing Management*, 21(3/4): 441–61.

Part VI

Individual Determinants of Tourist Behavior

12 Tourism Segmentation by Consumer-Based Variables

Sara Dolnicar and Byron Kemp

INTRODUCTION

The basis for successful marketing is to understand and satisfy consumer needs. Sometimes it is even possible to satisfy one individual customer's needs. In the tourism industry an individually customized tourism experience can be developed, but the market for such high-end tourism products is small. This does not, however, mean that the only alternative is to appeal to the mass market. The intermediate solution is to understand which groups of tourists have similar needs and develop tourism products that match group needs. This approach is referred to as market segmentation.

The aim of this chapter is to analyze market segmentation studies in tourism research over the past decade, review recent prototypical examples of different segmentation approaches, and discuss theoretical and methodological issues related to market segmentation studies. Recommendations are presented that provide guidance to researchers and students with respect to how to best avoid potential pitfalls that may lead to misinterpretations of segmentation solutions and, consequently, suboptimal strategic decisions.

SEGMENTING TOURISTS BY CONSUMER-BASED VARIABLES

Market segments are the result of splitting individuals according to a predefined rule. Consequently, many possible segmentation solutions exist for any given problem, depending on the predefined rule selected. Different segmentation solutions result from (1) different segmentation bases and (2) different segmentation methods. Figure 12.1 provides an overview of possible segmentation methods, including both conventional and alternative approaches.

Market segments can be defined using different segmentation bases (Wedel and Kamakura, 1998): tourists can be split into groups based on their country of origin, which arguably represents the most common market approach in tourism. Sociodemographic variables are frequently used in tourism as well: destinations may specialize in family vacations, thus trying to attract people with specific sociodemographic characteristics.

While geographic and sociodemographic segmentation is very popular in tourism, behavioral and psychographic segmentation criteria have received increasing attention since Haley (1968) introduced the concept of benefit segmentation. Behavioral variables of interest include ways in which different tourists organize their vacation (e.g., travel agent versus online) or tourists' vacation activities, which have direct impact on the tourism product design. Psychographic bases include benefits sought, travel motivations, and destination preferences. All these segmentation bases can be referred to as consumer-based variables because they are characteristics of each individual consumer: having or not having a specific trait leads to the classification of consumers into different market segments.

The approaches most frequently stated to be used in tourism research are referred to as Concept 1 and Concept 2 in Figure 12.1. Concept 1 is the *a priori* (Mazanec, 2000) or *commonsense* (Dolnicar, 2004a) approach where one single splitting criterion is selected in advance and consumers are split based on their characteristic of the respective consumer-based variables such as young versus old tourists (e.g., Reece, 2004), female versus male travelers (e.g., Kim, Jehto, and Morrison, 2007), or countries of origin (e.g., McCleary, Weaver, and Hsu, 2006). The advantage of this approach is that it is methodologically simple; possible disadvantages are that management may select an unsuitable or suboptimal splitting criterion, and that the splitting criterion may be used by many destinations or businesses, thus not providing a good basis for distinct image building and competitive advantage.

Concept 2 in Figure 12.1 is referred to as *post-hoc* (Myers and Tauber, 1977), *a posteriori* (Mazanec, 2000), or *data-driven* segmentation (Dolnicar, 2004a). The segmentation base is a set of variables. The advantage of this approach is that consumer-based variables, hypothesized to be associated more closely to destination or tourist business choice (such as benefits sought), can be used to determine market segments. Such segments may enable a more unique differentiation and thus offer a competitive advantage. The disadvantage is that the identification (Frank, Massy, and Wind, 1972; Myers and Tauber, 1977) or construction (Mazanec, 1997; Wedel and Kamakura, 1998) of segments is achieved by using statistical techniques involving methodological parameters to be chosen by the researcher which have a major impact on the final segmentation solution. These decisions will be discussed in detail next.

Alternative segmentation approaches are rarely declared as such. They involve—either implicitly or explicitly—two grouping steps. Concept 3 refers to the situation where both groupings are made based on a single criterion (e.g., senior travelers among cultural tourists are profiled). In Concept 4 studies, the first grouping is data-driven, followed by a commonsense segmentation (e.g., repeat visitors among vacation activity segments). Concept 5 studies start with a commonsense segmentation and then proceed to construct a data-driven grouping (e.g., benefit segments among German tourists). Finally, Concept 5 studies represent a sequence of two data-driven segmentation studies (e.g., vacation activity segments further segmented by benefits sought).

Note that studies initially appearing to be Concept 2 often turn out to be Concept 5 studies because the starting point is a subset of the total population. For instance, Sung (2004) used a subset of the population (the adventure traveler market) as the basis for a data-driven segmentation based on variables including sociodemographics, psychographics, and behavioral elements. When Concept 3, 4, 5, and 6 studies are conducted simultaneously rather then subsequently, they are referred to as Concept 7 studies. For example, an activity-based and a benefits-based segmentation are computed independently and then cross-tabulated to investigate resulting vacation styles (e.g., Dolnicar and Mazanec, 2000).

Finally, response-based approaches (Concept 8) have received significant attention in the marketing literature (Wedel and Kamakura, 1998), but have not been widely adopted in tourism. The difference between segmentation based on consumer characteristics and response-based segmentations is that the latter use consumer responses to specific marketing stimuli as the starting point. Thus, response-based segmentation is determined not only by consumer characteristics but by the interaction between marketing stimuli and consumer characteristics.

MARKET SEGMENTATION IN TOURISM

Due to the fact that a tourist population can be split in an endless number of ways, any of the segmentation approaches outlined in Figure 12.1 could suffer from the selection of a suboptimal segmentation base. The selection

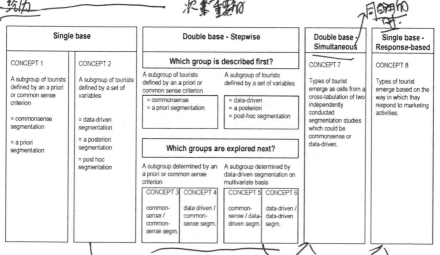

Figure 12.1   Segmentation approaches based on methods used for grouping.

of the segmentation base is a step in the segmentation process which has not received much research attention. One way to assess alternative segmentation bases would be to run simulations with alternative bases and, in so doing, empirically determine which segmentation base to choose. This, however, is not typically done. Usually the segmentation base is chosen in advance, based on managerial experience.

The second danger associated with all segmentation approaches at the profiling stage of the process is that group differences are frequently tested using independent tests for all variables of interest. Typically this is done by computing analyses of variance to test whether segments differ in metric variables (such as age, income, expenditure) and by computing chi-squared tests to assess whether differences between market segments in nominal, binary, or ordinal variables (such as gender, activities engaged in on vacation, country of origin) are significant. Because the same data set underlies all these tests, possible interactions between the variables are ignored, thus overestimating the significance of differences. This can lead to serious misinterpretations: marketing managers could falsely assume that the segments are highly distinct from each other in many ways. Correction for multiple testing or the use of a test that automatically accounts for multiple variables being tested simultaneously may, however, reveal that segments do not vary much at all and possibly do not even represent suitable target groups.

A third general problem is that changes over time are rarely accounted for. A segmentation solution is developed at a certain point in time and may then be used as the basis for strategic marketing for many years without reviewing changes in the segments over time. Approaches to take changes over time into account have been proposed by Wedel and Kamakura (1998) in the general area of market segmentation and Dolnicar (2004b) in the tourism context.

A final issue is the need to integrate segmentation strategies into the overall marketing strategy (including product positioning, segmentation, and competition). Only when all three strategic tools are well aligned can the optimal results be achieved. Optimally, a destination or a tourism business conveys an image which is distinctly different from the image of competitors and is in line with the market segment targeted. Typically, however, segmentation studies focus exclusively on identifying the most attractive segments. Rarely are positioning and competition issues taken into consideration. One exception is a segmentation method which uses brand image of tourists as the segmentation base and, in doing so, analyses all three aspects simultaneously. To date, this method, referred to as Perceptions Based Market Segmentation (Buchta, Dolnicar, and Reutterer, 2000; Mazanec and Strasser, 2000) or Perception-Based Analysis (Mazanec and Strasser, 2007), has not been widely adopted.

The following three sections review the predominant forms of segmentation studies by consumer-based variables in tourism. For this purpose, segmentation studies conducted in the past ten years that were published in the *Annals of Tourism Research, Tourism Management, Journal of Travel Research, Journal of Sustainable Tourism,* and *Journal of Travel and Tourism Marketing* were reviewed. Each study was coded as one case in SPSS including the variables sample size, type of segmentation, type of segmentation base, number of variables, data format, data structure investigation, data preprocessing, clustering algorithm, distance measure, number of clusters criterion, number of clusters, evaluation of validity, and evaluation of stability.

Single Base Commonsense/A Priori Segmentation (Concept 1)

Concept 1 segmentations require two steps: first, a splitting criterion is selected, typically by the marketing manager. Other indicators could come from prior literature as well as simulation. Each tourist is then classified as belonging to one of the segments based on their splitting criterion characteristic. Second, tests are conducted to assess whether the resulting segments differ significantly from each other in relevant dimensions, such as travel benefits sought and vacation activities or sources of information used during the destination-choice process. Such tests can either be conducted by independent chi-square tests and ANOVAs, in which case the resulting *p*-values have to be corrected to ensure that the significance is not overstated. Alternatively, discriminant analyses or regression models can be used in which the dependent variable is membership to a segment, and the independent variables are hypothesized to be significantly associated with being member of one of the segments.

The review of segmentation studies by consumer-based variables published in the last decade indicates that 56 percent of segmentation studies in tourism use the Concept 1 approach. Thirty four percent combine two segmentation bases to identify or construct market segments, and only 10 percent of studies use the pure single base data-driven approach. Concept 1 studies vary in the splitting criterion chosen as well as in the sample size used to profile the segment of interest. The average sample size was 2,080. The most frequently used splitting criteria (see Table 12.1) were behavioral (27 percent) and geographic (25 percent), followed by sociodemographic (23 percent) and psychographic (22 percent). Within the dominant group of behavioral characteristics, vacation activities and frequency of visit were most popular.

Single Base Data-driven/A Posteriori/Post-hoc Segmentation (Concept 2)

When using Concept 2 approaches, the expectation is that a quantitative method will identify which market segments exist in the data. This expectation implies that natural segments exist in the data, as depicted in Figure 12.2a. Although revealing the existence of natural clusters was clearly the intention of the pioneers of clustering in the social sciences, market

Table 12.1   Segmentation Variables used in Concept 1 Studies

Variable	Frequency	Percent
Segmentation base		
Behavioral	21	27%
Activities undertaken	8	10%
Frequency of visit	8	10%
Expenditure	5	7%
Geographic	19	25%
Sociodemographic	18	23%
Gender	7	9%
Age	4	5%
Lifecycle stage	2	3%
Disability	2	3%
Other sociodemographic	3	4%
Psychographic	17	22%
Values	5	7%
Motives	3	4%
Attitudes	3	4%
Expectations	2	3%
Other psychographic	4	5%
Mixed/Other	2	3%

segmentation and market structure analysis (Aldenderfer and Blashfield, 1984; Frank, Massy, and Wind, 1972; Myers and Tauber, 1977), segmentation researchers increasingly understand that survey data sets typically do not contain well-separated density clusters. This has led to a foundational paradigm shift whereby market segmentation is now viewed as construction of artificial groupings which are managerially useful (Mazanec, 1997; Wedel and Kamakura, 1998). Typical segmentations are therefore represented by the data illustrations in Figure 12.2b and 12.2c as opposed to 12.2a.

This has major practical implications: working with data as depicted in 12.2c means that every computation aiming at grouping tourists will result in a different solution. Consequently, methodological decisions made during the computation impact on the resulting segments. Solutions may still be managerially useful, but the data analyst and the manager using the segmentation solution as the basis for long-term strategic decisions need to be aware that they are essentially choosing a "random" solution. Sometimes

2a: True segment structure   2b: Pseudo structure   2c: No structure

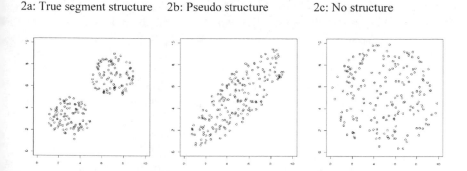

Figure 12.2   Examples of three data structures underlying a two-dimensional segmentation task (modified from Dolnicar & Leisch, 2001). Note: Figure 12.2 assumes only a two-dimensional segmentation problem, meaning that only two consumer-based variables are used as segmentation base. In reality, data-driven segmentation studies use significantly more variables than two.

data contains pseudo-structure, as depicted in 12.2b. Although natural segments do not exist, pseudo-structure leads to segmentation solutions that can be reproduced across replications, thus providing more confidence in the reliability of the solution.

With this in mind, the following steps are taken when a data-driven segmentation study is conducted: the starting point is the selection of the segmentation base. Then a suitable grouping algorithm needs to be identified. Grouping algorithms are not objective tools which help researchers to see the structure of the data; instead, they interact with data and have specific tendencies of constructing clusters of different shapes (Aldenderfer and Blashfield, 1984). The choice of algorithm affects the outcome. Everitt, Landau, and Leese (2001) discuss the way in which a range of clustering algorithms interacts with the data.

Next the number of segments to be constructed has to be chosen. Choosing the best number of clusters is an unresolved problem (Thorndike, 1953). A number of approaches have been proposed and compared in the past (Dimitriadou, Dolnicar, and Weingessel, 2002; Milligan and Cooper, 1985), but no single best solution has emerged. The authors prefer the approach of computing a number of segmentation solutions for each number of clusters and comparing how often each pair of respondents is grouped together across replications, an approach proposed by Dolnicar, Grabler, and Mazanec (1999).

Not that a large number of data-driven segmentation studies in tourism research use "factor cluster segmentation." This term describes a two-step approach whereby the original responses of tourists are factor analyzed, leading to a smaller subset of factors which are then used to cluster the data. This approach is not recommendable for market segmentation as demonstrated by Sheppard (1996) and Dolnicar and Grün (2008) because it does not help reveal heterogeneity based on consumer-based variables. These results are supported by a number of studies in management research and statistics (Aldenderfer and Blashfield, 1984; Arabie and Hubert, 1994; Ketchen and Shook, 1996; Milligan, 1996).

Concept 2 studies show fairly uniform trends. Sample sizes range from 100 to 1,680, with an average of 498 respondents; the number of variables in the segmentation base range from five to thirty-seven with an average of seventeen. Surprisingly, no association exists between sample size and the number of variables (Pearson correlation coefficient is–0.115). The studies with the largest number of variables in relation to the sample size only had three times as many respondents as variables. Fourteen percent of studies have less than ten times as many respondents as they use variables to identify homogeneous patterns. Formann's rule for latent class analysis can be used to provide an idea of reasonable sample sizes. Formann (1984) recommends–assuming binary question format—a sample of at least 2k to segment respondents using k variables; preferably 5*2k. According to this rule, the studies reviewed would require, on average, 131,072 respondents. Although Formann's rule relates to parametric procedures, it provides guidance for exploratory market segmentation, as it highlights that the complexity of the grouping increases exponentially with more variables.

The segmentation base chosen by segmentation researchers in tourism was almost exclusively psychographic (64 percent) or behavioral (21 percent, see Table 12.2). Among the behavioral studies, vacation activities represented 14 percent of behavioral studies. Among psychographic studies, values were the most frequently used segmentation base (21 percent). Other psychographic bases included perceptions, motives, attitudes, mood, expectations, and benefits sought.

More than half of the segmentation studies used ordinal data, raising the question of which distance measure was used, as distance measures for ordinal data are not readily available, yet they form the basic computation underlying clustering algorithms. Only 14 percent of studies provide information about the distance measure used, making an assessment of the quality of the segmentation solution difficult.

Data structure was not investigated by any of the Concept 2 studies reviewed, nor did any study include a measure of stability, indicating that researchers were either not aware of the structure before grouping or that they did not report data structure. In any case, it is difficult to assess the validity of a study if it is not clear whether segments were identified or artificially constructed. External validity, however, is tested frequently: two-thirds of studies report differences between segments using ANOVA and chi-squared tests. Corrections for multiple testing are rarely computed.

Only a few clustering algorithms are used: 36 percent use k-means clustering and 21 percent use hierarchical cluster analysis. The majority of

Table 12.2 Methodological Characteristics of Concept 2 Studies

Variable		Frequency	Percent
Segmentation base used	Psychographic	9	64%
	Values	3	21%
	Other	6	43%
	Behavioral	3	21%
	Activities under-taken	2	14%
	Search behavior	1	7%
	Mixed bases	2	14%
Data format of variables	Ordinal	9	64%
	Binary	1	7%
	Metric	1	7%
	Mixed	1	7%
	Not stated	2	14%
Evaluation of data structure	Yes	0	0%
	No	14	100%
Method of prepro-cessing	No preprocessing	8	57%
	Factor analysis	6	43%
Number of factors identified	3	1	17%
	4	3	50%
	5	1	17%
	10	1	17%
Clustering algorithm chosen	K-means	5	36%
	Hierarchical (not further specified)	3	21%
	Other	6	43%

continued

Table 12.2 (*continued*)

Variable		Frequency	Percent
Distance measure	Stated	2	14%
	Not stated	12	86%
Method for determining the number of clusters	Personal judgment	5	36%
	Heuristic procedure	3	21%
	Dendrogram from hierarch. step	3	21%
	Not stated	3	21%
Number of segments (clusters) selected	2	2	14%
	3	2	14%
	4	5	35%
	5	2	14%
	7	2	14%
	10	1	7%
Evaluation of validity	ANOVA	3	21%
	ANOVA and chi-square combination	3	21%
	MANOVA	1	7%
	Discriminant analysis	1	7%
	Mixture of the above	1	7%
	Not evaluated	5	35%
Evaluation of stability	Yes	0	0%
	No	14	100%

studies used the raw data for computations, but 43 percent used factor analysis, typically resulting in between three and ten factors which are subsequently used as data for clustering. This is concerning because the segmentation is actually performed in a transformed space if original variables

---

Case Study 1. A Recent Concept 2 Segmentation Study

Dallen (2007) recently conducted a Concept 2 segmentation study investigating public attitudes towards a railway line. Complete linkage hierarchical cluster analysis was used to define psychographic segments. Nine ordinal attitudinal statements from 282 respondents served as segmentation base. The raw data were used for calculations. No information is provided about data structure investigations or the distance measure used. While not directly stated, it can be inferred that the decision about the number of clusters was based on heuristic procedures (Dallen, 2007: 189). The clusters identified were described on the basis of additional characteristics. Although chi-square tests were mentioned, no significance tests are reported to allow the reader to assess the distinctiveness of resulting segments. Also, no evidence of stability is presented. The final segmentation solution resulting from this study consists of five user segments: "Train Devotees," "Infrequent Enthusiasts," "Train Tolerators," "Contented Car Users," and "Last Resort Riders." Recommendations include targeting the "Infrequent Enthusiasts" by improving the train environment to take advantage of this segment's already favorable attitude towards rail travel. In addition, "Train Tolerators" could be convinced to continue using the train by showing how the mode is preferable to car travel with regards to congestion and parking.

---

are not used. The methods for choosing the best number of clusters range from not mentioning how this selection was made (21 percent) to using heuristics and personal judgment.

Two key findings result from this review: (1) Concept 2 studies are not as frequent as anticipated, because many studies use a subset of tourists as a staring point. (2) There still is room for improvement with respect to the theoretical and methodological underpinnings of these studies. Many appear to use a process following a formula which is based on prior work, suggesting that researchers may not be fully aware of the impact of methodological choices which affect the outcome of the study.

Double-base Stepwise Segmentation Approaches (Concepts 3–7)

Double-base segmentations are combinations of the two pure forms of market segmentation discussed previously. Typically, they are conducted in a stepwise manner (Concepts 3–6) by first selecting a subset of tourists and then undertaking another grouping. Often the preselection of tourists is not declared as an intrinsic part of the segmentation process, thus leading to the possible misclassification of such approaches as purely data-driven (Concept 2). A few studies have also been published which use two segmentation approaches simultaneously (Concept 7). This can be achieved by choosing two splitting criteria or segmentation bases (gender and age),

Case Study 2: A Recent Concept 5 Segmentation Study

Sung (2004) selected a subset of 892 adventure travelers and then conducted a data-driven segmentation using twenty-six sociodemographic, psychographic (perceptions), and behavioral variables (trip-related factors including frequency of trip, expenditure, information sources) measured on different answer formats. Data structure was not investigated. Data were standardized before clustering, a reasonable decision given that variables with different scales were used. K-means clustering was the algorithm chosen. The number of clusters (6) was determined using information such as "distances between final cluster centers, iteration history, final cluster centers, number of cases in clusters and an ANOVA table" (Sung, 2004: 348). Resulting segments were labeled "General Enthusiasts," "Budget Youngsters," "Soft Moderates," "Upper High Naturalists," "Family Vacationers," and "Active Soloists" and differed on factors such as household size, income and perceptions of adventure. Management recommendations were provided. For example, "General Enthusiasts" were found to be more likely to appreciate and participate in adventurous activities, whereas "Soft Moderates" were less likely to perceive adventure as highly. Therefore, differing marketing activities were recommended depending on the segment. The validity of this final cluster solution was investigated using discriminant analysis. The stability of the cluster solution was not investigated.

splitting the data set separately using both criteria and then cross-tabulating the results to arrive at combined segments.

Because double-base segmentations are combinations of commonsense and data-driven segmentations, they involve the same steps as the pure Concept 1 and 2 segmentations consequently also being endangered by the same methodological problems. Our review of segmentation studies indicates that double-base stepwise segmentation studies are conducted in a very similar way to Concept 2 studies (see Table 12.3): the average sample size was 1,180 with a average number of twenty-seven variables used. One study used as many as 157 variables with only 850 respondents. More than two-thirds used psychographic criteria (mostly traveler motives). All other studies used either behavioral variables (mostly vacation activities) or mixed variables. Most variables were ordinal in nature. Three studies could be identified which did investigate data structure prior to segmentation (Bloom, 2005; both studies in Dolnicar and Leisch, 2003).

Factor analysis was the most frequently used method of preprocessing (60 percent). Standardization of data occurred in only three studies, with the remainder of studies (34 percent) not carrying out any preprocessing. K-means (42 percent) and Ward's hierarchical clustering (17 percent) or a combination of the two (9 percent) represented the most popular algorithms. Of the forty-seven Concept 3–7 studies, only thirteen stated the distance measure used. The primary method stated was squared Euclidean

Table 12.3   Methodological Characteristics of Double-base Segmentation Studies

Variable		Frequency	Percent
Segmentation base used	Psychographic	34	72%
	Motives	17	36%
	Benefits sought	5	11%
	Perceptions	4	9%
	Preferences	2	4%
	Attitudes	2	4%
	Other psychographic	4	9%
	Behavioral	9	19%
	Activities undertaken	7	15%
	Other behavioral	2	4%
	Mixed Bases	4	9%
Data format of variables	Ordinal	33	70%
	Binary	3	6%
	Metric	2	4%
	Nominal	1	2%
	Mixed	4	9%
	Not stated	4	9%
Evaluation of data structure	Yes	3	6%
	No	44	94%
Method of preprocessing	No preprocessing	16	34%
	Factor analysis	28	60%
	Standardization	3	6%
Number of factors identified	3	3	10%
	4	6	21%

continued

Table 12.3 (continued)

Variable		Frequency	Percent
	5	11	38%
	6	3	10%
	8	4	14%
	10	1	3%
	34	1	3%
Clustering algorithm chosen	k-means	20	42%
	Ward's	8	17%
	Combination of k-means and Ward's	4	9%
	Hierarchical (not further specified)	4	9%
	Other	5	11%
	Not stated	5	11%
Distance measure	Stated	13	28%
	Not stated	38	72%
Method for determining the number of clusters	Personal judgment	12	26%
	Heuristic procedure	10	21%
	Dendrogram from hierarch. step	6	13%
	Other	2	4%
	Not stated	17	36%
Number of segments (clusters) selected	2	6	13%
	3	11	24%
	4	15	32%
	5	9	19%
	6	5	9%
	7	1	2%

continued

Table 12.3 *(continued)*

Variable		Frequency	Percent
Evaluation of validity	ANOVA and chi-square combination	13	28%
	Discriminant analysis	7	15%
	Chi-squared testing	6	13%
	ANOVA	5	11%
	Comparison with external variables	3	6%
	None	7	15%
	Mixture of the above	6	13%
Evaluation of stability	Yes	3	6%
	No	44	94%

distance, a method not suitable for ordinal answer formats. Thirty six percent did not report the method used to determine the number of clusters; when reported, personal judgment (26 percent) or some sort of heuristic procedure (21 percent) were more common. Concept 3–7 studies resulted in between two and seven segments. External validity was tested in 85 percent of cases, mainly using ANOVAs (11 percent), chi-squared tests (13 percent), a combination of both (28 percent), or discriminant analysis (15 percent). Three of the Concept 3–7 studies evaluated the stability of results (two studies reported in Andreu et al., 2005; Dolnicar and Leisch, 2003).

CONCLUSION AND IMPLICATIONS

The main results of this review indicate that segmentation research in tourism is still dominated by commonsense segmentation (Concept 1) studies. Such studies are sometimes viewed as "less sophisticated" but in fact represent the simplest model if tourism managers know which splitting criterion matters. Tests indicating how segments resulting from the split actually differ from each other should be provided to give tourism managers confidence that the splitting criterion does in fact lead to distinctly different segments. Data-driven segmentation studies are heavily utilized in tourism research, both in their pure form (Concept 2) and as part of double-base segmentation studies (Concepts 4–6). Psychographic and behavioral variables are most frequently used as segmentation bases. A number of methodological aspects have been identified which could be improved in future segmentation studies, including a data-driven component.

1. The number of variables should be reasonable given the sample size. Formann's rule can be used as a guide.
2. The structure of empirical data sets should be explored before clustering in order to be able to communicate to the end users whether naturally occurring segments were revealed, stable artificial clusters were constructed, or unstable artificial clusters are presented.
3. Data should not be factor analyzed before clustering. Instead, the raw data should be used where possible.
4. Cluster solutions should be validated using both stability and external validity measures.
5. The detailed parameters of the computations should be reported, including the precise algorithm chosen, distance measure used, and the approach taken for choosing the number of clusters.
6. Finally, it would be advantageous if segmentation studies would take into consideration positioning and competition issues. Currently they are treated as stand-alone components of strategic marketing, which does not mirror the reality that tourism destinations and businesses face.

Surprisingly, the picture that emerges from this review of segmentation studies published in the last decade mirrors previous findings of review studies. This is surprising because previous reviews have made explicit recommendations about how segmentation studies could be improved in the future. Specifically, Sheppard (1996) emphasized the need for caution when selecting factor analysis as a means of preprocessing, asserting that cluster analysis on raw item scores produces more accurate data-driven results.

Frochot and Morrison (2000) recommended selecting the most discriminating criteria for inclusion into the segmentation base, as practiced by Gitelson and Kerstetter (1990), who eliminated variables that were considered unimportant by more than 90 percent of respondents. This approach helps researchers reduce the number of variables without conducting factor analysis. Dolnicar (2002) recommended that the number of variables should be carefully selected relative to the sample size and that stability should be evaluated for obtaining a reliable solution. The issue of stability was raised by Dolnicar and Leisch (2003), who presented a method (bagged clustering) that automatically accounts for stability, and by Frochot and Morrison (2000), who recommended repeated measurements as the method of choice. Dolnicar et al. (1999) pointed out the importance of strategic integration of market segmentation, product positioning, and competition aspects.

It can be concluded that tourism research has come a long way with respect to acknowledging that consumers are not one homogenous mass which can be expected to enjoy the same tourism product. A large number of segmentation studies have been conducted over the past decade which acknowledge differences between consumers and attempt to learn how to best match consumer needs of specific subsegments. There is, however, still significant room for improvement.

REFERENCES

Aldenderfer, M. S. & Blashfield, R. K. (1984). *Cluster analysis*, Beverly Hills: Sage.
Andreu, L., Kozak, M., Avci, N. & Cifter, N. (2005). Market segmentation by motivations to travel: British tourists visiting Turkey. *Journal of Travel and Tourism Marketing*, 19(1): 1–14.
Arabie, P. & Hubert, L. (1994). Cluster analysis in marketing research. In R. Bagozzi (Ed.), *Advanced Methods of Marketing Research*. Cambridge: : Blackwell.
Bloom, J. (2005). Market segmentation, a neural network application. *Annals of Tourism Research*, 32(1): 93–111.
Buchta, C., Dolnicar, S. & Reutterer, T. (2000). *A nonparametric approach to perceptions-based market segmentation*, vol. 2. Berlin: Springer.
Dallen, J. (2007). Sustainable transport, market segmentation and tourism: The Looe Valley branch line railway, Cornwall, UK. *Journal of Sustainable Tourism*, 15(2): 180–99.
Dimitriadou, E., Dolnicar, S. & Weingessel, A. (2002). An examination of indexes for determining the number of clusters in binary data sets. *Psychometrika*, 67(1): 137–60.
Dolnicar, S. (2002). Review of data-driven market segmentation in tourism. *Journal of Travel and Tourism Marketing*, 12(1): 1–22.
———. (2004a). Beyond "commonsense segmentation"—a systematics of segmentation approaches in tourism. *Journal of Travel Research*, 42(3): 244–50.
———. (2004b). Tracking data-driven market segments. *Tourism Analysis*, 8(2–4): 227–32.
Dolnicar, S., Grabler, K. & Mazanec, J. A. (1999). A tale of three cities: Perceptual charting for analyzing destination images. In A. Woodside (Ed.), *Consumer psychology of tourism, hospitality and leisure*, pp. 39–62. New York: CABI.
Dolnicar, S. & Grün, B. (2008). Challenging "factor cluster segmentation." *Journal of Travel Research*, 47: 63–71.
Dolnicar, S. & Leisch, F. (2001, 5–8 July). *Knowing what you get—a conceptual clustering framework for increased transparency of market segmentation studies*. Paper presented at the Marketing Science, Wiesbaden, Germany.
———. (2003). Winter tourist segments in Austria—identifying stable vacation styles for target marketing action. *Journal of Travel Research*, 41(3): 181–93.
Dolnicar, S. & Mazanec, J. A. (2000). Holiday styles and tourist types: Emerging new concepts and methodology. In W. C. Gartner & D. W. Lime (Eds.), *Trends in outdoor recreation, leisure and tourism*, pp. 245–55. New York: CABI.
Everitt, B. S., Landau, S. & Leese, M. (2001). *Cluster analysis*. London: Arnold.
Formann, A. K. (1984). *Die latent-class-analyse: Einführung in die theorie und anwendung*. Weinheim, Germany: Beltz.
Frank, R. E., Massy, W. F. & Wind, Y. (1972). *Market segmentation*. Englewood Cliffs, NJ: Prentice-Hall.

Frochot, I. & Morrison, A. M. (2000). Benefit segmentation: A review of its application to travel and tourism research. *Journal of Travel and Tourism Marketing,* 9(4): 21–45.

Gitelson, R. J. & Kerstetter, D. L. (1990). The relationship between sociodemographic variables, benefits sought and subsequent vacation behavior: A case study. *Journal of Travel Research,* 28(3): 24–29.

Haley, R. J. (1968). Benefit segmentation: A decision oriented research tool. *Journal of Marketing,* 32(30): 35.

Ketchen, D. J. J. & Shook, C. L. (1996). The application of cluster analysis in strategic management research: An analysis and critique. *Strategic Management Journal,* 17: 441–58.

Kim, D., Jehto, X. Y. & Morrison, A. M. (2007). Gender differences in online travel information search: Implications for marketing communications on the Internet. *Tourism Management,* 28: 367–78.

Mazanec, J. A. (Ed.). (1997). *International city tourism: Analysis and strategy.* London: Pinter/Cassell.

Mazanec, J. A. (2000). Market segmentation. In J. Jafari (Ed.), *Encyclopedia of tourism.* London: Routledge.

Mazanec, J. A. & Strasser, H. (2000). *A Nonparametric approach to perceptions-based market segmentation: Foundations.* Berlin: Springer.

———. (2007). Perceptions-based analysis of tourism products and service providers. *Journal of Travel Research,* 45(4): 387–401.

McCleary, K. W., Weaver, P. A. & Hsu, C. H. (2006). The relationship between international leisure travellers' origin country and product satisfaction, value service quality, and intent to return. *Journal of Travel and Tourism Marketing,* 21(2/3): 117–30.

Milligan, G. W. (1996). Clustering validation: Results and implications for applied analyses. In P. Arabie & L. Hubert (Eds.), *Clustering and classification.* River Edge, NJ: World Scientific Publications.

Milligan, G. W. & Cooper, M. C. (1985). An examination of procedures for determining the number of clusters in a data set. *Psychometrika,* 50(2): 159–79.

Myers, J. H. & Tauber, E. (1977). *Market structure analysis.* Chicago: American Marketing Association.

Reece, W. (2004). Are senior leisure travellers different? *Journal of Travel Research,* 43(1): 11–18.

Sheppard, A. G. (1996). The sequence of factor analysis and cluster analysis: Differences in segmentation and dimensionality through the use of raw and factor scores. *Tourism Analysis,* 1: 49–57.

Sung, H. H. (2004). Classification of adventure travellers: Behavior, decision making and target markets. *Journal of Travel Research,* 42(4): 343–56.

Thorndike, R. L. (1953). Who belongs in the family? *Psychometrika,* 18(4): 267–76.

Wedel, M. & Kamakura, W. (1998). *Market segmentation: Conceptual and methodological foundations.* Boston: Kluwer Academic Publishers.

13 Emotions and Affective States in Tourism Behavior

Juergen Gnoth and Andreas H. Zins

INTRODUCTION

Emotions in tourism behavior have gained increasing interest amongst researchers and managers alike. The reason is simple: tourism is all about recreating, feeling better both mentally and physically. Despite the recent surge in, for example, "wellness centers," it appears, however, that the emotional side of tourists' experiences in general has seemingly been ignored while the focus of competition between destinations continues to be on price and supply by way of second-guessing what tourists most desire to enhance their experience.

Instead of looking at price or product, the present chapter looks at some of the most important drivers and benefits tourists seek: emotions both as the stimulant towards activity as well as the outcome of experiences. Emotions are therefore discussed as the impetus, drive, compulsion, or simply a distinct energy that moves people either towards a destination experience or moves a person away from it (De Rivera, 1977). The chapter sets out why emotions are important for tourism researchers, and how we may study and understand them. It thereby reveals that emotions are by far not totally understood, including the fact that the difference between cognitions and emotions is not clear-cut. The chapter would also like readers to appreciate that emotions are symbolic experiences as they indicate both qualities of ensuing *actions* as well as those of *reactions*. Emotions thereby illustrate the relationship between the subject and object of a situation. After the development and discussion of the construct of emotions, the chapter finishes off with an overview of emotion research in tourism and calls for a more critical and more systematic treatment of emotions in tourism research.

WHY ARE EMOTIONS IMPORTANT?

Indeed, emotional responses to supply and experience elements in tourism have yet to be appropriately addressed in research. We have little understanding of how the actual interaction or the interplay between tourist and new environment is experienced, whereby "new" can mean anything from the experience of "familiar" to "exotic" attractions and across all tourism supply elements. The latter dichotomy highlights that the allocentric seeks out different amenities and levels of service to the psychocentric tourist (Plog, 1974), and every unexpected variation may impact the tourist's satisfaction for better or for worse. Yet, despite all progress, we still lack the right theories and tools to determine what exactly creates surprises or satisfaction, and to detail the role of expectations in the process of experiencing.

Consequently and as the vignettes indicate, emotion research dovetails with tourism motivation and expectation research (Gnoth, 1997). In particular, it links up with Pearce and Moscardo's (1985) notion of tourists' travel career as well as with Adler's (1989) notion of role play. The first concept deals with the skills tourists acquire when traveling repeatedly; as they "learn how to travel" they strive for higher need satisfaction, according to Maslow's hierarchy (1957). Yet how this is actually accomplished in experiential terms still eludes us and the concepts of experience and travel efficacy remain vague.

Likewise, the notion that "tourists play roles" when traveling relates to the different behaviors tourists display as they "live out their fantasies" and conceptions of what are desirable destinations and ways of traveling. Yet, there is as yet no way of knowing how tourists came to "play the role" in terms of acculturation (Berry and Sam, 1997; Rudmin, 2006) and how they adapt their feelings as they are doing it. We also lack deeper insights as to whether they experience known feelings in new surroundings or whether they experience new feelings in new surroundings, thus increasing their emotional repertoire (O'Malley and Gillette, 1984).

The difficulty that lies at the root of a lack of more rapid progress in this central concern of tourism research is, however, perplexing: What are emotions really? For example, Kleinginna and Kleinginna (1981a, b) found ninety-two different definitions of emotions and 102 different ones of motivation. This chapter details the phenomenon of emotions and related constructs (including affect, feeling states, mood, and traits). We then discuss emotion and affective response research in tourism and the emphases that have been chosen thus far. We close with a brief outline of further related and implicated constructs that are of importance to cross-cultural emotion research, including the link of emotions to schemata, values, and acculturation.

Understanding emotions is particularly important to researchers and marketers alike as tourism is all about the search for pleasure. Harking back to the beginnings of tourism in the modern world, traveling was ostensibly all about education and learning. Likewise but contrary to the intense intellectual stimulation of educational tourism just mentioned, there is the hedonic holiday, the one which is focusing on physical pleasure, be it resting on the beach or physical exertion on a mountain bike in lush bush or on mountain ridges. Emotions can be both, the natural response to felt needs as well as goals of activities. They are a response to the workaday's life (e.g.,

Parker, 1983), boredom, or a goal in the sense of wanting to "feel good," a desire for self-completion or fulfillment. They are part of processes as well as of states of being. Emotions are therefore also a central element in Csiksentmihalyi's (1975) concept of "flow," a feeling state that signals a perfect balance between a person's personal challenges and capabilities. Flow is like "riding the crest of a wave" or feeling in command of something that used to be precariously close to one's personal limits.

But while the popular understanding of emotions is relatively clear, researchers often grapple with the precise connotations of the term. How can an emotion be both a response and a goal? How can it be part of a process as well as an outcome? If learning through traveling is strongly dependent on cognitive activity, how does that link up with emotions? While we have some control over cognitions, can we control emotions? How do they differ and what have they got in common? Indeed, Prof. James's question put in the late 1800s is still awaiting a full answer, "What is an Emotion?" (1884).

Tourism management deals with the provision of experiences for the benefit of recreation, education, and entertainment. Consumption emotions are a response to these experiences. However, both managers and behavioral researchers in tourism require a deep understanding of how the generation of core affect (Russell, 2003) that is common to all humans links up with emotions as a reaction to contextualized circumstances. In order to help facilitate a better understanding of emotions in tourism experiences, this chapter will help develop an understanding of emotions in the context of sociocultural situations that typifies tourism.

THE PHENOMENON OF EMOTIONS

Emotions are psychophysical phenomena (Frijda, 1986) and may also be measured electronically as well as biochemically. Emotions may reach from subconscious reactions to stimuli in the environment (e.g., *dangerous* traffic, *towering* waves, . . .), to responses towards one's physical needs (e.g., nourishment, love, shelter). Psychologists often distinguish between basic and complex emotions. For example, Plutchik (1980) lists *acceptance, anger, anticipation, disgust, joy, fear, sadness, surprise* as basic emotions, while Izard (1977) also lists *interest, guilt,* and *distress,* neglecting others listed by Plutchik (for comparisons see Ortony and Turner, 1990). Parrot (2001), following Plutchik and others, lists primary, secondary, and tertiary emotions as combinations of the former primary emotions such as *love* (primary), *affection* (secondary), and *adoration* (tertiary). Emotions are often considered as either (a) feeling states, (b) motoric expressions that are generated by evaluative processes, or (c) outcomes of interpretations of physiological arousal.

One of the major issues with affective states is the role of time (cf. Figure 13.1). Feeling states can relate to any awareness of affect, whether it is

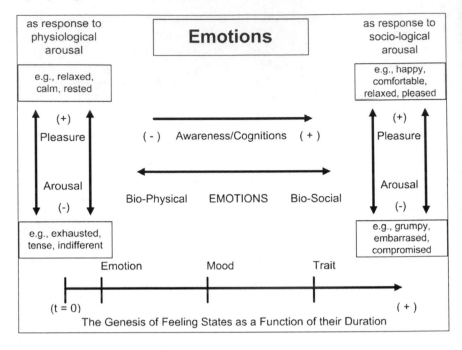

Figure 13.1 Emotions as responses.

the short, sharp feeling of pain when cutting your finger or when feeling bubbly, energetic, and outgoing. The first instance is classed as an *emotion* while the latter is referred to as *mood*. Yet, when a mood lasts for a long time or is persistent, people call it a *trait* (Allport, 1937; Plutchik and Kellerman, 1989). This common usage, however, lacks the precision that scientists require, thus still causing confusion within psychology (see Kleinginna and Kleinginna, 1981a) but also other disciplines, such as marketing (Bagozzi, Gopinath, and Nyer, 1999).

Motoric expressions relate to subconscious and nonvoluntary reactions in the body. Affective motoric expressions reach from instinctive responses to semiconscious physical responses. Yet, this can create confusion as it raises the question whether an instinctive reaction can be called an evaluation of a situation. If an evaluation takes place in a given situation (e.g., "does this person/situation/object pose a danger to me?"), then there is cognition involved, albeit at a primitive level. If this is not the case, then we are dealing with a clear distinction between emotion and cognition as two separate mechanisms that determine behavior. In psychology, some authors argue that emotions always follow cognitions (Lazarus, 1984) while others argue that affect does not always need cognition to instigate reactions (Zajonc, 1984). Again, the problem lies with classification and what the criteria are by which we classify an episode as cognitive (Kleinginna and Kleinginna, 1985).

Case Study 1. Stereotypical Emotions

There are some two hundred tourists milling around the shore of Milford Sound on the western side of an ancient forest in the Southern Alps, one of the biggest attractions of New Zealand's South Island. German, Japanese, and American tourists are taking photos, dipping their toes into the water, kayaking, or watching dolphins frolicking in the water. Against the backdrop of gray and green, mountainous rocks rise steeply from the sea, creating the fiord's gigantic passageway out to sea some eight kilometers away. When asked how they feel, the Germans mention the *overwhelming* size, the *sense of remoteness* and wilderness that emphasizes the *feeling of insignificance* of humans. The Americans just *love the contrast* of snow-capped mountains which, unlike in the United States, are so close to the sea. They also remark on the *quaint presentation of service facilities and the feeling of home-grown and unspoiled, genuinely friendly people* helping them on and off the coaches and into the boats that cruise out to sea and back. The Japanese, however, are showing their happiness of *having made it to one of New Zealand's most famous places* despite the *arduous trip* along bumpy roads and through the *eerie*, roughly hewn Homer Tunnel through which traffic has to thread in single file.

The seemingly easiest emotional category is the feeling state created by physiological arousal. This relates to evaluations of physical states whereby the state indicates a certain need or desire, or their satisfaction. Emotions appear to be highly subjective experiences that may or may not be under the influence of cultural learning rather than universal in their experience, expression, and form.

Another relevant distinction, especially for tourism researchers, is therefore that of dividing emotions into *biophysical and biosocial emotions*. Biophysical emotions refer to emotions that serve the functional or physical survival of beings. They are biophysical because the action-tendencies they evoke (Izard, 1977) are related to a genetic programming that favors survival. They relate to what is happening in the feeling body and what behavior they might trigger.

However, problems remain in clearly defining this set of emotions. Cognitions include knowledge, awareness, judgment, reasoning, and perception, and while the example of a victim's protective hand gesture in view of a falling baton may be an instinctive reaction, it appears to be learned and based on cognitions, albeit primitive ones. Nevertheless, the distinction may be more based on definitions and conventions than a true understanding of the nature of emotions.

The focus of biophysical emotions is the feeling person. Yet, there is often no sense in discussing emotions without reference to the environment that they arise in or that induces an emotional reaction. And it is precisely the complexity of the interaction between the individual being and the environment that appears to be the reason for the emergence of more sophisticated emotions over time. Viewed in their context, many emotions can therefore be classified as biosocial, which means they have developed in conjunction with the functions of hegemony and territorialism as ways of surviving and competing for resources (see, for example, van den Berghe, 1974).

Biosocial emotions have multiplied as a function of the development of more and more complex organisms that are now human beings, and because of the more and more complex roles humans play. In true fashion of emotions in general, biosocial emotions are mechanisms that help in the adaptation to the environment (Lazarus, 1991). They are considered as responses to stimuli by the appraisal school of thought (see Scherer, 1999). Both the struggle with the elements for survival and the struggle within one's social environment have created extensive and sophisticated emotional sensitivities and nuanced or highly differentiated behaviors.

It is at this point of cultural and social developments that we begin to differentiate simple emotions into more and more refined responses which we can name or describe. For example, the feeling of joy is a form of physical exultation. It can be further differentiated into delight, happiness, bliss, pleasure or ecstasy. Depending on the context, these terms contain different nuances in the meaning of joy that may signal socially relevant information as to its appropriateness. For example, one may feel happiness to be finally in the Sistine Chapel, in Rome's Vatican, but to feel ecstatic would most likely be considered inappropriate. *Biosocial emotions* are therefore those that have cognitive elements attached to their meaning and experience which they cannot be separated from. They differ across sociocultural settings and situations.

This leads us to a further differentiation, the difference between *emotions* and *cognitions*. The synonymous use of "feeling and thinking" indicates that there is a qualitative difference. . We can be aware of a feeling which suggests that a feeling can have a cognitive structure (Rollenhagen and Dalqvist, 1989). Conversely, we can have sad thoughts or listen to rousing poetry which may create the very feeling it tries to provoke. It is created entirely cognitively by a quasi-experience of the meaning of the words used. Yet it also appears that emotions have the capacity to be instantiated automatically (Kahnemann and Treisman, 1984), that is, without being paid attention as a function of cognition, or as a stimulus-response event. The emotional system may therefore be related to the cognitive system and partially overlap but also function as a system of its own. These factors permit the generation of new emotional experiences as well as cognitive growth.

At its extremes, the difference between cognitions and emotions reminds us of the one between the sign and the signified. The emotion of sadness signifies a certain feeling state that is a response to an evaluation of a situation for which we have the name (sign) of sadness. Thinking allows us to consider "sadness" without feeling it. The emotion of sadness can only be felt but not thought. It appears therefore that the human capacity of reflection, of critically observing one's own feelings, thought processes, and behavior, has facilitated at least two consequences. Firstly, it allows a more efficient way of solving problems by abstraction from situations so that logical thinking rather than trial-and-error processes can create solutions. Secondly, it facilitated the symbolic differentiation of situations; this refined distinguishing of the experiential elements of situations then permits the creation of defining terms. In other words, new emotion terms come into existence.

It is in this context that tourism researchers may find emotion research helpful in the analysis of behavior and experiences. Tourists come to new destinations with a set or repertoire of emotions that have been learned or associated with certain situations and in certain sociocultural contexts. The changes in the environment as well as the change in mental perspective from a workaday world to a holiday world permit not only cognitive but also emotional learning. The juxtaposition of one's own emotional profile or repertoire and new situations creates possibilities for expanding the adaptive capacity of both one's behavior and one's emotions. The emotional experience of (touristic) situations may be entirely new or expanding into new directions in quality and intensity, while new behavior is acquired.

Case Study 2. Pleasure and Arousal

Today is the great day! Finally, eleven-year-old Peter, his younger sister Sonja, mum, pop, and nana are going to the theme park with roller coasters and spooky caves. Peter has been *longing for* this day for weeks now and is quite *excited* as he tries to wriggle himself out of his father's *tensioning* hand. Nana looks up at the sheer height of the roller coaster and her *blood seems to drain* from her head so that she feels quite *dizzy*. Only mum and Sonja seem quite calm. They are quite *surprised* by the variety of activities and *enjoy* the colorful surroundings. Only dad feels *tired* and his arm has begun to *hurt* from Peter's persistent pulling. He simply cannot understand how Peter could be just so *full of anticipation*. Instead of Peter's *desire* for the sensations of *thrill* and *horror*, dad is *looking forward* to a *tasty* beer under the *cooling* shade of the trees while mum and nana, no doubt, will *quench their thirst* with a soft drink and *marvel* at Peter's seemingly insatiable *hunger* for extreme sensations that make him feel *exhilarated* but the women feel nauseated. Only Sonja is quite *calm* and *controlled* as she is *quite sure* that the *soothing* ride across the fairy-tale lake in a *softly cushioned* swan-like boat will be nothing like the *blood-curdling*, stomach-*wrenching* escapades her brother is sheer mad about.

EMOTIONS IN TOURISM RESEARCH

When using the terms *emotion, mood,* or *affect* for a literature search on CABI's Leisure and Tourism Abstracts, more than two hundred references can be identified. More than two-thirds of the publications emerged in the realm of sports, therapeutic, and other recreational research. About seventy-five papers address more tourism-related issues. The database covers more than twenty-five years of publications. About 10 percent of the identified contributions appeared in the eighties, roughly 20 percent in the nineties, and the overwhelming majority in the first seven years of the new millennium. This explosion reflects the increasing interest and maybe relevance of the topic in tourism research. Overall, four major areas can be differentiated.

Emotions in Satisfaction and Loyalty Research

About 20 percent of the accessible research (based on CABI abstracts) discusses the role of emotions for explaining customer satisfaction and loyalty aspects. In general, the core question focuses on identifying the most relevant emotional responses during the consumption/experience of different tourism services to explain satisfaction and repeat patronage. Studies cover tourists in general or in a particular destination (e.g., Baloglu, 2001; Chang, 2008; Hernández Maestro, Muñoz Gallego, and Santos Requejo, 2007), in the accommodation sector (e.g., Barsky and Nash, 2002; Han and Back, 2007; Wang and Wen, 2005), and the restaurant sector (Mattila, 2000; Ryu and Jang, 2007). Other studies addressed theme park (Bigné, Andreu, and Gnoth, 2005) and zoo visitors (Tsaur, Chiu, and Wang, 2006), cruise passengers (Sirakaya, Petrick, and Choi, 2004), and travel agency customers (Gilbert and Gao, 2005). Only a limited number of studies make use of previously tested inventories of consumption emotions, such as the PAD scale (Lehto, Douglas, and Park, 2007), the Consumption Emotion Set (Han and Back, 2007), or the consumption experience–elicited emotions (Zins, 2002).

Affective Attribution and Destination Image Research

The most significant share of scholarly contributions in this area addresses destination image: its structure, its formation, its impact on decision making. In contrast to these dominant domains, it appears that the focus is not the person/traveler who is to be characterized but the capacity of an object (in most cases here: destinations) to arouse emotions. Tourists evaluate constructions, projections, or experiences of environments and situations that destinations may generate. This evaluation is based on attributes (mostly moods and traits) which follow the aforementioned continuum of emotion terms as a function of their duration (see Figure 13.1).

Hence, the majority of destination image studies try to find out which category of attributes weighs more: for decision making prior to the visit (e.g., Lin, Morais, Kerstetter, and Hou, 2007; Phillips and Jang, 2007; San Martín and Rodríguez del Bosque, 2008) or explain repeat-visit intention during or after the trip (e.g., Chen and Tsai, 2007; MacKay and McVetty, 2002). Others are more interested in the psychographic properties per se that reflect on emotional responses (e.g., Baloglu and Love, 2004; Kim and Yoon, 2003). Only a small number of studies—in the present context—focus on the role of images in a competitive environment where destination managers have to identify an appropriate positioning strategy (e.g., Morgan and Pritchard, 1999; Pike and Ryan, 2004). A few papers incorporate the idea that perceived images differ according to different motivations and cultural backgrounds (e.g., San Martín and Rodríguez del Bosque, 2008) or through different consumption emotions during the visit (Tran Tuan, Schneider, and Gartner, 2006).

Experiences and Emotions

Defining and finally studying tourism experiences seem to be a rather new and emerging field of studies. Experiences are sometimes narrowed to some key elements of the entire leisure or holiday setting. Therefore, landscape perceptions (Hull and Revell, 1989; Pralong, 2006), the sense of a place (Stokowski, 2002), and experiences at a penguin-watching attraction (Schänzel and McIntosh, 2000) or at a Maori village (McIntosh and Johnson, 2004) appear as reference object to study the role of emotional responses to these particular exposures. The degree of host-guest interactions varies in these examples. However, the following three articles particularly focus on the role and impact of mood management: through the intervention of adventure guides (Sharpe, 2005) or waiters in a restaurant (Wildes, 2002) or other staff in nightclubs (Berkley, 1997).

Other Topics

Examples of this category include emotions, moods, or other kinds of affective responses as focal part of the research question. One common topic appeared as investigating the role of emotions or emotional mind-sets prior to traveling or other leisure activities: for example, Winiarski (1988) validated a seven-forces tourist-motivation scale comprising activity, catharsis, health, society, emotion, ambition, and knowledge; Leiper (1983) explored mental (cognitive and affective states among these) and nonmental factors of travel motivation; Gnoth, Zins, Lengmüller, and Boshoff (2000) tried to measure the trait concept of static versus dynamic orientation in order to explain travel motivations. Value-related research is almost nonexistent in the tourism context. Nevertheless, some studies related to ethical and/or environmental issues can be identified (e.g., Becken, 2004; LaPage, 2004).

Terror-related risks have been addressed by Uriely, Maoz, and Reichel (2007), while McIntyre (2007) developed the so-called Survival Theory of tourist consumption to explain tourists' learning experiences as a coping mechanism to the exposure of limited risks.

CONCLUSION AND IMPLICATIONS

Emotions are considered to be responses to internal or external stimuli. They express themselves in brief reactions (e.g., pain, joy) or in longer lasting experiences called moods and traits. Their importance for tourism researchers lies with their function in determining the experiential processes and outcomes of tourism activities. They help determine the quality of touristic pull as well as tourist-based push elements. A brief discussion of the fluidity of the terms involved, that is, the somewhat fuzzy distinction between emotions, moods, and traits, as well as the difference between cognition and emotion, is further complicated by the fact that emotions are determining experiences and outcomes as much as they help determine processes and goals.

The brief overview of emotions in tourism research shows a wide variety of application; alas, the authors miss a more critical and more systematic treatment of (the theory of) emotions. Rather, emotion research in tourism is very much based on a popular rather than scientific distinction. We therefore call for research that links emotions with motivation research in order to help determine the emotional qualities of what drives tourists to travel as well as how this impacts perceptions and experiences. Furthermore, as hedonic goals, emotions can also be configured as values that consumers strive to live by. Values are, in this sense, biosocial emotions or super-symbols to which tourists react as well as strive for.

Emotions also play a role in the creation and instantiation of schemata (Bartlett, 1932). As emotions set up action-tendencies they determine perceptions and expectations of processes and outcomes. Since tourism involves often new experiences in new situations, it appears as a fruitful goal to study how the experiencing tourist adjusts to new environments and alters as well as develops his/her emotional repertoire. Likewise, although the study of acculturation (Berry and Sam, 1997) focuses mainly on the impact and change of majorities on minorities, it can also involve the impact of minorities (tourists) on the emotional experience of hosts (majority). All in all, despite its central role emotion research in tourism is still in its beginnings.

REFERENCES

Adler, J. (1989). Travel as performed art. *American Journal of Sociology*, 94(6): 1366–91.
Allport, G. (1937). *Personality: A psychological interpretation*. New York: Holt.

Bagozzi, R. P., Gopinath, M. & Nyer, P.U. (1999). The role of emotions in marketing. *Journal of the Academy of Marketing Science*, 27(2): 184–207.
Baloglu, S. (2001). An investigation of a loyalty typology and the multidestination loyalty of international travelers. *Tourism Analysis* 6(1): 41–52.
Baloglu, S. & Love, C. (2004). A cognitive-affective positioning analysis of convention cities: An extension of the circumplex model of affect. *Tourism Analysis*, 9(4): 299–308.
Barsky, J. & Nash, L. (2002). Evoking emotion: Affective keys to hotel loyalty. *Cornell Hotel and Restaurant Administration Quarterly*, 43(1): 39–46.
Bartlett, F. C. (1932). *Remembering: An experimental and social study.* Cambridge: Cambridge University Press.
Becken, S. (2004). How tourists and tourism experts perceive climate change and carbon-offsetting schemes. *Journal of Sustainable Tourism*, 12(4): 332–45.
Berkley, B. J. (1997). Preventing customer altercations in nightclubs. *Cornell Hotel and Restaurant Administration Quarterly*, 38(2): 82–94.
Berry, J. W. & Sam, D. L. (1997). Acculturation and adaptation. In J. W. Berry, M. H. Segall, & C. Kigitcibasi (Eds.), *Handbook of cross-cultural psychology*, 2nd ed., Boston: Allyn & Bacon, pp. 291–326.
Bigné, J. E., Andreu, L. & Gnoth, J. (2005). The theme park experience: An analysis of pleasure, arousal and satisfaction. *Tourism Management*, 26(6): 833–44.
Chang, J. (2008). Tourists' satisfaction judgments: An investigation of emotion, equity, and attribution. *Journal of Hospitality & Tourism Research*, 32(1): 108–34.
Chen, C. & Tsai, D. (2007). How destination image and evaluative factors affect behavioral intentions? *Tourism Management*, 28(4): 1115–22.
Csikszentmihalyi, M. (1975). *Beyond boredom and anxiety*, San Francisco: Jossey-Bass.
De Rivera, J. (1977). *The structural theory of the emotions: Psychological issues.* Monograph 40. New York: International Universities Press.
Frijda, N. H. (1986). *The emotions. Studies in emotion and social interaction.* New York: Cambridge University Press.
Gilbert, D. & Gao, Y. (2005). A failure of UK travel agencies to strengthen zones of tolerance. *Tourism and Hospitality Research*, 5(4): 306–21.
Gnoth, J., Zins, A. H., Lengmüller, R. & Boshoff, C. (2000). Emotions, mood, flow and motivations to travel. *Journal of Travel and Tourism Marketing*, 9(3): 23–34.
Han, H. S. & Back, K. J. (2007). Assessing customers' emotional experiences influencing their satisfaction in the lodging industry. *Journal of Travel and Tourism Marketing*, 23(1): 43–56.\
Hernández Maestro, R. M., Muñoz Gallego, P. A. & Santos Requejo, L. (2007). The moderating role of familiarity in rural tourism in Spain. *Tourism Management*, 28(4): 951–64.
Hull, R. B. I. & Revell, G. R. B. (1989). Issues in sampling landscapes for visual quality assessments. *Landscape and Urban Planning*, 17(4): 323–30.
Izard, C. E. (197&). *Human emotions.* New York: Plenum Press.
James, W. (1884). What is an emotion?. *Mind*, 9: 188–205.
Kahnemann, D. & Treisman, A. (1984). Changing views of attention and automaticity. In R. Parasuraman & D. R. Davies (Eds), *Varieties of attention*, pp. 29–61.Orlando, FL: Academic Press.
Kleinginna, P. R. & Kleinginna, A. M. (1985). Cognition and affect: A reply to Lazarus and Zajonc. *American Psychologist*, 40(4): 470–71.
———. (1981a). A categorized list of emotion definitions, with suggestions for a consensual definition. *Motivation and Emotion*, 5(4): 345–79.

————. (1981b). A categorized list of motivation definitions, with suggestions for a consensual definition. *Motivation and Emotion,* 5(3): 263–91.

Kim, S. & Yoon, Y. (2003). The hierarchical effects of affective and cognitive components on tourism destination image. *Journal of Travel and Tourism Marketing,* 14(2): 1–22.

LaPage, W. (2004). Parks for life—an emotion-based park ethic for everyone. *Parks and Recreation (Ashburn),* 39(11): 8–10.

Lazarus, R. S. (1984). On the primacy of cognition. *American Psychologist,* 39: 124–29.

————. (1991). *Emotion and adaptation.* New York: Oxford University Press.

Lehto, X. R., Douglas, A. C. & Park, J. K. (2007). Mediating the effects of natural disasters on travel intention. *Journal of Travel and Tourism Marketing,* 23(2/4): 29–43.

Leiper, N. (1983). *Why people travel: A causal approach to tourism.* Working Paper, Travel and Tourism Division, School of Business and Administrative Studies, Sydney Technical College, New South Wales, Australia.

Lin, C., Morais, D. B. Kerstetter, D. L. & Hou, J. (2007). Examining the role of cognitive and affective image in predicting choice across natural, developed, and theme-park destinations. *Journal of Travel Research,* 46(2): 183–94.

Maslow, A. H. (1954). *Motivation and personality.* New York: Harper.

Mattila, A. (2000). When does mood matter? An examination of two types of hospitality service encounters. *Journal of Hospitality and Leisure Marketing,* 7(3): 55–65.

MacKay, K. J. & McVetty, D. (2002). Images of first-time visitors to Queen Charlotte Islands and Gwaii Haanas National Park reserve. *Journal of Park and Recreation Administration,* 20(2): 11–30.

McIntosh, A. J. & Johnson, H. (2004). Exploring the nature of the Maori experience in New Zealand: Views from hosts and tourists. *Tourism (Zagreb),* 52(2): 117–29.

McIntyre, C. (2007). Survival theory: Tourist consumption as a beneficial experiential process in a limited risk setting. *International Journal of Tourism Research* 9(2): 115–30.

Morgan, N. J. & Pritchard A. (1999). Managing destination image: The promise of mood branding. *Papers de Turisme,* 25: 141–49.

O'Malley, M. N., and Gillette, C. S. (1984). "Exploring the relations between traits and emotions." *Journal of Personality,* 52 (3): 274–84.

Ortony, A. & Turner, T. J. (1990). What's basic about basic emotions? *Psychological Review,* 97: 315–31.

Parker, S. L. (1983). *Leisure and work.* London: Allan & Unwin.

Parrott, W. (2001). *Emotions in social psychology.* Philadelphia: Psychology Press.

Pearce, P. L. & Moscardo, G. M. (1985). The relationship between travellers' career levels and the concept of authenticity. *Australian Journal of Psychology,* 37(2): 157–74.

Phillips, W. and S. C. Jang (2007). "Destination image and visit intention: examining the moderating role of motivation." ITourism Analysis *12 (4): 319–26.*

Pike, S. & Ryan, C. (2004). Destination positioning analysis through a comparison of cognitive, affective, and conative perceptions. *Journal of Travel Research,* 42(4): 333–42.

Plog, S. C. (1974). "Why Destination Areas Rise and Fall in Popularity," *The Cornell H.R.A. Quaterly.* 14 (4): 55–60.

Plutchik, R. (1980). *Emotion: A psychoevolutionary synthesis.* New York: Harper and Row.

Plutchik, R. & Kellerman, H. (Eds.). (1989). *Emotion: Theory, research, and experience,* vol. 1, pp. 3–33. New York: Academic.

Pralong, J. P. (2006). Geotourism: A new form of tourism utilising natural landscapes and based on imagination and emotion. *Tourism Review*, 61(3): 20–25.
Rollenhagen, C. & Dalkvist, J. (1989). *Cognitive aspects of emotion awareness.* Technical Report, Department of Psychology, University of Stockholm.
Rudmin, F. W. (2006). Debate in science: The case of acculturation. *AnthroGlobe Journal.* Retrieved 20 March, 2008, from http://malinowski.kent.ac.uk/docs/rudminf_acculturation_061204.pdf or http://www.anthroglobe.ca/docs/rudminf_acculturation_061204.pdf.
Russell, J. A. (2003). "Core Affect and the Psychological Construction of Emotion." *Psychological Review* 110 (1): 145–72.
Ryu, K. S. & Jang, S. C. S. (2007). The effect of environmental perceptions on behavioral intentions through emotions: The case of upscale restaurants. *Journal of Hospitality and Tourism Research*, 31(1): 56–72.
San Martín, H. & Rodríguez del Bosque, I. A. (2008). Exploring the cognitive-affective nature of destination image and the role of psychological factors in its formation. *Tourism Management*, 29(2): 263–77.
Schänzel, H. A. & McIntosh, A. J. (2000). An insight into the personal and emotive context of wildlife viewing at the Penguin Place, Otago Peninsula, New Zealand. *Journal of Sustainable Tourism*, 8(1): 36–52.
Scherer, K. R. (1999). Appraisal theory. In T. Dalgleish & M. J. Power (Eds.), *Handbook of emotion and cognition*, pp. 637–63. Hillsdale, NJ: Erlbaum.
Sharpe, E. K. (2005). Going above and beyond: The emotional labor of adventure guides. *Journal of Leisure Research*, 37(1): 29–50.
Sirakaya, E., Petrick, J. & Choi, H. (2004). The role of mood on tourism product evaluations. *Annals of Tourism Research*, 31(3): 517–39.
Stokowski, P. A. (2002). Languages of place and discourses of power: Constructing new senses of place. *Journal of Leisure Research*, 34(4): 368–82.
Tran-tuan, H., Schneider, I. E. & Gartner, W. C. (2006). Image of Vietnam held by US tourists: Initial inquiry. *Asia Pacific Journal of Tourism Research*, 11(2): 147–59.
Tsaur, S., Chiu, Y. & Wang, C. (2006). The visitors' behavioral consequences of experiential marketing: An empirical study on Taipei Zoo. *Journal of Travel and Tourism Marketing*, 21(1): 47–64.
Uriely, N., Maoz, D. & Reichel, A. (2007). Rationalising terror-related risks: The case of Israeli tourists in Sinai. *International Journal of Tourism Research*, 9(1): 1–8.
Van den Berghe, P. L. (1974). Bringing the beasts back in: Toward a biosocial theory of aggression. *American Sociological Review*, 39: 777–88.
Wang, C. & Wen, B. (2005). An empirical study of the emotion patterns of hotel guests. *China Tourism Research*, 1(1): 17–35.
Wildes, V. J. (2002). Unique training: The mood indicator is an employee's tool. *International Journal of Contemporary Hospitality Management*, 14(4): 193–96.
Winiarski, R. (1988). The questionnaire on tourist motivation /QTM/: Construction and psychometric characteristics. *Problemy Turystyki*, 11(2): 50–60.
Zajonc, R. B. (1984). On the primacy of emotions. *American Psychologist*, 39: 117–23.
Zins, A. H. (2002). Consumption emotions, experience quality and satisfaction: A structural analysis for complainers versus non-complainers. *Journal of Travel and Tourism Marketing*, 12(2/3): 3–18.

Part VII

Environmental Determinants of Tourist Behavior

14 E-Tourist Behavior
The Influence of IT on Consumers

Christine Petr

INTRODUCTION

E-tourism refers to the activities undertaken on the Web and on mobiles by consumers dealing with travel inquiries and decisions. E-tourism covers all electronically mediated activities carried out by consumers from their very first intention to get away up to their return. This large spectrum of e-tourism implies that e-tourists are not merely Internet shoppers but that they are more generally Internet surfers, whether they surf on the Web or through mobiles. Consequently, tourism Web sites and mobile services are regularly and strikingly challenged by consumers who request products, services, information, and guidance at every stage of their vacation process: future traveler, traveler, vacationer on the spot, and posttraveler.

At the same time, computer and mobile Internet technologies are dramatically changing the tourism sector and the practices of professionals, and not only the "travel agency" subsector. Thanks to Internet technologies, today professionals are able to target directly their potential consumers and to enlarge their traditional offers. For instance, airlines sell plane tickets and complementary services such as lodging, entertainment ticketing, and car rentals. These expanding and direct opportunities provided by Internet technologies have hybridized the tourism sector and dematerialized offers.

To better understand and forecast the changes brought about by the digital revolution, this chapter focuses on the consumer side. More precisely, this chapter reveals the main features of the vacation decision process in the Internet era. According to the "grand model" (Sirakaya and Woodside, 2005) designed by Engel, Kollat, and Blackwell (1968), once consumers have decided to go on holiday (i.e., after the "need recognition" preliminary step has occurred and was solved by the elicitation of a vacation departure), their decision process follows six main steps: (1) search for information, (2) evaluation of alternatives, (3) purchase, (4) delivery, (5) consumption, and (6) postconsumption feedback.

For tourism-related decisions in the Internet technologies era, this traditional six-stage decision-making process is converted into: (1) pretrip information search, (2) evaluation of alternatives, (3) booking, ordering, and

Table 14.1   New Services and Behaviors Offered to E-tourists

Consumer decision model	Tourism decision stages	New opportunities offered by Internet technologies (Web and mobile)
1. Information search	Pretrip information search	New way to search for information about destinations and packages An opportunity to receive customized information about offers and promotions
2. Evaluation of alternatives	Evaluation of alternatives (transportation, lodging, attractions)	A possibility to compare prices and products/to search for the best price
3. Purchase	Booking, ordering, and purchase	A complementary transaction channel to purchase travel products
4. Delivery	Delivery of tickets and vouchers	A quick and easy-to-use distribution channel for getting tickets and vouchers
5. Consumption	On-trip consumption and information search	An informational channel about attractions at the vacation spot
6. Postconsumption	Postconsumption (satisfaction, complaints, word of mouth)	A new way to express satisfaction and complaints A powerful media to spread word of mouth ("word of mouse": Gelb and Sundaram, 2002)

purchase, (4) delivery of tickets and vouchers, (5) on-trip consumption and information search, (6) and postconsumption. In each step, Internet technologies offer new opportunities and services for the consumer. As synthesized in Table 14.1, vacation planning behavior is altered in many ways.

SEARCH PRETRIP INFORMATION

Once the consumers have made their decision to take a trip, they search for information about offers and destinations. In this first stage, Internet technologies operate as a new communication channel that perfectly fits the intangible, complex, and interdependent nature of tourism. The Internet acts as the lifeblood of customers' motivation and ability to travel since it provides "the right information, at the right time, in the right place to the right individuals." In fact, information is quickly available anytime and anywhere, twenty-four hours a day, seven days a week.

Looking for Information

Data regularly confirm the important role of the Internet as a communication channel. For instance, Lake (2001) explained that 95 percent of Web users searched the Internet to gather travel-related information, with 93 percent looking for information through tourism Web sites. The impact of the Internet during the consumers search, together with the opportunity for destinations to be online to provide immediate, cost-effective information for travelers, has led numerous researchers to investigate the qualities and effectiveness of Web-based interfaces.

Travelers expect Web sites to be informative, interactive, and attractive (Chu, 2001). They are looking for reduced waiting time during browsing, which implies good page-loading speed and navigation efficiency. They consider ease of use, usefulness, information content, security, responsiveness, and personalization as key quality factors (Kim and Lee, 2004). And they appreciate finding everything on the Web site: editorial content and some value-added services. A good example of value-added service is offering, thanks to mash-up technology, direct and contextualized access to other Web sites (e.g., connection to GoogleMaps).

Also, the format of information (like color combination) influences the information search and the purchase intentions. For instance, some contextualized information makes Web site browsing pleasant and increases the intention to purchase products since the concept of store atmospherics is relevant when applied to online retailing (Eroglu, Machleit, and Davis, 2003).

However, procedural qualities are required to process information online; these are mainly cognitive and functional processes (Lehto, Kim, and Morrison, 2005; Pan and Fesenmaier, 2006). The three factors for an online information search to be successful are (1) information ease of access, (2) ease of use and (3) reliability.

Regarding the importance ease of access, accessibility should be the focus for destination and travel-related suppliers. Indeed, many Web users are unable to access sites because they use particular hardware and software. Williams and Rattray (2005), running the Bobby Web Accessibility Checker on a sample of UK lodging sites, found that 81 percent of hotel sites contain critical problems that impede accessibility. If the search is too time-consuming, Web users move to other Web sites.

The Hyper-choice Peril

The tremendous quantity of Web information is a double-edged sword. When future tourists look for information about offers and destinations, the Internet offers the opportunity to compare alternatives. Consumers have more choice within a larger area. Theoretically, the greater and better information on the Internet should lead to better decision making. But Peterson and Merino (2003) noticed that few studies dealt with this assumption. Usually, they neglected such situations, although "information overload" is crucial in the consumer decision process (Jacoby, 1984).

In contrast to intuitive and initial qualities associated with the Internet, the tremendous quantity of opportunities and information available can lead consumers to face hyper-choice situations. In fact, if there are too many offers to compare, consumers become unable and unwilling to evaluate all the alternatives in a rational way because the information search costs are too high (Ratchford, 1982). Overload situations are due either to the abundance of offers or to task overload (Otnes, Lowrey, and Shrum, 1997). Several factors contribute to tourism decision overload on the Internet:

- Regarding the general concept of choice sets (awareness, unawareness, evoked, inert, inept), studies show the need for a limited choice set and the use of a funnel-like procedure by consumers (Sirikaya and Woodside, 2005). Consumers seek to eliminate alternatives progressively so as to narrow down their choices. But the hypertext functions of the Internet provide more and more choices at every browsing click.
- This harmful overload increases when browsing starts in a generic search engine (like Yahoo). Every link containing the key words used to run the search is potentially listed. The links are displayed without any order or relevance hierarchy. Hence, the huge list of Web sites does not help consumers. They do not examine only the relevant sources and they do not ignore the irrelevant ones.
- Vacation planning online follows a hierarchical structure of decision episodes and chapters (Pan and Fesenmaier, 2006: 825). Consequently, consumers have to cope with overload during each phase of the vacation decision.
- Travel preparation is always a constructive and dynamic process; consumers often change their plans (Stewart and Vogt, 1999). Although consumers act as rationally as possible, the tourism psychology framework differs from the rationality paradigm. For instance, travelers may exert "triggering events" at some time in their vacation planning and information search, which will impact the consecutive vacation process (Decrop, 1999). These triggering events can occur during browsing through online promotional alerts or banner advertisements. Instead of being reassuring, they may induce consumers to constantly reinterpret their convictions.

As a consequence of overload situations, consumers will feel mixed emotions during the decision process. Since they are pleased to prepare their vacation, they should have positive feelings like joy and excitation, but they may have negative ones like anger, stress, and disappointment. This is called the ambivalence concept (Otnes, Lowrey, and Shrum, 1997). When consumers exert such mixed emotions in the marketplace, here the marketspace, they cope through several strategies:

Simplification: Due to limited brain capabilities, when consumers are confronted with complex situations, they adopt satisfying rules rather than maximizing ones. They will not search for the optimal solution but rather choose what can satisfy their main requests. This suggests that travel-related suppliers who are online should: (a) be among the most renown (to increase brand identification within the search result pages); (b) be well referenced (to be displayed on the first result pages), which implies finding the key words used by consumers rather than those exhibited by tourist organizations, since consumers' and institutions' word choices may differ (Pan and Fesenmaier, 2006); and (c) use simple domain names like the emerging ".travel" (Wagner, 2007) and provide an evocative title page (like "www.parisinfo.com" for the official City Tourist Board). This requirement for meaningfulness and simplicity is growing. Internet interfaces and browsing scenarios must be made simple, especially for mobile environments (Mahmoud and Yu, 2006).

Seeking assistance: E-tourists may seek assistance in three ways. First, they can use electronic agents (comparison-shopping agents) that run as recommenders. Second, they can ask friends and relatives, either in the real word (i.e., word of mouth) or on the Web (i.e., "word of mouse"; Gelb and Sundaram, 2002). Thanks to Web 2.0, an improved form of the World Wide Web where users can generate and distribute content, electronic word of mouth is expanding. The main Web 2.0 supports available are virtual communities (like Couchsurfing), travel blogs (personal or corporate), and travel wiki (like TripAdvisor Inside). They allow consumers to share experiences, to compliment and complain about travel-related suppliers, and to comment on hotels, attractions, restaurants, locations, and so on. Credibility is the main issue in these social networks and collaborative Web sites. In fact, since they are means of tourism marketing communication, consumers generally attribute a lower level of authoritativeness to them than to traditional word of mouth (Mack, Blose, and Pan, 2008). And finally, tourists can seek assistance from "brick-and-mortar" travel agents. In fact, traditional travel agencies will have to focus on specialized services in the disintermediated e-tourism environment (Dolnicar and Laesser, 2007) and change their roles as travel counselors or travel consultants (Bennett and Chi-Wen, 2005).

Extensive information search: Even if an extensive information search is synonymous with information overload, another coping strategy is to go on further into the search. These consumers will not use only online browsing. They will favor destination and tour operator brochures, for instance. Paradoxically, the Internet can rejuvenate the role and potential of traditional media in the digitalized era.

PERSONALIZED AND INTERACTIVE COMMUNICATIONS

Internet communications serve to process interactivity and personalization. The Internet offers the opportunity to customize available information about offers and promotions (Ansari and Mela, 2003). These customization opportunities are detailed here with a distinction between "push communication" (i.e., the organization sends information to clients and prospects) and "pull communication" (i.e., clients and prospects seek specific information from the organizations that have caught their attention).

Interactive Web Site Contents

The era of simple broadcasting of information has passed. Today, consumers can interact with the Web site content. It is a way to engage them with the Web site, to create interest and a desire to return to the site, and an opportunity to gain information about their preferences. Knowing users preferences allows the Web site contents to be customized for their next visit and to provide personalized communications and services that can meet their needs. Regarding travel planning theory, this examination of the preinformation search is also interesting for understanding complex travel behavior (Soo, Vogt, and MacKay, 2007). For this customer relationship marketing (CRM) purpose, Webmasters use tracking protocols to create personal profiles with the special needs for each Web user visiting the site. Cookies are good examples of such tracking technologies. These are little text files that store information about the Web users and their visits on the site. When the Web user comes back to the site, this information is reloaded in order to propose better adapted contents. For instance, if a Web user has checked weather forecasts during a previous visit on a destination site, this kind of information, or either the link to these specific pages of the Web site, should be presented directly on the home page for this Web user. In this way, content can be optimized for each visitor.

Newsletters, E-mails, and RSS Feeds

Regarding newsletters, many tourism organizations and travel suppliers collect information to personalize their newsletters. In a general context of consumers who are willing to provide significant personal information in exchange for recognition and better services, it is an opportunity to personalize the offers. When consumers prepare a specific trip, the opportunity to receive customized news and offers through e-mails serves their utilitarian consumer behavior perfectly. "RSS feeds" provide consumers with personalized information instantly on their computers. This technology makes up for consumers' shortage of time since they do not need to visit their favorites to check for news and updates. After subscription to the site, Web users are ensured to be automatically notified about updates and about the publishing of the precise information sought. In the vein of personalized services driven by advanced customer relationship management systems, customers accept to give their preferences and requirements in order to receive what they requested.

EVALUATION OF ALTERNATIVES

During the consumer-decision process, an important step is the evaluation phase. This evaluation consists in comparing offers regarding their scores on some important attributes. These attributes are derived from the utility function of each "consumer-decision problem" dyad.

The Recommendation-seeking Model

Some Internet software tools allow consumers to lessen the effort linked to the information search and to the evaluation of alternatives (Häubl and Murray, 2003). They are electronic decision aids that screen the vast array of offers on the Web. But, conversely to many Web search engines that sort the results on an alphabetically ordered list or by key-word match, these aids function as *recommender systems* (Ricci and Werthner, 2006). They are designed to assist customers in making their purchase decisions by providing an ordered list from the most to the least promising regarding consumers preferences and profiles. Acting as a super-salesperson with excellent knowledge of the qualities of the inventory and the tastes of the buyer, these screening agents provide prescriptions for consumers preparing a trip (Diehl, Kornish, and Lynch, 2003). According to microeconomists, the generic principle of shopping agents is to approximate the consumers' utility function. Since the utility function is correctly modeled, it is easier to restrain the display to offers that closely match the consumers' needs (Alba et al., 1997; Häubl and Trifts, 2000).

Regularly used by Web users, numerous online shopping comparison sites are dedicated to consumers travel activities and decisions. A nonexhaustive list is Expedia, Fastbooking, Illicotravel, Liligo, Planigo, Ratestogo, and Venere. These online shopping comparison sites propose to use the attributes that are common to most or all available products. For instance, to check for a flight, the attributes listed are departure and arrival dates and location, airline companies, class (economy, business, and first class), and some specific requirements like direct flights only. If consumers select one of the offers listed on the search-result pages of their online shopping comparison engine, they receive reverse fees from the product provider (hotel, airline company, car rental, etc.). The strategy of such e-travel retailers is therefore to increase the role of objective product information and their retailer brand credibility (Bo-Chiuan, 2007).

The model of comparison-shopping agents, also called "shopbots," is quite ancient since BargainFinder, the most widely recognized shopping agent, was developed in 1995 (but later abandoned). As the name of this premonitory tool proclaimed, the main service is price comparison. Price-comparison shopping is synonymous with both saving money and having fun (Marmorstein, Grewal, and Fishe, 1992). Nonetheless, shopping agents should not be price-dominated. Qualitative differentiation between the offers is increasingly requested. Responding to consumers' need, more personalized and integrative software tools are regularly implemented to increase marketing efficiency, which points to the upcoming expansion of electronic recommendation tools with qualitative comparison.

Towards More Price Sensitivity?

At the beginning of the Internet, it seemed the Web would lower consumers search costs and lead to greater price sensitivity. Further research shows conversely that the Internet can have a differentiating advertising effect due to the ease of access and processing of quality information, which turns into lower price sensitivity (for a review, see Dielh et al., 2003). Since the debate is not closed, some transitory elements should be noticed.

First, despite the assumption that Web screening on quality should decrease consumer price sensitivity and increase prices paid, recent research shows the opposite. Dielh et al. (2003) found that consumers faced with a price-ordered list from a screening agent will make many good choices with nearly comparable quality. So, price is more likely to play a deciding role. In fact, they showed that consumers paid lower prices when recommendations are ordered (ordered versus random agents). They also observed a learning process by Web users of recommendation agents: users gained in ability to find a low price. This suggests tourists will in the future be able to select the most suitable offers (of an average or optimal quality) at the best price.

Second, information search via the Internet is a major vehicle for comparison shopping. In this vein, recall that price is still the main criteria for ordering the results list on recommendation agents. Consequently, because the price attribute is easier to process, it is more prominent: when easy to process, price weighs more in decision making (Häubl and Murray, 2003). Concerning the diffusion of price-comparison tool usage among the whole population, Kocas (2002) analyzed the impact of the increasing numbers of price-comparison shoppers. His model forecasts a general tendency to bring down prices with an increase in the price dispersion up to a peak, after which the price range will decrease.

Third, pricing strategies on the Web are a major issue for firms in the tourism sector. The Internet makes it possible to reduce the recruiting costs of a consumer since the average transaction costs on an electronic distribution channel are much lower than on other channels. For instance, lodging and transport suppliers can improve pricing strategies and yields (Lockyer,

2005) taking into account their desire not to offer lower prices than their intermediaries, as they possibly fear "commercial retaliation." At the same time, when pricing formulas are correctly designed, the Internet lessens the suppliers' dependence on intermediaries, discounters, or traditional channels (Carvell and Quan, 2008). All these elements converge towards efforts to engage consumers through online and mobile channels and to determine why some are still not willing to use the Internet.

Fourth, the growth of no-frills airline companies and last-minute travel offers has accustomed travelers to dealing with low-cost tourism (Buhalis and Law, 2008). Regularly confronted with price deals, consumers have become bargain seekers. Indeed, Internet tourists value lower prices in many ways. For example, "the value for money of the package tour" is the most important factor affecting consumers' choice of a travel agency (Tak and Wan, 2005). Similarly, Wong and Law (2005) noted over 90 percent of the respondents they interviewed would consider booking hotel rooms through the Internet as long as there was a discount of at least 6 percent. These price promotions and "last-minute" offers are often not suitably considered in academic research about tourists' consumer behavior, although they dramatically impact the decision process; this point calls for additional investigation (Sirakaya and Woodside, 2005).

PURCHASING AND DELIVERY IN A DIGITAL WORLD

As anticipated, the use of the Internet for booking travel-related services is growing tremendously. In the European Community, 23 percent of

---

Case Study 1. E-tourists: Lookers, and Shoppers

Eric has practiced fun boarding during holidays since he was an adolescent. Now, he his married, and he has to balance his invading passion with the requests of his wife and now his baby. Last holiday, he found by himself the ideal spot on a very windy destination. To find this lodging close to beaches and windsurf material renters but with a swimming pool and some facilities for babies, he spent a lot of time to chat with other fun boarders on specialized e-forums and community Web sites. For next holiday, he has not much time to prepare the trip. He decides to book online a package from a tour operator specialist in windsurf holiday trips (e.g., "sportaway. com"). Everything will be prepared and scheduled. He has only to check availability and price. As demonstrated, Eric changes his decision process according to situations: When he uses the Internet to get information, he is an e-tourist "looker" (i.e., an Internet browser interested in tourism); when he looks for information and then shops online, he behaves as a "pure" e-tourist (i.e., a looker and a shopper).

over-sixteen-year-old Internet users have ordered products for personal use by Internet. Nevertheless, data show that Internet surfers are much more lookers than purchasers (Suskind, Bonn, and Dev, 2003).

The Multichannel Tourists Strategy: More Lookers than Purchasers

Many Web users are still not confident about security on the Internet and prefer to purchase off-line, that is, through traditional channels such as travel agents. As an illustration, Cunningham and colleagues (2005) found Internet airline reservation systems are perceived as riskier than traditional airline reservation shopping. Consequently, consumers use multiple channels when making arrangements for travel, accommodation, and attractions (Pearce and Schott, 2005). Future tourists search for pretrip information on the Web, receive information about Web-only fares and rates, approximate price boundaries of offers, learn from the "must" elements regarding the destination, and so on. Although many tourists actively use the Internet to find information to prepare their trips, only a minor part are actually shopping (payment with credit card) on the Web.

Regarding the differences between online and off-line shoppers, personal characteristics are a first set of explaining factors. The second one is prior experience with the destination and Web use experience. The third set is linked to attitudes toward Internet shopping and more precisely, attitudes toward outcomes of purchasing on the Web. The fourth set of factors refers to the quality of the online search experience. For instance,

---

Case Study 2. The Hybrid Tourist Decision Behavior

Marie and Jean-Michel are music festival organizers living in France. They have decided to go on holiday to Thailand for their summer break with their daughter. They do not want to prepare too much for their trip but have already booked a one-week stay in a hotel on Phuket Island for the first quarter of their Asian stay. They have found and purchased this lodging online from a French tour operator. For the rest of their four-week holiday, they found a lot of documentation about diverse places to visit. They have not booked anything, because they are persuaded they will find lots of interesting last-minute offers, online or off-line, when they undergo their research in Bangkok. For that purpose, when browsing Thai destination organization Web sites they have created a list of favorite Web sites to consult from their mobile phones when on the spot. They also think they will be recommended to check other interesting last-minute offers (transportation, visits, and lodging) by either local residents or tourists. For their holiday, Marie and Jean-Michel are combining online information search and off-line information search. Using online and off-line services and information as well, they are "hybrid" e-tourists.

Wong and Law (2005) reported that the three factors most affecting (68.3 percent of the intention to purchase variance) the intention to make a booking and to purchase for hotels on the Web are (1) the information quality (number of hotel Web features, links to other sites, useful information, visually attractive, price information); (2) the sensitivity content (sending sensitive information, competitive price); and (3) time (time required to fill in room-booking information and time required to search for a hotel Web site).

The Evidence of Digitalized Distribution

Numerous researches on retailing insist on the dematerialization of delivery created by electronic digitalization. This dematerialization is particularly manifested in the tourism sector. Since the product is consumed on spot at the destination, tourists need only tickets or vouchers to prove they have purchased the products. Since there is no physical delivery necessary to get tourism packages, Internet technologies are perfect to distribute travel products. Connecting to Web or mobile portals organized by category with contact details or links to the third-party operator, new contextualized and location-based services (LBS) allow consumers to book hotel rooms, airline tickets, and car rentals and to retrieve information about transportation schedules, travel guides for destinations, and dining guides wherever they are at the moment they need specific information.

Internet technologies appear to be very relevant when the decision choice is limited and routinized, as for domestic vacation decisions. They offer the opportunity to counter the growing impatience of consumers who want to find immediate answers to their travel questions (Buhalis and Law, 2008). Nowadays, more and more self-service technologies (SSTs) are implemented for digital distribution in the tourism disintermediated world. They are technological interfaces that enable customers to produce a service without involving direct service employees (Meuter et al., 2000). As a result, tourists can submit an on-screen reservation form to receive, nearly immediately on their mobile for instance (Tyler, 2000), the ticket or the voucher delivering the purchase.

To ensure tourism products enter the "marketspace" ("a virtual realm where products and services exist as digital information and can be delivered through information base channels" as defined by Rayport and Sviolka (1994: 14), some pragmatic advice is available. For instance, Kim and Kim (2004) established that after convenience, safety, and price, the next most important factor was the ease of information search. This calls for Web sites that are carefully designed. For example, a consumer-friendly Web site enables visitors to find important information "within two clicks" (frequently requested information should be displayed on the first page with hyperlinks); the transaction function (ordering functionality) is simple; current customers can easily retrieve and make modifications on their initial command (even ordered from another channel).

When following such recommendations for more consumer-orientated Web sites, the Internet represents an easy-to-use and successful complementary transaction channel for consumers. Under certain conditions of multiple-channel presence, the Internet also becomes efficient from the producer side (Lal and Sarvary, 1999): it can complement the traditional commercial environment, decrease price competition, and even increase consumer loyalty.

CONCLUSION AND IMPLICATIONS

Since the early form of the Internet, used in the 1960s by the armed forces for sending messages, the WWW has become a vast network of computer networks. Today, this technological tool that allows connecting individuals and cultures has dramatically changed the shape of the tourism industry and the way consumers make their vacation decisions. Today, tourists can build their tourism experience by bundling their products dynamically on the Web. They can form their individualized package of travel products (accommodation, transportation, etc.) without having to rely on intermediaries such as tour operators and global distribution systems.

Consequently, the Internet has empowered consumers. They are becoming more knowledgeable, independent, and sophisticated, which has dramatically changed tourism consumer behavior and even created a "new" tourist (Buhalis and Law, 2008). This "new" tourist, or "e-tourist," has gained bargaining power thanks to instant access to information about market offers and conditions and to the postconsumption testimonials of preceding tourists.

The Internet is persistently and dramatically changing the tourism industry. Facing the numerous alterations brought about by the Internet, every supplier and intermediary, either traditional or electronic, needs to adapt to remain competitive. But professionals do not have to abandon their current practices and know-how. Rather, they have to adapt and integrate the Internet and mobile technologies as complementary media and distribution channels in their global consumer-orientated strategy. Indeed, the Internet fits in well with traditional commerce and channels. It leads to hybrid distribution formats (the "click-and-mortar" model) and supports multimodality in the consumption process of tourists. Henceforth, the proliferation of the Internet and mobile technologies underlines the need for research on functional features for assessing effectiveness (ideal interfaces) and on Web literacy shortcomings. Additionally, studies should identify the technological and marketing procedures for ensuring consumers have greater confidentiality and privacy on the Web.

To conclude, e-commerce initially referred to the selling and purchasing of goods and services through computer-mediated Internet networks. Thanks to new networks mediated by mobile phones, e-commerce is now embracing mobile technology. Mobile phones are cheaper, easier to use, and more widespread than computers. In 2007, about 1.3 billion people had landline telephones and 2.2 billion had mobile phones (International Union of Telecommunications, UIT). In 2006, 33 percent of the world population had access to mobile-mediated networks and only 16 percent had Internet access. Given the multichannel strategies and mobile-marketing applications ("m-marketing" as called by Balasubramanian et al., 2002), mobile-mediated networks will tremendously expand the digitalized informational and commercial space of the Internet, leading to modifications of the offers and to new business practices. Indeed, all broadcasters agree that cell phone technology will play a major role in future e-commerce.

REFERENCES

Alba, J. et al. (1997). Interactive home shopping: Consumer, retailer, and manufacturer incentives to participate in electronic marketplaces. *Journal of Marketing*, 61: 38–53.
Ansari, A. & Mela, C. (2003). e-Customization. *Journal of Marketing Research*, 40: 131–45.
Balasubramanian, S., Peterson, R. A. & Jarvenpaa, S. L. (2002). Exploring the implications of M-Commerce for markets and marketing. *Journal of the Academy of Marketing Science*, 30(4): 348–61.
Bennett, M. M. & Chi-Wen, K. L. (2005). The impact of the Internet on travel agencies in Taiwan. *Tourism and Hospitality Research*, 6(1): 8–23.
Bo-Chiuan, S. (2007). Consumer e-tailer choice strategies at on-line shopping comparison sites. *International Journal of Electronic Commerce*, 1(3): 135–59.
Buhalis, D. & Law, R. (2008). Progress in information technology and tourism management: 20 years on and 10 years after the Internet—the state of etourism research. *Tourism Management*, 29(4): 609–23.
Carvell, S. A. & Quan, D. C. (2008). Exotic reservation—low-price guarantees. *International Journal of Hospitality Management*, 27(2): 162–69.
Chu, R. (2001). What online Hong Kong travellers look for on airline/travel websites? International *Journal of Hospitality Management*, 20(1): 95–100.
Cunningham, L. F., Gerlach, J. H., Harper, M. D. & Young, C. (2005). Perceived risk and the consumer buying process: Internet airline reservations. *International Journal of Service Industry Management*, 16(4): 357–72.
Decrop, A. (1999). Tourists decision-making and behavior processes. In A. Pizam & Y. Mansfeld (Eds.), *Consumer behavior*, pp. 103–33. New York: The Haworth Press.
Diehl, K., Kornish, L. J. & Lynch, J. G., Jr. (2003). Smart agents: When lower search costs for quality information increase price sensitivity. *Journal of Consumer Research*, 30: 56–71.
Dolnicar, S. & Laesser, C. (2007). Travel agency marketing strategy: Insights from Switzerland. *Journal of Travel Research*, 46(2): 133–46.
Engel, J. F., Kollat, D. J. & Blackwell, R. D. (Eds.). (1968). Consumer Behavior. New York: Holt, Rinehart & Winston.
Eroglu, S. A., Machleit, K. A. & Davis, L. M. (2003). Empirical testing of a model of online store atmospherics and shopper responses. *Psychology and Marketing*, 20(2): 139–50.
Gelb, B. D. & Sundaram, S. (2002). Adapting to word of mouse. *Business Horizons*, 45(4): 15–20.

Häubl, G. & Murray, K. B. (2003). Preference construction and persistence in digital marketplaces: The role of electronic recommendation agents. *Journal of Consumer Psychology*, 13(1–2): 75–91.

Häubl, G. & Trifts, V. (2000). Consumer decision making in online shopping environments: The effects of interactive decision aids. *Marketing Science*, 19: 4–21.

Jacoby, J. (1984). Perspectives on information overload. *Journal of Consumer Research*, 10(4): 432–35.

Kim, W. G. & Kim, D. J. (2004). Factors affecting online hotel reservation intention between online and non-online customers. *International Journal of Hospitality Management*, 23(4): 381–95.

Kim, W. G. & Lee, H. Y. (2004). Comparison of web service quality between online travel agencies and online travel suppliers. *Journal of Travel and Tourism Marketing*, 17(2/3): 105–16.

Kocas, C. (2002). Evolution of prices in electronic markets under diffusion of price-comparison shopping. *Journal of Management Information Systems*, 19(3): 99–119.

Lake, D. (2001). Americans go online for travel-information. CNN, 14 June.

Lal, R. & Sarvary, M. (1999). When and how is the Internet likely to decrease price competition? *Marketing Science*, 18(4): 485–503.

Lehto, X. Y., Kim, D. Y. and Morrison, A. M. (2005). The effect of prior destination experience on online information search behaviour, *Tourism and Hospitality Research*, 6 (2), 160–78.

Lockyer, T. (2005). The perceived importance of price as one hotel selection dimension. *Tourism Management*, 26: 529–37.

Mack, R. W., Blose, J. E. & Pan, B. (2008). Believe it or not: Credibility of blogs in tourism. *Journal of Vacation Marketing*, 14(2):133–34.

Mahmoud, Q. H. & Yu, L. (2006). Havana agents for comparison shopping and location-aware advertising in wireless mobile environments. *Electronic Commerce Research and Applications*, 5(3): 220–28.

Marmorstein, H., Grewal, D. & Fishe, R. (1992). The value of time spent in price-comparison shopping: survey and experimental evidence. *Journal of Consumer Research*, 19(1): 52–61.

Meuter, M. L., Ostrom, A. L., Roundtree, R. I. & Bitner, M. J. (2000). Self-service technologies: Understanding customer satisfaction with technology-based service encounters. *Journal of Marketing*, 64: 50–64.

Otnes, C., Lowrey, T. M. & Shrum, L. J. (1997). Toward an understanding of consumer ambivalence. *Journal of Consumer Research*, 24(1): 80–93.

Pan, B. & Fesenmaier, D. R. (2006). Online information search: Vacation planning process. *Annals of Tourism Research*, 33(3): 809–32.

Pearce, D. G. and Schott, C. (2005). Tourism Distribution Channels: The Visitors' Perspective, *Journal of Travel Research*, 44 (1), 50–63.

Peterson, R. A. & Merino, M. C. (2003). Consumer information search behavior and the Internet. *Psychology and Marketing*, 20(2): 99–121.

Ratchford, B. T. (1982). Cost-benefit models for explaining consumer choice and information seeking behaviour. *Management Science*, 28(2): 197–202.

Rayport, J. F. & Sviolka, J. J. (1994). Managing in the marketspace. *Harvard Business Review*, 72(6): 141–50.

Ricci, F. & Werthner, H. (2006). Recommender systems. *International Journal of Electronic Commerce*, 11(2): 5–9.

Sirakaya, E. & Woodside, A. G. (2005). Building and testing theories of decision making by travellers. *Tourism Management*, 26: 815–32.

Soo, H. J., Vogt, C. A. & MacKay, K. J. (2007). Relationships between travel information search and travel product purchase in pretrip contexts. *Journal of Travel Research*, 45(3): 266–74.

Stewart, S. & Vogt, C. (1999). A case-based approach to understanding vacation planning. *Leisure Science*, 21: 79–95.

Suskind, A., Bonn, M. & Dev, C. (2003). To look or book: An examination of consumers apprehensiveness toward internet use. *Journal of Travel Research*, 41: 256–65.

Tak, K. H. & Wan, D. (2005). Factors affecting consumers' choice of a travel agency: The case of Singapore. *Journal of Travel and Tourism Marketing*, 19(4): 1–12.

Tyler, C. (2000). Ticketing and distribution in the airline industry, *Travel and Tourism Analyst*, 2, 83–105.

Wagner, D. (2007). Advantages of travel as a top-level domain. *Tourism and Hospitality Research*, 7(3/4): 282–83.

Williams, R. and R. Rattray. (2005). UK Hotel web page accessibility for disabled and challenged users, *tourism and Hospitality Research*, 5 (3), 255–67.

Wong, J. & Law, R. (2005). Analysing the intention to purchase on hotel websites: A study of travellers to Hong Kong. *International Journal of Hospitality Management*, 24: 311–29. ✓

15 The Role of Media Products on Consumer Behavior in Tourism

Maria Månsson

INTRODUCTION

It has been suggested that tourists' imagination and consumption of destinations are no longer primarily influenced by destinations' promotion material such as brochures and advertisements. Contemporary tourists are influenced by media products like literature and film to a much higher degree in Western societies (Morgan and Pritchard, 1998). For instance, Rosslyn Chapel receives literary pilgrims paying tribute to *The Da Vinci Code* and New Zealand has experienced a boom of tourist arrivals after the film release of *The Lord of the Rings* trilogy. The connection is not new: the romance between art, literature, and travel has existed since the Grand Tour Period. What is new is the increased commercial sophistication of the merging between tourism and various popular media products.

Film and tourism industries are both products of a modern era where mass communication to consumers on a global market is possible (Sydney-Smith, 2006). They are also two industries feeding off each other in an intricate network, where the entertainment industry influences the tourism industry and vice versa. Popular cultural media products like *The Da Vinci Code* by Dan Brown (2004) are no longer just novels in themselves, as books and films are parts of a global entertainment industry where film production companies cooperate with destination marketing organizations as a means to get consumers' awareness.

In this chapter I intend to elaborate upon the role and effect of intertwined media products on tourism behavior. Previous studies of popular media products and tourism have, to a large extent, focused on one product at a time and treated this phenomenon as a niche tourism segment—an example being film tourism. I will therefore begin with an overview of some popular cultural media products like photographs and film in relation to tourists' behavior. This will be followed by an attempt to bring these media products together to be discussed as part of one and the same phenomenon, namely, mediatized tourism. *The Da Vinci Code* will be used throughout to illustrate media products influence on tourists' consumer behavior.

MEDIA PRODUCTS AND TOURIST BEHAVIOR

Media products may influence each stage of tourist behavior, from image formation to final decisions. Tourists can be inspired by a number of popular cultural media products, to various degrees, at the same time. Certain media products can inspire tourists differently depending on whether they are consumed before, during, or after a journey (Dann, 1996). This section outlines research that has been done in relation to the impact of various popular cultural media products on tourists' image of destinations and on their behavior. The first popular cultural media product I will discuss is paintings, to be followed by literature, film, guidebooks, and finally photographs, each having in common that they reproduce places and attractions although only guidebooks are produced specifically for tourists.

All media products are important for tourists in creating an awareness of depicted places or attractions as well as being a tool for tourists' image formation. These images are what tourists dream of seeing in real life. Hence, media products could be a determining factor in the decision-making process in relation to which destination to visit next time. Further, media products also influence the actual visit as they guide tourists to how places and attractions are viewed. After the return home the media products are still influential for the postconsumption behavior as a tool for sharing or remembrance. The chosen media products are examples of the phenomenon this chapter is intended to discuss—the convergence between media products and tourists' consumer behavior.

Paintings have been influencing tourists for a long time—this can be traced back to the Grand Tour Period. Artists framed images of people and of landscapes in paintings of places far away. These artist-created images were subsequently shown to people at home. The same images were repeated over and over again, which enabled recognition as discussed in Cherry's (2003) study of Algeria. Thus, when tourism started to grow in the nineteenth century, tourists often went to places associated or previously envisioned in paintings—the English fondness for certain places in Italy being a good example. However, paintings are not just media products that were popular in the beginning of the nineteenth century since they continue to have an impact on tourists and their approach to locations. For example, the Louvre has received an influx of visitors who come after they have read or seen *The Da Vinci Code* (Marjavaara, 2005). In a tourism context, the distinction between high art and popular culture does no longer seem valid, because in the case of the Louvre, for instance, tourists are influenced by a popular cultural media product to visit a museum with high art.

Literature is a media product which has a long tradition of being an influence on tourists' behavior. Literary tourism is usually connected to writers' lives and their work, and there are several potential reasons that tourists may decide to visit literary places. For instance, tourists are attracted by places which are connected to writers' lives, special dramatic events in the writers' lives, or the settings of a novel, Beatrix Potter and Hill Top Farm in The Lake District, England, being a prime example. Real places are embedded with special meanings derived from the authors' books (Herbert, 2001). Tourists also visit literary places to gain a deeper understanding of scenes in novels, including heightened emotional experiences triggered by books, even though the feelings they experience are not directly connected to the story in itself, such as childhood memories (Herbert, 2001). In Iwashita's (2006) study about Japanese tourists to the UK, it was evident that literature read as a child often influenced tourists' perception of and behavior at the destination.

Literary tourism has often been associated with literary pilgrims, that is, tourists who wish to visit places connected to a writer's life. However, the number of tourists who visit literary places out of curiosity or with a general interest outnumber the literary pilgrims (Herbert, 2001). Literary pilgrims might visit far-off locations but in general the setting is very important for tourists. A literary setting has to be located on a general tourist route close to other attractions and facilities in order to be visited. Interest in visiting literary sights has grown in recent years and so has the use of writers and their work to promote regions or towns by marketing organizations with the aim of attracting visitors. As an example, the author Mankell's detective novels about Kurt Wallander are used to promote Ystad, Sweden, in order to attract tourists to the town (Ystad kommun, 2007). This has been noted by Herbert, who argues that "Literary places are no longer accidents of history, sites of a writer's birth or death; they are also social constructions, created, amplified, and promoted to attract visitors (tourists)" (Herbert, 2001: 313). Thus, literature is influential for tourists' consumer behavior and a medium that can be used in all stages of a trip, for example, as a guidebook or as a memento.

Film and TV are high impact popular cultural media products when it comes to tourists' consumer behavior. The influence of film and TV is expected to grow, particularly in the case of film, which is perceived to take over the role formerly held by literature by some researchers (Kim and Richardson, 2003). Hudson and Ritchie (2006) defined film tourism as involving tourists who visit a destination or attraction as a result of the destination being featured on television, video, DVD, or the cinema screen. Film tourism could be seen as a new phenomenon, though Butler (1990 in Connell, 2004: 764) argues that film tourism can be placed in "a historical continuity . . . [of] . . . promotion through visual media, including high art, postcards, photographs and posters, traceable from the Grand Tour period." Whether it is new or not, film and TV tourism is enjoying a burgeoning interest within tourism research.

Previously conducted research in film tourism can be divided into four different fields of interest. First, the influence of film on the decision to travel (Riley, Baker, and Van Doren, 1998; Tooke and Baker, 1996). Second, research that focuses on the visitors to film locations, that is, film tourists (Macionis, 2004; Singh and Best, 2004). Third, sustainable destination issues with the impact of film tourism on visitation numbers and on residents (Beeton, 2005; Connell, 2005). Finally, destination marketing activities related to film (Hudson and Ritchie, 2006). Film tourism as analyzed in prior research is seen as a niche tourism segment where film and TV provide tourists with destinations, landscapes, icons, or stories to be consumed. Places therefore become commodities ready to be consumed by film tourists. Thus, film and TV's influence on destinations is confirmed, although there are still a limited number of studies made of the actual people who are influenced by these media products.

Although a different genre from the media products discussed before, guidebooks are the next item to be discussed. Guidebooks are much connected to tourists both as a tool for preparation and as a guide to the places that are visited. These books could be anything from educative, informative to read as pure entertainment. In the wake of tourism in the nineteenth century, guidebooks in the Baedeker style accompanied tourists and they showed which sights to see at a destination. Today the guidebook market is diversified and varied with anything from generic regional guidebooks to special interests like *Fodor's Guide to The Da Vinci Code: On the Trail of the Bestselling Novel* (Fodor Travel Publications, 2006). However, guidebooks are still influential to tourists' behavior and the books show how, when, and where to look while traveling (Urry, 1990). This is confirmed in a study of German tourists' use of guidebooks in Sweden. It showed that guidebooks had the highest influence on tourists' decisions to which places or attractions to visit (Zillinger, 2006).

Guidebooks might create mass tourism to certain attractions and destinations with the corollary that if a place or attraction doesn't exist in a guidebook, few tourists will go there. The influence of guidebooks could be seen as fomenting a herd mentality in tourists as the guidebook readers all travel to the same places and look at the sights through the same prism of the text. In contrast, Sørensen and Therkelsen (2005) argue that guidebooks help tourists to be individual travelers and to experience things on their own instead of being part of an arranged package tour. In this context, the guidebook is just a tool for helping the tourist to select between displayed places and attractions. Thus, guidebooks support the individual tourist's consumer behavior while at the same time upholding the beaten track and steering tourists' gaze.

Finally, photographs are products with many similarities to paintings as they are both visual media but also with some key differences. Recently, photographs have gained a growing place in tourism research. Although photographs and paintings are both visual media, tourists are more likely to take an active part in photographing a destination. Photography is closely linked with tourism and has been ever since the technology was developed.

It is one of these rituals of a trip that has to be done while being a tourist (Larsen, 2004). All these circulating photos, private as well as professional shots, are, in O'Barr's (1994) opinion, influencing what people go to see at a destination as well as how things are viewed. Larsen (2004) questions this argument, as he sees photos as a creation of memories to be consumed again and again by tourists. He claims it is an emphasis on family and relations and not just about imitating and repeating images seen elsewhere.

Photography is a practice which is not confined to tourists, as there are also professional photographers who sell their pictures on a global market. Photos surround people all the time—they can be part of promotional material, magazines, on postcards and private collections. Photographs have therefore many purposes other than in tourism; nonetheless, this might be the occasion when people are most active in the practice of photography themselves. With today's technology it is possible to instantly share moments and sights on a journey using mobile phones with Internet access. Thus, tourists are not passive consumers of media products because tourists are active in creating and distributing media products themselves. Furthermore, these tourist-created media products are circulating and consumed by other tourists as well as influencing other media products.

Thus, there are many different media products circulating simultaneously which affects tourists' consumer behavior. When media products circulate it is difficult to distinguish between images created by a specific media product since they intertwine and are in process simultaneously. This is reiterated by Busby and Klug (2001), who see literature and film as interchangeable. Hav-

---

Case Study 1: Visit Scotland's Da Vinci Code Campaign

The novel *The Da Vinci Code* by Dan Brown (2004) is estimated to be printed in 60 million copies worldwide (Wikipedia, 2008). The global factor of the book and the release of the film in forty countries in 2006 encouraged Visit Scotland, Maison De La France, and Visit Britain to cooperate in a global marketing campaign with the film production company, Sony Pictures, and its global partner Eurostar to show locations, destinations, and attractions associated with the film and the book (Visit Scotland, 2006). This campaign had many elements—one of them was www.visit-davincicode.com, which was a Web page with information covering the different attractions in the book as well as film locations. The site launched at the same time as the film premiered. The global press was very interested to write about this film because it had well-known actors in the lead roles, namely, Tom Hanks and Audrey Tautou. Visit Scotland has estimated that they gained £6 million worth of global publicity thanks to *The Da Vinci Code* (Scotsman, 2006). This joint venture shows how it is possible for the tourism industry to collaborate with the media industry before a film has premiered in order to stimulate visitor demand.

Case Study 2: Consuming Rosslyn Chapel

The Scottish setting for *The Da Vinci Code* is Rosslyn chapel, just outside Edinburgh. In 2006 it was one of Scotland's top 20 attractions with 170,000 visitors. This figure represented an increase of 48 per cent in just one year (Visit Scotland, 2007). The influx in visitor figures happened the same year the film was released, although the increase of visitors was already noticeable after the book was published in 2003 (*Scotsman*, 2006). Visitors have a number of reasons for coming to Rosslyn Chapel and it does not necessarily have to be connected to the book or the film. Nonetheless, as I noticed when I talked to tourists at the chapel, even visitors who had not read or seen *The Da Vinci Code* were aware of the connection because they had heard of the film, book, or been exposed to the media buzz. Despite this, there is a lack of visible references to *The Da Vinci Code* in the entrance building or in the chapel, and it is not until you reach the gift shop that a connection is made. With this case in mind, I can illustrate media influences on tourist behavior, as the book (and the film in this case) influences an attraction in both direct and indirect ways.

---

ing said that, it is not just these two products that are interchangeable, as popular cultural media products in general are intertextual and the boundaries between them are blurred. A novel like *The Da Vinci Code* has been turned into a film, documentaries, spin-off books, computer games, board games, tours for tourists, and guidebooks as well as much other merchandise. Where one product ends and another begins for the tourist is impossible to say because they are consumed concurrently. Hence, popular cultural media products are part of the same phenomenon, mediatized tourism, and I will exemplify this along the case of *The Da Vinci Code*. This case intends to show how popular cultural media products influence tourists' consumer behavior in a greater perspective than previously understood.

MEDIATIZED TOURISM

Tourism is seen as a ritual separated from everyday life and binary divisions like the ordinary–extraordinary, work–leisure, and home–away are in focus while discussing tourists' behavior (Urry, 1990). Leisure tourism has for those reasons focused on the week or fortnight tourists who go away on holiday. However, it is problematic to view tourism as an activity with a specific beginning or end because it creates a limiting perspective. The journey to a destination is preceded by talking to friends, reading novels and guidebooks, watching television programs or films, and so on, which are all sources for influencing imaginary landscapes that guide tourists' understanding of the things they are going to see and experience at a certain destination (Franklin and Crang, 2001). Take, for instance, a tourist to Rosslyn Chapel; his or her consumer behavior started already with the first contact with a *Da Vinci Code*–related product. All the combined inputs from various sources are accompanying the tourist to the actual visit and hereafter the process continues at home. Thus, in order to understand tourists' behavior it is necessary to view tourism as ongoing process with no clear beginning or end. Tourists' consumer behavior has therefore neither spatial nor temporal boundaries as it becomes inextricably linked with media consumption.

Destinations have no fixed meaning because they are dependent on whom and in which circumstance they are observed. This means that people create their own imaginary places with both internal and external influences like popular culture. Places, spaces, and landscapes are constructed through various influences like visual, textual, and symbolic media representations (Urry, 1990). It is these representations that are consumed and not the reality, and it is through these representations that knowledge of the world is created. Thus, the consumption of Rosslyn Chapel is not based on just the real place in itself because tourists will create their own imaginary experience. Novels, newspapers, Web pages, and talking to friends could, for instance, construct tourists' representations of Rosslyn Chapel.

The media in all forms have a prominent role in representations and constructions of places and tourist destinations. This can only increase as postmodern media surround everybody with fragments, narratives, and representations, which tourists can incorporate or reject (Campbell, 2005). There is a high level of intertextuality between different signs and images and "when we read a text, consciously or unconsciously, we place it in wider frames of reference of language and knowledge, cross-fertilizing a particular reading with other discourses drawn from our own socially, culturally and historically situated experiences" (O'Donohoe, 1997: 235). It is characteristic of postmodern society that consumers' lives are formed of webs of signs, and there is a rapid circulation of images with self-referential systems that are created and re-created on a constant basis (Jansson, 2002b). Tourists consume these circulating images and use them to construct an understanding of the world to experience as a tourist.

Modern technology can spread these circulating webs of signs rapidly to consumers in a global arena where popular culture reinforces and reflects patterns of communication and consumption for a mass audience. Because popular culture media products have a great impact on people's knowledge and image of destinations, they could be factors that determine which destination to visit next time, given that tourists are highly media literate. Therefore, to be a tourist is not an isolated state separate from other things going on in people's lives but rather is always present to some extent.

In the previous section, each popular cultural media product was discussed on its own. At this point, I shall look at them together to expand on the intertwining of media products and tourism. *The Da Vinci Code* case discussed earlier is intended to partly illustrate how partnerships between the media and the tourism industry are developed and also to highlight the impact of media products on consumer behavior in tourism. These examples show that different popular cultural media products work together at the same time—it may be films, paintings, novels, or marketing materials that influence tourists' consumer behavior. In many cases, films, which are used to promote destinations, such as *The Da Vinci Code, Arn: The Knight Templar,* and *The Lord of the Rings,* are based on a literary original.

Furthermore, film locations and literary attractions are listed in guidebooks like any other attraction. Still shots from media production and tourists' own photographs of these locations circulate, creating a blur of popular cultural related media products, which tourists then go on to consume. If a large proportion of tourism and tourist behavior is stimulated by media representations, it is important to study the convergence of popular cultural media and tourism itself. Thus, tourism is going through a mediatization process in which tourism and media consumption are inextricably linked. The ways in which people engage in media products have many similarities to tourism activities.

In Crouch, Jackson, and Thompson's (2005) understanding, tourism and media are linked through the tourist's imagination. This is a bridging concept between media and tourism, and it should be seen as a personal mode of understanding and feeling about the world. Issues of the tourist gaze and authenticity are highlighted through this concept. Jansson (2002a) also discusses the tourist gaze, which he considers has become intertwined with the consumption of media images, even if tourists also consume mediated representations. Thus, it is hard to separate media and tourism because they are so highly connected. This raises questions about fiction and reality.

Authenticity was one aspect discussed by Crouch et al. (2005)—it is a complicated concept, because the notion of real and fiction is highly personal. For some consumers, the meaning of a place is created through imaginary worlds. However, these imaginary worlds are not seen as fictional, because they are real to the beholder (Herbert, 2001). Another study where this is a relevant issue is Couldry's (2005) research into motivations of visitors to the set of the TV series *Coronation Street.* Although it is a fictitious place, it is perceived as real for tourists/visitors to the set. The set is the place where filming takes place and therefore is considered to be a real place by visitors. Some researchers stretch this even further and describe couch tourists or television tourists (cf. Davin, 2005; Gibson, 2006). They surmise that it is no longer necessary to travel to be a tourist, because the process starts while watching a TV program or reading a book.

The borderline between viewing a television program and being a tourist is blurring, because we are tourists all the time. Some researchers fear that imaginary tourism will replace visiting actual places, but Jansson (2002a) has noted that mediatized tourism is not replacing real traveling—on the contrary, it triggers an interest in firsthand experiences. The ongoing development of consumer motivations for tourism and the potential impact of media on them is worthy of continued study in order to challenge preconceptions of tourism and to analyze popular cultural media products in the context of relations to tourist behavior.

CONCLUSION AND IMPLICATIONS

The unclear dividing lines of creator and consumer and the blur of fictional and real call for a broader perspective to understand the new tourism—what Iwashita (2006) calls popular media-induced tourism. Busby and Klug (2001) call it media-related tourism. These terms are limiting, because they continue to view media and tourism as separate phenomena. I therefore suggest *mediatized tourism.* In my understanding, all tourism activities are in some way related to media products. While the media industry and the tourism industry are converging, so are the activities influencing consumer behavior in tourism. Media consumption weaves together with other forms of consumption (Jansson, 2002b) such as tourism consumption—as this overlap grows it should be studied in order to inform future approaches to the tourism experience.

Mediatized tourism is not a new label of niche tourist activity like film tourism. It should rather be understood as a converging concept to understand how media and tourism are related to each other. By this I mean there is an increased media commercialization in our society that affects tourist behavior. This is based on the growing number of cooperative ventures between media and tourism industries as in the projects of selling *The Da Vinci Code* and the related locations to potential consumers and tourists. Another characteristic element of mediatized tourism is the circulation of signs. Different popular cultural media products are circulating in marketing as well as among tourists themselves. Tourists consume these circulating signs which in turn affect new signs in a continuous process. The circulating signs influence tourists' consumer behavior in cases of decision making, motivation, representation of destinations, and so forth.

In mediatized tourism, the tourists are also co-constructers of the places they are visiting. For instance, Rosslyn Chapel is not just made of the buildings and the surroundings that can be seen in reality. The tourists bring their own signs to the actual visit which together form the construction and the reading of the place. Tourists' own imaginary worlds are therefore influencing their behavior at a destination.

Finally, what consequences will the intertwining of media and tourism take in tourism consumption? Consumers will take an active role when tourism and media-related products are merging. Tourists' own media products such as films, photographs, and travelogues are, for instance, created and shared with other tourists at community sites on the Internet. These communities have global reach and tourists can therefore live anywhere in the world and still share the same products. Thus, customer-to-customer communities are important for tourist behavior. When tourism is no longer seen as something detached from everyday life, it is necessary to further study tourism consumption in a broader popular cultural media perspective.

REFERENCES

Beeton, S. (2005). *Film-induced tourism*, Clevedon, UK: Channel View Publications.

Brown, D. (2004). *The Da Vinci code*. London: Corgi Books.

Busby, G. & Klug, J. (2001). Movie-induced tourism: The challenge of measurement and other issues. *Journal of Vacation Marketing*, 7(4): 316–32.

Campbell, N. (2005). Producing America: Redefining post-tourism in the global media age. In D. Crouch, R. Jackson, & F. Thompson (Eds.), *The media and the tourist imagination*, pp. 198–214. New York: Routledge.

Cherry, D. (2003). Algeria in and out of the frame: Visuality and cultural tourism in the nineteenth century. In D. Crouch & N. Lübbren (Eds.), *Visual culture and tourism*, pp. l 41–58. New York: Berg.

Connell, J. (2004). Toddlers, tourism and Tobermory: Destination marketing issues and television-induced tourism. *Tourism Management*, 26: 763–76.

———. (2005). "What's the story in Balamory?" The impacts of a children's TV programme on small tourism enterprises on the isle of Mull, Scotland. *Journal of Sustainable Tourism*, 13(3): 228–55.

Couldry, N. (2005). On the actual street. In D. Crouch, R. Jackson, & F. Thompson (Eds.), *The media and the tourist imagination*, pp. 60–75. New York: Routledge.

Crouch, D., Jackson, R. & Thompson, F. (Eds.). (2005). *The media and the tourist imagination*. New York: Routledge.

Dann, G. M. S. (1996). *The language of tourism: A sociolinguistic perspective*. Wallingford, UK: CABI.

Davin, S. (2005). Tourists and television viewers: Some similarities. In D. Crouch, R. Jackson, & F. Thompson (Eds.), *The media and the tourist imagination*, pp. 170–82. New York: Routledge.

Fodor Travel Publications. (2006). *Fodor's guide to The Da Vinci code: On the trail of the bestselling novel*. London: Ebury Press.

Franklin, A. & Crang, M. (2001). The trouble with tourism and travel theory. *Tourist Studies*, 1(1): 5–22.

Gibson, S. (2006). A seat with a view. Tourism, im(mobility) and the cinematic-travel glance. *Tourist Studies*, 6(2): 157–78.

Herbert, D. (2001). Literary places, tourism and the heritage experience. *Annals of Tourism Research*, 28(2): 312–33.

Hudson, S. & Ritchie, B. (2006). Promoting destinations via film tourism: An empirical identification of supporting marketing initiatives. *Journal of Travel Research*, 44: 387–96.

Iwashita, C. (2006). Media representation of the UK as a destination for Japanese tourists. Popular culture and tourism. *Tourist Studies*, 6(1): 59–77.

Jansson, A. (2002a). Spatial phantasmagoria. The mediatization of tourism experience. *European Journal of Communication*, 17(4): 429–43.

———. (2002b). The mediatization of consumption. Towards an analytical framework of image culture. *Journal of Consumer Culture*, 2(1): 5–31.

Kim, H. & Richardson, S. L. (2003). Motion picture impacts on destination images. *Annals of Tourism Research*, 30(1): 216–37.

Larsen, J. (2004). *Performing tourist photography*. PhD thesis, Department of Geography and International Development Studies, Roskilde University, Denmark.

236   *Maria Månsson*

236   *Maria Månsson*

Macionis, N. (2004). Understanding the film-induced tourist. In W. Frost, G. Croy, & S. Beeton (Eds.), *International tourism and media conference proceedings*, pp. 86–97. Melbourne: Tourism Research Unit, Monash University.

Marjavaara, N. (2005). Bestialiska mord och mystiska koder. Available HTTP: http://www.aftonbladet.se/resa/europa/frankrike/article276118.ab (accessed 16 June 2006).

Morgan, N. & Pritchard, A. (1998). *Tourism, promotion and power: Creating images, creating identities.* Chichester, UK: Wiley.

O'Barr, W. (1994). *Culture and the ad.* Boulder, CO: Westview Press.

O'Donohoe, S. (1997). Raiding the postmodern pantry. Advertising intertextuality and the young adult audience. *European Journal of Marketing*, 32(3/4): 234–53.

Riley, R. W., Baker, D. & Van Doren, C. S. (1998). Movie induced tourism. *Annals of Tourism Research*, 25(4): 919–35.

Scotsman. (2006). *Da Vinci code* translates into £6m boost for Scots tourism. Available http://heritage.scotsman.com/topics.cfm?tid=542&id=1532032006 (accessed 18 January 2007).

Singh, K. & Best, G. (2004). Film-induced tourism: Motivations of visitors to the Hobbiton movie set as featured in *The Lord of the Rings*. In W. Frost, G. Croy, & S. Beeton (Eds.), *International Tourism and Media Conference Proceedings*, pp. 98–111. Melbourne: Tourism Research Unit, Monash University.

Sørensen, A. & Therkelsen, A. (2005). Guidebook: Tourists' ways of reading and relating to guidebooks. *The Journal of Tourism Studies*, 16(1): 48–60.

Sydney-Smith, S. (2006). Changing places. Touring the British crime film. *Tourist Studies*, 6(1): 79–94.

Tooke, N. & Baker, M. (1996). Seeing is believing: The effect of film on visitor numbers to screened locations *Tourism Management*, 17(2): 87–94.

Urry, J. (1990). *The tourist gaze.* London: Sage.

Visit Scotland. (2006). Promoting Scotland through *The Da Vinci code*. Available http://www.scotexchange.net/news_item.htm?newsID=39425 (accessed 30 May 2006).

Visit Scotland. (2007). Kelvingrove and Edinburgh Castle top Scottish visitor attractions. Available http://www.visitscotland.org/news_item.htm?newsID=45123 (accessed 8 May 2007).

Wikipedia. (2008). *The Da Vinci code*. Available http://en.wikipedia.org/wiki/The_Da_Vinci_Code (accessed 22 July 2008).

Ystad kommun. (2007). Kurt Wallander. Available http://www.ystad.se/Ystadweb.nsf/AllDocuments/BB304A3B6D259B9DC1256ED600260956 (accessed 25 June 2007).

Zillinger, M. (2006). The importance of guidebooks for the choice of tourist sites: A study of German tourists in Sweden. *Scandinavian Journal of Hospitality and Tourism*, 6(3): 229–47.

16 Cross-Cultural Differences in Tourist Behavior

Yvette Reisinger

INTRODUCTION

The tourism and travel industry has been experiencing an extraordinary increase in international tourism in the past decade. Worldwide international travel arrivals increased from 536 million in 1995 to nearly 900 million in 2007, with a 4.1 percent average growth per year. It has been predicted that this number will reach 1.6 billion by the year 2020 (WTO, 2007). These figures indicate continued and significant growth in international travel in the future. International travel patterns around the world have also changed in the last decade. The mature destinations, such as Europe and the Americas, show slower-than-average growth. Enormous growth is noticed in emerging markets and developing economies of Asia and the Pacific, the Middle East, and Africa. These regions are forecasted to record high growth in the future. The major future tourism regions will be Asia and the Pacific, China, India, Eastern and Central Europe, including Russia, and Latin America.

It seems that travelers from culturally different and non-English-speaking backgrounds will dominate the international marketplaces. Thus, there is a need to improve the ability of those who will be working in the tourism industry to understand and appreciate differences in culturally different tourist behavior and to translate that understanding into effective communication and interaction and appropriate management and marketing strategies. Some cultural differences, such as different ways of life, customs, dress, music, or cuisine, may be experienced by international tourists directly at a destination and generate interest. Other cultural differences such as kinship systems or many day-to-day practices that are hidden deeply in culture and cannot be experienced directly will require prolonged social contacts with locals and immersion in culture and can generate difficulties in adaptation to a foreign culture. The higher the demand for international tourism and more opportunities for cross-cultural contact, the greater the potential for cultural difficulties and meeting the demands of tourists and achieving their satisfaction.

CHALLENGES FOR THE TOURISM INDUSTRY

Such continued growth in international tourism and changes in travel patterns propose significant implications for the tourism industry. One of the most significant challenges for the industry will be meeting the needs and expectations of diverse cultural groups of international tourists, and dealing with cultural misunderstanding and even conflicts. The fundamental differences in philosophies, values, and social organizations make intercultural encounters prime candidates for colliding expectations (Burgoon, 1995). The needs and expectations of future international travelers will be influenced by their national cultures—the most powerful force that shapes people's behaviors. National cultures affect how tourists think, communicate, and understand. Tourists from different national cultures have distinct cultural values, norms, customs, rules of social behavior, beliefs, attitudes, needs, expectations, experiences, motivations, and communication styles. They perceive things differently, develop different meanings, and behave differently. Those from very different cultures will have the biggest difficulties in interacting and communicating with each other.

CULTURAL DIMENSIONS

A variety of dimensions have been identified as essential in differentiating and explaining differences in national cultures (e.g., Hall, 1976; Hofstede, 1980, 2001; Hofstede and Bond, 1984; Kluckhohn and Strodtbeck, 1961). These dimensions provide ways to understand how people behave and communicate across different cultures. Particularly significant are Hofstede's (1980, 2001) and Hofstede and Hofstede's (2005) dimensions of individualism/collectivism (IDV), uncertainty avoidance (UAI), power distance (PD), and masculinity/femininity (MAS), all of which were found to be very useful in distinguishing among culturally different societies and their behaviors. These dimensions are briefly discussed next.

Individualism/collectivism (IDV) refers to the extent to which individual goals and needs take primacy over group goals and needs. According to Hofstede (1991), individualism refers to "societies in which the ties between individuals are loose: everyone is expected to look after himself or herself or an immediate family" (p. 51). Conversely, collectivism refers to "societies in which people . . . are integrated into strong, cohesive in-groups, which throughout people's lifetime protect them in exchange of unquestioned loyalty" (Hofstede, 1991: 51). Thus, people from an individualistic culture tend to view themselves as independent of others in that their own individual goals are most important, whereas people from a collectivist culture tend to view themselves as connected to others and value the group's goals over their own.

Uncertainty avoidance (UAI) refers to the extent to which a society feels threatened by ambiguity and uncertainty and avoids risk. Individuals from high-uncertainty-avoidance cultures tend to avoid ambiguity and risk (e.g., new ideas, strangers) as opposed to individuals from low-uncertainty cultures. Power distance (PD) refers to the extent to which a society accepts class differences and social inequality. Individuals from a high-power-distance culture follow the orders of superiors and requests of elders, whereas individuals from a low-power-distance culture focus on equality and opportunity for everyone. Masculinity/femininity (MAS) refers to the extent to which a society emphasizes aggressiveness, competition, and gender inequality, versus quality of life and work, and gender quality. Individuals from a high-masculine culture tend to be competitive, achievement oriented, and assertive, as opposed to individuals from a feminine culture.

In order to evaluate Hofstede's findings, Michael Bond, with a group of Hong Kong and Taiwanese researchers, developed the Chinese Culture Connection (CCC) (1987) Value Survey. One of the dimensions identified which did not correlate with Hofstede's dimensions was Confucian work dynamism, which described patterns that are consistent with the teachings of Confucius (social order, unequal relationships between people, importance of family, education, proper social behavior, hard work, patience). This dimension significantly differentiated people in Asian countries from people in Western cultures. This dimension was added to Hofstede's model and called long- versus short-term orientation (LTO) (Hofstede and Bond, 1984). The LTO dimension differentiates societies according to their "time horizon" and approach to the past and present. Individuals from the long-term-oriented societies value long-term commitments and planning; focus on the past; and prescribe strong work ethics, perseverance, and persistence. Individuals from the short-term-oriented societies value short-term commitments and focus on the present rather than the past.

Table 16.1 presents an evaluation of various countries on Hofstede and Hofstede's (2005) value orientations. Based upon the previously mentioned classifications put forth by Hofstede, Western societies are most often associated with low or moderate uncertainty avoidance (except for Belgium, France, Germany, and Spain) and low power distance (except for Belgium, France, Italy, Spain, and the United States) and are generally individualistic (except for Spain) and short- or medium-term oriented, with mixed masculinity characteristics. On the other hand, Asian societies are most often associated with high collectivism and power distance, a long-term orientation, but are mixed in terms of masculinity and uncertainty-avoidance characteristics.

Although Hofstede's cultural dimensions have often been criticized for not being able to compare the values of individuals, measuring work values in a single industry, and not taking into account changing values over the longer period of time, they have been accepted as an international guide to understanding the differences in cultures between countries. Hofstede's

---

Case Study 1. Japanese Understanding

In Japanese culture, real understanding depends on understanding the meanings of words and expressions. There is a distinction between *tatamae* (what one feels must be said to maintain face) and *honne* (honest motives and real intentions). It is not *what* is said that is important but *how* it is said. There are three levels of the Japanese language: (1) low level, for addressing subordinates and younger people; (2) intimate level, for family members and close friends, and (3) a high level for superiors and elders. There is a special style of language for different genders. In introduction the use of first names is not accepted. The exchange of name cards is followed by a bow. There are informal, formal, and the highest forms of bowing. There are rules on when, how long and low, and how many times to bow. Shaking hands, favored by Westerners, is perceived as distasteful although it has been recently accepted for dealing with Westerners.

---

study has been replicated many times and the results confirmed on different samples. Hofstede's cultural dimensions have been successfully used in tourism research to differentiate among national cultures of tourists (e.g., Crotts and Erdmann, 2000; Litvin, Crotts, and Hefner, 2004; Litvin and Goh, 2004; Money and Crotts, 2003).

DIFFICULTIES IN MEETING THE TOURISTS' NEEDS

Cultural differences among international societies will make the task of meeting the needs of culturally different tourists difficult. The main difficulties experienced by international tourists usually develop from different value and belief systems, different rules of social behavior (e.g., proper introduction, greetings, self-disclosure, conversation codes, expression of opinions, showing respect, networking, making or refusing requests, and even eating habits), and communication style. Miscommunication occurs due to differences in the ways in which verbal cues (e.g., language fluency, polite language usage, expressing attitudes, feelings, or emotions) and nonverbal cues (e.g., facial expressions, eye gaze, spatial behavior, touching, posture, or gesture) are used. Differences in cultural values, beliefs, rules of social behavior, and communication style can cause irritations and be grounds for misinterpretation, misunderstanding, inaccurate perceptions, confusion, friction, and even conflicts.

The larger the cultural differences between international tourists and locals at a destination, the more difficulties experienced by tourists at the destination and the higher the probability of misunderstanding and tensions between tourists and locals. Destinations which are known and popular among international tourists can experience the most difficul-

Table 16.1 Evaluation of Selected Countries on Hofstede's (2005) Five Value Dimensions

Country	Power Distance	Uncertainty Avoidance	Individualism	Masculinity	Long Orientation
Australia	Low	Medium	Very high	High	Low
Austria	Very low	High	Medium	High	Low
Belgium	High	Very high	High	Medium	
Canada	Low	Medium	Very high	Medium	Low
China	Very high	Low	Low	High	Extremely high
Croatia	High	Very high	Low	Medium	Very low
Czech Republic	Medium	High	Medium	Medium	
Denmark	Very low	Low	High	Very low	Medium
Finland	Low	Medium	High	Low	Medium
France	High	Very high	High	Medium	Low
Germany	Low	High	High	High	Low
Greece	High	Extremely high	Low	Medium	
Hong Kong	High	Low	Low	Medium	Very high
Hungary	Medium	Very high	Very high	Very high	Medium
India	High	Medium	Medium	Medium	High
Indonesia	High	Medium	Very low	Medium	
Italy	Medium	High	High	High	Low
Japan	Medium	Very high	Medium	Very high	Very high
Malaysia	Extremely high	Low	Low	Medium	
New Zealand	Low	Medium	High	Medium	Low
Norway	Low	Medium	High	Very low	Medium
Philippines	Very high	Medium	Low	High	Very low
Russia	Very high	Very high	Low	Low	
Singapore	High	Very low	Low	Medium	Medium
South Korea	High	Very high	Low	Low	High
Spain	Medium	Very high	Medium	Medium	Very low
Sweden	Low	Low	High	Very low	Low
Switzerland					

continued

Table 16.1 (continued)

Country	Power Distance	Uncertainty Avoidance	Individualism	Masculinity	Long Orientation
French	High	High	High	Medium	
German	Low	Medium	High	High	
Taiwan	Medium	High	Very low	Medium	Very high
Thailand	High	High	Low	Low	Medium
Turkey	High	Very high	Low	Medium	
United Kingdom	Low	Low	Very high	High	Low
United States	Medium	Medium	Very high	High	Low
Vietnam	High	Low	Low	Medium	Very high

Source: Hofstede and Hofstede (2005).
*Countries were evaluated by assigning scores. A high score on the dimension indicates a high evaluation on that dimension. Scores 1–19 = very low evaluation, 20–39 = low evaluation, 40–59 = moderate evaluation, 60–79 = high evaluation, 80–99 = very high evaluation, 100 and above = extremely high evaluation.

ties in meeting the tourists' needs due to the very many opportunities for experiencing cultural differences in behavior of tourists and locals. Samovar and Porter (1991) reported that the largest differences among cultural groups are between Asian and Western cultures. This means that visitors from Asia to the West or vice versa have the least commonalities with each other and that meeting the needs of Asian tourists by Western hosts or meeting the needs of Western tourists by Asian hosts can be the most difficult. This also means that the social interaction and communication between the members of Asian and Western cultures can generate the largest cultural conflicts.

The potential for avoiding cultural conflicts and effective social interaction and communication between tourists and hosts depends upon the cultural knowledge both parties have of each other. The more cultural knowledge locals have of international tourists and international tourists have of locals and the more they know about their behavior, the better they can predict each others' behavior and more easily enter into social relationships and communicate. As a result, studying behavioral differences among different cultural groups, understanding and appreciating culturally different tourist markets, and accepting the differences between cultures are professional obligations of those who work in the tourism and hospitality industry. Cross-cultural education is the only way to get ahead in the world today in order to avoid and/or reduce tensions and build mutual understanding among countries with different cultural values.

CULTURAL DIFFERENCES IN TOURISM STUDIES

To date, research in the area of cross-cultural differences has identified numerous behavioral differences among tourists from different cultural groups. For example, cultural differences have been identified in the following categories: tourist motivation (Jang and Cai, 2002; Kozak, 2002); preferences for travel services (Crotts and Erdmann, 2000); information search (Chen, 2000; Money and Crotts, 2003); destination perceptions (Reisinger and Mavondo, 2006a); image (Litvin et al., 2004); social interaction (Reisinger and Turner, 2002a, b); perceptions of travel risk (Reisinger and Mavondo, 2006a, b); travel behavior (Litvin et al., 2004); travel patterns (Sussmann and Rashcovsky, 1997); perceptions and stereotypes of tourists (Pizam and Sussmann, 1995; Pizam, Jansen-Verbeke, and Steel, 1997); perceptions and satisfaction with service quality (Tsang and Ap, 2007; Weiermair, 2000); perceptions of hotel facilities (Mattila, 1999a); and consumption patterns (Rosenbaum and Spears, 2005).

Numerous studies identified cultural differences among international tourists in attaching importance to accommodation (Becker and Murmann, 1999; McClearly, Cho, and Weaver, 1998; Sussmann and Rashcovsky, 1997), travel information (Sussmann and Rashcovsky, 1997), service (Mattila, 1999b, c), service in hotels (Armstrong et al., 1997), restaurants and food establishments (Becker and Murmann, 1999; Sheldon and Fox, 1988), and many others. The aforementioned studies have suggested that various cultural groups of tourists have different behavioral strategies than those of other cultural groups. Next are the examples of some studies that have identified cultural differences in tourist behavior.

CULTURAL DIFFERENCES IN TOURIST BEHAVIOR

The quality of the international tourists' experiences in a culturally different environment influences their holiday satisfaction. The understanding how cultural differences in tourist behavior influence tourist experiences allows the managers of the tourism and hospitality industry to better differentiate their tourism products and services for international tourists depending on the tourists' cultural needs as well as improve their social relations with international tourists. The examples of the major cultural differences in tourist behavior identified in the current tourism literature are presented next.

Importance of Food

Research has suggested that international tourists differ in attaching importance to food when on vacation. For example, for British and Japanese tourists, food is the most important part of a good vacation. For

Australians it is ranked third, for Germans it is fifth, and for the French food is not at all important (Sheldon and Fox, 1988). International tourists also differ in eating habits. For example, Americans like to eat fish and chips, French like snails, and Chinese like rice.

Perceptions of Tourists

Pizam and Sussmann (1995) proposed that Japanese, French, Italian, and American tourists differ in eighteen out of twenty behavioral characteristics related to social interactions, activity preferences, bargaining, knowledge of destination, and commercial transactions. Japanese tourists are perceived to be the most distinctive, whereas Italian tourists are the most like the other nationalities. The Italians and French are very similar to each other in their behavior, followed by the Americans and Italians. French and American tourists are the least similar.

Differences Between Asian Tourists and Western Hosts

Asian tourists (Indonesian, Japanese, Korean, Mandarin-speaking Chinese, Thai) differ from Australian service providers in cultural values, rules of social behavior, perceptions of service, preferences for social interaction, and satisfaction with tourist-host contact. These differences appear in seventy-three out of 117 (62.4 percent) areas of measurement (Reisinger and Turner, 2002a, b). For example, eighteen differences out of thirty-six areas of measurement were identified in cultural values, twenty-two out of thirty-four in rules of social interaction, twenty-three out of twenty-nine in perceptions of service, seven out of eleven in forms of social interaction, and three out of seven in satisfaction (see Table 16.2).

Travel Behavior

Korean tourists differ from Japanese tourists. Although Korean tourists travel as part of a group and use the packaged tour because it is an easy and quick way to arrange travel (Kim and Prideaux, 1998), Korean tourists take more risk and are more adventurous than the Japanese in choosing tourism activities and more impulsive in purchasing (March, 1997). Korean tourists have also significantly shorter decision time frames than Japanese travelers (Iverson, 1997).

Trip Characteristics

The mainland Chinese and the American visitors to Hong Kong differ in their trip characteristics. Mainland Chinese visitors to Hong Kong engage in shorter trips; their total trip duration is about four nights, whereas American visitors have total trip duration of more than thirteen nights. The

Table 16.2 Significant Differences Between Australian Hosts and Asian Language Groups

Group indicators	Max	Australian Total Asian	Australian Indonesian	Australian Japanese	Australian Korean	Australian Mandarin	Australian Thai
Cultural values	36	18	14	26	26	12	14
Rules of interaction	34	22	24	22	18	18	20
Perceptions of service	29	23	18	23	20	15	24
Forms of interaction	11	7	5	8	7	6	3
Satisfaction	7	3	3	4	3	2	3
Total	117	73	64	83	74	53	64

Source: Reisinger and Turner (2002a).

Mainland Chinese visitors also spend less money on services and shopping than the American visitors (Yoo, McKercher, and Mena, 2004).

Travel Motivation

The Mainland Chinese and the Americans have different motivations for traveling to Hong Kong. While Mainland Chinese visit Hong Kong for business purposes, Americans visitors come to Hong Kong for vacation and leisure purposes (Yoo et al., 2004). British and German tourists have different motivations for and satisfaction levels with visits to Mallorca and Turkey (Kozak, 2001, 2002). The Asian and Caucasian visitors have different motivations for attending a Cultural Expo in Korea (Lee, 2000).

Service-quality Perceptions

Numerous studies identified cultural differences in service-quality perceptions. Asian tourists give significantly lower ratings for all the relational quality-service attributes compared to their Western counterparts. Western customers place more emphasis on goal completion, efficiency, and time savings (Tsang and Ap, 2007). Japanese tourists demand more constant attention and care than American tourists (Ahmed and Krohn, 1992).

Service-quality Dimensions

It was found that customers from different cultures assign different importance weightings to the five SERVQUAL dimensions of service quality (Furrer, Liu, and Sudharsham, 2000). Customers with a Western cultural background rely more on tangible cues from the physical environment than customers with an Asian cultural background. The hedonic dimension of the consumption experience is more important for Western consumers than for Asians (Winsted, 1997).

Service Expectations

Tourists from Great Britain, the United States, Australia, Japan, and Taiwan have different expectations for hotel service quality. British tourists have the highest expectations, followed by tourists from the United States, Australia, Taiwan, and Japan. Japanese tourists have the lowest expectations for the tangible and the empathy dimensions of service quality. The Taiwanese tourists also have lower expectations for the empathy dimensions in terms of providing, caring, and giving individual attention to the tourist. A great cultural distance exists between Taiwan and Japan, and small differences among tourists from the United States, Great Britain, and Australia (Mok and Armstrong, 1998).

Preferences for Service Timing

Guests in casual restaurants have different preferences for service timing. The American tourists perceive a higher acceptable time to wait prior to seating, whereas guests from Hong Kong perceive a higher acceptable time to wait for the check upon the conclusion of the meal. U.S. guests perceive a prolonged wait for the check to be a sign of neglectful service (Becker and Murmann, 1999).

Complaint Behavior

Guests in hotel restaurants in Hong Kong, SAR, and Houston, Texas, differ in their complaint behavior. The Hong Kong guests complain more about the noise level, while the Houston guests complain more about temperature and décor of hotel restaurants. Service efficiency, greetings, attentiveness, and helpfulness are also rated differently; the Hong Kong guests rate "greetings" higher than the Houston guests (DeFranco et al., 2005).

Importance of Social Status

The personalization of service is important for American diners' satisfaction, whereas individual recognition and personalization are less important for Korean diners. Koreans avoid unnecessary involvement in service encounters and "out-group" interactions, and they do not

---

Case Study 2. Japanese Polite Behavior

In Japan, polite behavior is regulated by many "display rules" related to human interaction and situation. Japanese control themselves more in public because more things are prohibited in public. The have many behavioral rules regulating relations with supervisors, about obedience, loyalty, and group harmony. Patience (*nintai*) is essential; displaying impatience is a rude behavior. Restraining emotions and suppressing natural feelings are musts. Criticizing or complaining in public is a serious breach of social etiquette. Conflict is avoided in order to save one's own and others' face and maintain harmony in interpersonal relations. A humble, apologetic attitude is an important element of the person's character. Apologies for the reasons of admitting guilt, or for demonstrating humility and regret, seem to be illogical to Westerners. Openly expressing emotions is rude. Westerners are regarded as too cold, too objective, and uncaring about the emotional aspect of personal relations. Those who talk too much and raise their voices are perceived to be insincere and creating friction. In contrast, expressing feelings and thoughts in public and praising good talkers is a normal practice in the West.

desire familiarity with service providers whose social status differs from their own. Respect for social distance and recognition of status require Korean service providers to avoid expressions of familiarity, which is in contrast to Americans (Kong and Jogaratnam, 2007). Routine Western customer-employee service encounters do not satisfy Korean guests because they ignore the importance of status differences. Koreans expect a formal relationship in a service encounter, especially in the upscale, expensive restaurants.

Tolerance for Service Quality

It was found that the larger the cultural distance between countries, the higher the tolerance level for service quality and valuation of service criteria such as waiting times, queuing, added service components, and the choice of transportation mode (Becker and Murmann, 1999). For example, tourists from German-speaking and other EU countries have higher tolerance levels for non-EU countries in all areas of tourism activity and service quality dimensions (Weiermair and Fuchs, 1999a, b).

Behavior of Casino Guests

Further, research suggested differences in behaviors of casino customers from five cultural groups: Japanese, Korean, Chinese (mainland Chinese, Taiwanese, Hong Kong Chinese), Westerners (U.S. Americans and Europeans). and others (mainly Sri Lankan, Filipino, Bangladeshi, Thai, and Malaysian). The Chinese exhibit the most disruptive behavior, while the Japanese are the least disruptive. The Japanese and Koreans have the greatest tendency to tip the dealer, and the Japanese are the most likely to tip the drink waitresses, while the Chinese and minority guests rarely give tips. Chinese guests also have the highest tendency to purchase drinks from the bar, whereas Japanese guests prefer to order drinks from waitresses. Japanese guests are also the most likely to consume alcoholic drinks in contrast to Chinese guests (Kim, Prideaux, and Kim, 2002).

Responsible Tourist Behavior

Moreover, Korean, Australian, and British tourists differ in attitudes towards responsible tourist behaviors. The Korean tourists are the most likely to spend time before they travel studying or collecting information about the environment of the destination, the lifestyle of the local residents, and environmentally friendly tours and places to stay. They also seek to participate in environmental education programs while traveling and agree to spend some money on environmental conservation and preservation (Kang and Moscardo, 2006).

CULTURAL DIFFERENCES USING HOFSTEDE'S DIMENSIONS

Numerous studies examined cultural differences in tourist behavior using Hofstede's cultural dimensions. The IDV dimension was assessed as the major dimension differentiating cultures in the area of social behavior, communication, attitudes to others, developing human relationships, expressing emotions and feelings, complaining and complimenting, and many others. In tourism, the IDV dimension was found to have a significant influence on perceptions of service quality, travel-information search, or gift-giving. The UAI dimension was found to influence travel characteristics and patterns, information search, complimenting and complaining behavior. The MAS dimension was found to influence tourists' loyalty and travel satisfaction.

Individualism/Collectivism and Service Quality

Tourists from individualistic cultures are more likely to demand more efficient, prompt, and error-free service when compared to customers in collectivist cultures, where sincerity shown by service employees is the most important concern. Individualistic customers have higher expectations of assurance from service providers than collectivist customers because they expect service providers to give them confidence about the service they are receiving (Donthu and Yoo, 1998). Individualists maintain a distance between themselves and the service providers, and tangibles are a means to reduce the closeness of the interaction (Furrer and Sudharshan, 2000).

Individualism/Collectivism and Travel-information Search

When seeking external travel information, business travelers from highly collectivist Japan and Korea rely heavily on tour companies, corporate travel offices, travel guides, and advice from friends and relatives. Business travelers from the individualistic Australian society prefer obtaining their information directly from the airlines and state/city travel offices. Japanese and Australian leisure visitors show individualistic tendencies in their search strategies while Korean visitors evoke collectivist information-search behaviors (Chen, 2000).

Individualism/Collectivism and Gift-giving

In addition, tourists from collectivist cultures such as Korea buy more gifts, give gifts on more occasions, especially cash gifts, have a higher gift budget, and give more gifts at the workplace. On the other hand, Americans who are from individualistic cultures are under less pressure to reciprocate and thus have fewer gift-giving occasions, give gifts on more voluntary occasions, and have more flexibility in gift budgeting (Park, 1998).

Uncertainty Avoidance and Travel Characteristics

Tourists from low UAI cultures (Germany) and tourists from high UAI cultures (Japan) differ in information-search patterns, trip-planning-time horizons, travel-party characteristics, and trip characteristics. Japanese travelers engage in risk/uncertainty-reducing behaviors by seeking pretrip information from travel channel members, purchasing prepaid tour packages, traveling in larger groups, staying for shorter periods, and visiting fewer destinations than the Germans, who take more risk, travel independently, stay for longer periods of time, and visit more destinations (Money and Crotts, 2003).

Uncertainty Avoidance and Travel-information Search

Tourists from Japan, South Korea, and Australia to the United States have different preferences for external information sources (Chen, 2000). Tourists from the high UAI cultures (e.g., Japanese and Greek) acquire more information from friends, relatives, state and city travel offices, and tour operators than tourists from low UAI cultures (e.g., the Germans and British), who use travel guides and information obtained from marketing-dominated sources, such as advertisements on TV and radio (Litvin et al., 2004).

Uncertainty Avoidance and Travel Patterns

Those from high UAI cultures spend fewer days on trip planning, whereas those from low UAI cultures spend more time in arranging travel details, traveling alone, or traveling with fewer parties than tourists from high UAI cultures. Those from high UAI cultures purchase significantly more pre-packaged travel tours, whereas those from low UAI cultures are more likely to rent cars. Also, high UAI tourists visit fewer destinations and spend fewer nights in the visited country and during the length of their journey, as compared with low UAI tourists (Litvin et al., 2004).

Uncertainty Avoidance and Complimenting and Complaining Behavior

Although compliments in high-uncertainty-avoidance cultures are avoided because they are considered to cause embarrassment and loss of "face," other tourists from higher-uncertainty-avoidance cultures have usually a higher intention to praise the service providers if they experience positive service quality. However, if they experience a problem, they show a lower intention to switch to another service provider, to give negative word of mouth, or to complain (Liu and McClure, 2001). Those from high-uncertainty-avoidance cultures avoid negative emotions and opinions, criticism, complaints, and conflicts in all interpersonal relations. Criticism and complaints are considered rude and damaging to social harmony.

Table 16.3 Major Areas of Cultural Differences in Tourist Behavior

Areas of cultural differences in tourist behavior	Authors
Behavior of casino guests	Kim, Prideaux, and Kim, 2002
Complaining and complimenting behavior	DeFranco, Wortman, Lam, and Countryman, 2005; Liu and McClure, 2001
Consumption patterns	Rosenbaum and Spears, 2005
Cultural values	Reisinger and Turner ,2002a, b
Decision making	Park and Jun, 2003
Decision time frames	Iverson, 1997
Destination perceptions	Reisinger and Mavondo, 2006a
Destination image	Litvin, Crotts, and Hefner, 2004
Differences between Asian tourists and Australian service providers	Reisinger and Turner, 2002a, b
Forms of social interaction	Reisinger and Turner 2002a, b
Gift giving	Park, 1998
Importance attached to accommodation	Becker and Murmann, 1999; McClearly, Choi, and Weaver, 1998; Sussmann and Rashcovsky, 1997
Importance of social status and satisfaction with service	Kong and Jogaratnam, 2007; Furrer, Liu, and Sudharsham, 2000
Loyalty and travel satisfaction	Crotts and Erdmann, 2000
Perceptions and stereotypes of tourists	Pizam and Sussmann, 1995; Pizam, Jansen-Verbeke, and Steel, 1997
Perceptions of hotel facilities	Mattila, 1999a
Perceptions of travel risk	Reisinger and Mavondo, 2006a, b
Preferences for service timing	Becker and Murmann, 1999
Preferences for travel services	Crotts and Erdmann, 2000
Responsible tourist behavior	Kang and Moscardo, 2006
Rules of social interaction	Reisinger and Turner 2002a, b
Service perception	Ahmed and Krohn, 1992; Mattila, 1999b, c; Tsang and Ap, 2007
Service quality dimensions	Furrer, Liu, and Sudharsham, 2000; Winsted, 1997
Service in hotels	Armstrong, Mok, Go, and Chan, 1997
Service in restaurants and food establishments	Becker and Murmann, 1999; Sheldon and Fox, 1988
Service expectations	Mok and Armstrong, 1998; Donthu and Yoo, 1998

continued

Table 16.3   (continued)

Areas of cultural differences in tourist behavior	Authors
Service perception and satisfaction	Reisinger and Turner 2002a, b; Tsang and Ap, 2007; Weiermair, 2000
Social interaction	Reisinger and Turner 2002a, b
Tolerance for service quality	Weiermair and Fuchs, 1999a ,b
Tourist motivation	Jang and Cai, 2002; Kozak, 2001, 2002; Lee, 2000
Travel activities	March, 1997
Travel arrangements	Kim and Prideaux, 1998
Travel behavior	Litvin, Crotts, and Hefner, 2004
Travel information search	Chen, 2000; Litvin, Crotts, and Hefner, 2004; Money and Crotts, 2003; Sussmann and Rashcovsky, 1997
Trip characteristics	Litvin, Crotts, and Hefner, 2004; Money and Crotts, 2003; Yoo, McKercher, and Mena, 2004

Masculinity and Loyalty and Travel Satisfaction

Tourists from less masculine cultures are more loyal when evaluating travel services, while tourists from more masculine societies report strong customer defection. Those from highly masculine societies who focus on success, performance, and excellence also have higher dissatisfaction than those from low to moderate masculine societies who focus on quality of life, welfare of others. and nurturing behavior (Crotts and Erdmann, 2000). A summary of the literature review results is presented in Table 16.3.

CONCLUSION AND IMPLICATIONS

Cultural differences in tourist behavior do exist and represent a very important assessment index of a social interaction and communication between international tourists and local hosts. Considering that the international tourist industry is expected to continue to grow and aim at diverse cultural groups of tourists, industry professionals must increasingly meet the needs and expectations of those cultural groups. As the industry grows, opportunities for misunderstanding of tourists' needs may be enhanced. In order to avoid cultural tensions and successfully deal with international tourists, industry practitioners must recognize and understand the importance of cultural differences in international tourist behavior to satisfy their needs.

Understanding cultural differences among international tourist markets is imperative for developing effective marketing strategies, creating awareness and appreciation of multiple cultures and one's own culture, enhancing the managers and marketers' abilities to develop a more favorable destination image, and developing a better communication strategy that ultimately delivers higher tourist satisfaction. Cultural differences should be used as very useful constructs for identifying cultural profiles of the international tourist markets, their segmentation, targeting and positioning, and determining promotional strategies that directly target a specific cultural market segment. It is hoped that more studies in the area of cultural differences in tourist behavior will be conducted.

REFERENCES

Ahmed, Z. & Krohn, F. (1992). Understanding the unique consumer behavior of Japanese tourists. *Journal of Travel and Tourism Marketing*, 1(3): 73–86.

Armstrong, R., Mok, C., Go, F. & Chan, A. (1997). The importance of cross-cultural expectations in the measurement of service quality perceptions in the hotel industry. *International Journal of Hospitality Management*, 16(2): 181–90.

Becker, C. & Murmann, S. (1999). The effect of cultural orientation on the service timing preferences of customers in casual dining operations: An exploratory study. *International Journal of Hospitality Management*, 18: 59–65.

Burgoon, J. (1995). Cross-cultural and intercultural applications of expectancy violations theory. *International and Intercultural Communication Annual*, 19: 194–214.

Chen, J.S. (2000). Cross-cultural differences in travel information acquisition among tourists from three Pacific-Rim countries. *Journal of Hospitality and Tourism Research*, 24: 239.

Crotts, J. & Erdmann, R. (2000). Does national culture influence consumers' evaluation of travel services? A test of Hofstede's model of cross-cultural differences. *Managing Service Quality*, 10(6): 410–22.

DeFranco, A., Wortman, J., Lam, T. & Countryman, C. (2005). A cross-cultural comparison of customer complaint behavior in restaurants in hotels. *Asia Pacific Journal of Tourism Research*, 10(2): 173–90.

Donthu, N. & Yoo, B. (1998). Cultural influences on service quality expectations. *Journal of Service Research*, 1(2): 178–86.

Furrer, O., Liu, B. & Sudharshan, D. (2000). The relationship between culture and service quality perceptions: Basis for cross-cultural market segmentation and resource allocation. *Journal of Service Research*, 2(4): 355–71.

Hall, E. (1976). *Beyond culture*. New York: Anchor.

Hofstede, G. (1980). *Culture's consequences: International differences in work-related values*. London: Sage.

———. (1991). *Cultures and organization: Software of the mind*. London: McGraw-Hill.

———. (2001). *Culture's consequences: Comparing values, behaviors, institutions and organizations across nations,* 2nd ed. Thousand Oaks, CA: Sage.

Hofstede, G. & Bond, M. (1984). Hofstede's culture dimensions: An independent validation of Rokeach's Value Survey. *Journal of Cross-Cultural Psychology*, 15: 417–33.

254   *Yvette Reisinger*

Hofstede, G. & Hofstede, G. J. (2005). *Cultures and organizations: Software of the mind.* Revised and expanded 2nd ed. New York: McGraw-Hill.

Iverson, T. (1997). Japanese visitors to Guam: Lessons from experience. *Journal of Travel and Tourism Marketing,* 6(1): 41–54.

Jang, S. & Cai, L. (2002). Travel motivations and destination choice: A study of British outbound market. *Journal of Travel and Tourism Marketing,* 13(3): 111–33.

Kang, M. & Moscardo, G. (2006). Exploring cross-cultural differences in attitudes towards responsible tourist behavior: A comparison of Korean, British and Australian tourists. *Asia Pacific Journal of Tourism Research,* 11(4): 303–20.

Kim, S. & Prideaux, B. (1998). Korean inbound tourism to Australia—a study of supply-side deficiencies. *Journal of Vacation Marketing,* 5(1): 66–81.

Kim, S., Prideaux, B. & Kim, S. (2002). A cross-cultural study on casino guests as perceived by casino employees. *Tourism Management,* 23(5): 511–20.

Kluckhohn, F. & Strodtbeck, F. (1961). *Variations in value orientations.* New York: Harper & Row.

Kong, M. & Jogaratnam, G. (2007). The influence of culture on perceptions of service employee behavior. *Managing Service Quality,* 17: 275–97.

Kozak, M. (2001). Comparative assessment of tourist satisfaction with destinations across two nationalities. *Tourism Management,* 22(4): 391–401.

———. (2002). Comparative assessment of tourist motivations by nationality and destinations. *Tourism Management,* 23: 221–32.

Lee, C. (2000). A comparative study of Caucasian and Asian visitors to a cultural expo in an Asian setting. *Tourism Management,* 21: 169–76.

Litvin, S., Crotts, J. & Hefner, F. (2004). Cross-cultural tourist behaviour: A replication and extension involving Hofstede's uncertainty avoidance dimension. *International Journal of Tourism Research,* 6: 29–37.

Litvin, S. & Goh, W. (2004). Individualism/collectivism as a moderating factor to the self-image congruity concept. *Journal of Vacation Marketing,* 10(1): 23–32.

Liu, R. & McClure, P. (2001). Recognizing cross-cultural differences in consumer complaint behavior and intentions: An empirical examination. *The Journal of Consumer Marketing,* 18(1): 54–75.

March, R. (1997). Diversity in Asian outbound travel industries: A comparison between Indonesia, Thailand, Taiwan, South Korea and Japan. *International Journal of Hospitality Management,* 16(2): 231–38.

Mattila, A. (1999a). An analysis of means-end hierarchy in cross-cultural context: What motivates Asian and Western business travellers to stay at luxury hotels? *Journal of Hospitality and Leisure Marketing,* 6(2): 19–28.

———. (1999b). The role of culture in the service evaluation process. *Journal of Service Research,* 1(3): 250–61.

———. (1999c). The role of culture and purchase motivation in service encounter evaluations. *Journal of Service Management,* 13(4/5): 376–89.

McClearly, K., Choi, B. & Weaver, P. (1998). A comparison of hotel selection criteria between U.S. and Korean business travelers. *Journal of Hospitality and Tourism Research,* 22(1): 25–38.

Mok, C. & Armstrong, R. (1998). Expectations for hotel service quality: Do they differ from culture to culture? *Journal of Vacation Marketing,* 4(4): 381–91.

Money, R. B. & Crotts, J. C. (2003). The effect of uncertainty avoidance on information search, planning, and purchases of international travel vacations. *Tourism Management,* 24: 191–202.

Park, C. & Jun, J. (2003). A cross-cultural comparison of Internet buying behavior effects of Internet usage, perceived risks, and innovativeness. *International Marketing Review,* 20: 534–53.

Park, S. (1998). A comparison of Korean and American gift-giving behaviors. *Psychology and Marketing*, 15: 577–93.

Pizam, A. & Sussmann, S. (1995). Does nationality affect tourist behavior? *Annals of Tourism Research*, 22(4): 901–17.

Pizam, A., Jansen-Verbeke, M. & Steel, L. (1997). Are all tourists alike regardless of nationality? The perceptions of Dutch tour guides. *Journal of International Hospitality, Leisure and Tourism Management*, 1(1): 19–40.

Reisinger, Y. & Mavondo, F. (2006a). Cultural consequences on travel risk perception and safety. *Tourism Analysis*, 11(4): 265–84.

———. (2006b). Cultural differences in travel risk perception. *Journal of Travel and Tourism Marketing*, 20(1): 13–31.

Reisinger, Y. & Turner, L. (2002a). Cultural differences between Asian tourist markets and Australian hosts Part 1. *Journal of Travel Research*, 40(3): 295–315.

———. (2002b). Cultural differences between Asian tourist markets and Australian hosts Part 2. *Journal of Travel Research*, 40(4): 374–84.

Rosenbaum, M. & Spears, D. (2005). Who buys what? Who does what? Analysis of cross-cultural consumption behaviours among tourists in Hawaii. *Journal of Vacation Marketing*, 11(3): 235–47.

Samovar, L. A. & Porter, R. E. (1991). *Communication between cultures*. Belmont, CA: Wadsworth Publishing Company.

Sheldon, P. J. & Fox, M. (1988). The role of foodservice in vacation choice and experience: A cross-cultural analysis. *Journal of Travel Research*, 27(3): 9–15.

Sussmann, S. & Rashcovsky, C. (1997). A cross-cultural analysis of English and French Canadians' vacation travel patterns. *International Journal of Hospitality Management*, 16(2): 191–208.

Tsang, N. & Ap, J. (2007). Tourists' perceptions of relational quality service attributes: A cross-cultural study. *Journal of Travel Research*, 45: 355–63.

Weiermair, K. (2000). Tourists' perceptions towards and satisfaction with service quality in the cross-cultural service encounter: Implications for hospitality and tourism management. *Managing Service Quality*, 10(6): 397–409.

Weiermair, K. & Fuchs, M. (1999a). *The impact of cultural distance on perceived service quality gaps: The case of Alpine tourism*. Proceedings of the 9th Workshop on Quality Management in Services, European Institute for Advanced Studies in Management, Gothenberg, Sweden, 2–17 April.

———. (1999b). *The effect of cultural distance on perceived service quality gaps in Alpine tourism: Implications for IT-based intercultural communication strategies*. Paper presented at the First International Conference of the Service Operations Management Association (SOMA), 22–25 August, Waltham, Massachusetts.

Winsted, K. (1997). Evaluating service encounters: A cross-cultural and cross-industry exploration. *Journal of Marketing Theory and Practice*, 7(2): 106–23.

WTO. (2007). United National World Tourism Organization. *Facts and figures*. Available at *http://unwto.org/facts/eng/vision.htm*.

Yoo, J., McKercher, B. & Mena, M. (2004). A cross-cultural comparison of trip characteristics: International visitors to Hong Kong from Mainland China and USA. *Journal of Travel and Tourism Marketing*, 16(1): 65–77.

Contributors

Bodil Stilling Blichfeldt teaches all aspects of marketing as well as product/service/enterprise development, entrepreneurship, innovation, and philosophy of science/methodology. Research areas are consumer behavior, branding, and new service/product development. Apart from qualitative research focusing on consumers' travel motivations and experiences, present research emphasizes destination branding and hospitality. Department of Business Communication and Information Science, University of Southern Denmark, Niels Bohrs Vej 9, 6700 Esbjerg, Denmark. E-mail: bsb@sitkom.sdu.dk.

Antónia Correia is Assistant Professor of Economics in the Faculty of Economics at the University of the Algarve, Portugal. Her research interest is on consumer behavior in tourism. She has previously published a number of articles in some of the leading tourism and business journals, including *Annals of Tourism Research, Journal of Travel Research, Tourism Economics*, and *Journal of Business Research*. Faculty of Economics, University of Algarve, Campus de Gambelas, 8000–117 Faro, Portugal. E-mail: acorreia@ualg.pt.

Alain Decrop is Professor of Marketing at the Louvain School of Management and a member of CeRCLe at the University of Namur, Belgium. He holds master degrees in history and economics, and a PhD in business administration. His major research interests include consumer decision making and behavior, qualitative interpretive methods, and tourism marketing. Faculty of Business and Economics, University of Namur, and Louvain School of Management, Belgium. E-mail: alain.decrop@fundp.ac.be.

Sara Dolnicar is Professor of Marketing at the University of Wollongong, Australia. She holds degrees in psychology (University of Vienna) and business administration (Vienna University of Business Administration) and was awarded her PhD in business administration in 1996. Her primary research interests are in market segmentation, marketing research methodology, and tourism. Marketing Research Innovation Centre (MRIC), School of Management and Marketing, University of

Wollongong, Northfields Ave., 2522 Wollongong NSW Australia. E-mail: sara_dolnicar@uow.edu.au.

Teoman Duman is an Assistant Professor of Marketing in the School of Hotel, Restaurant and Tourism Administration, Gaziosmanpasa University, Turkey. He gained his PhD degree in leisure studies at the Penn State University, USA. He specializes in different areas of tourism marketing such as destination marketing, consumer behavior in tourism, service value, and special-interest tourism. Dincerler School of Tourism and Hotel Management, Gaziosmanpasa University, Zile, Tokat 60400, Turkey. E-mail: teomanduman@yahoo.com.

Clare I. Foster is a Research Associate for the Tourism Research Intelligence Partnership (TRIP) based within the Christel DeHaan Tourism and Travel Research Institute at the University of Nottingham. Her main research interests are in consumer behavior in tourism, narratives and storytelling, and cultural identity. She is currently working towards completion of her PhD on tourist evaluations of package holiday experiences. Christel DeHaan Tourism and Travel Research Institute, Nottingham University, UK. Email: Clare.foster@nottingham.ac.uk.

Juergen Gnoth is Associate Professor at the Department of Marketing, the University of Otago, New Zealand. He teaches and searches tourists' and general consumer behavior but also place branding and networking. In recent years, he has also developed an interest in social marketing and is involved in values research and the consumption of common or public goods. Department of Marketing, University of Otago, Dunedin, New Zealand. E-mail: jgnoth@business.otago.ac.nz.

Frank M. Go is Professor and Director of the Centre for Tourism Management at the Rotterdam School of Management, Erasmus University, the Netherlands. His research focus is on the co-evolution of marketing, ICT and organization practices, sustainable business development, destination images and brand identity, and technology-enhanced learning contexts. Centre for Tourism Management, Rotterdam School of Management, Erasmus University, Netherlands. E-mail: fgo@rsm.nl.

Robert Govers is Assistant Professor Marketing and Strategy in the Master in Tourism Program at the University of Leuven, Belgium. He also acts as visiting faculty at the IULM University, Milan; the Hotel School, The Hague; the Emirates Academy of Hospitality Management and Ehsal, Dubai. Prior to returning to the Benelux in 2003, Robert worked in Dubai for four years. University of Leuven, Belgium. E-mail: rgovers@geo.kuleuven.be.

Kenneth F. Hyde is Senior Lecturer in Marketing at AUT University and an Associate Director of the New Zealand Tourism Research Institute. His research interests include consumer behavior in tourism, independent travel, tourist decision making, and vacation planning. His research has been published in the *Journal of Travel Research, Journal of Travel and Tourism Marketing, Tourism Analysis and Qualitative Market Research*. AUT University, Private Bag 92006, Auckland, New Zealand. E-mail: ken.hyde@aut.ac.nz.

Byron Kemp is Research Assistant in the School of Management and Marketing at the University of Wollongong, Australia, where he has worked with research teams on topics in the areas of brand image measurement, market segmentation, and environmentally sustainable tourism. He completed his bachelor of commerce (marketing) in 2007 and is currently undertaking Honours research. Marketing Research Innovation Centre (MRIC), School of Management and Marketing, University of Wollongong, Northfields Ave., 2522 Wollongong NSW Australia. E-mail: byron_kemp@uow.edu.au.

Inès Kessler presently researches tourism consumer behavior with special focus on at-destination decision making. Further research areas are information communication technology and experience economy, using quantitative as well as qualitative research methods. Department of Business Communication and Information Science, University of Southern Denmark, Niels Bohrs Vej 9, 6700 Esbjerg, Denmark. E-mail: Kessler@sitkom.sdu.dk.

Metin Kozak is Professor of Marketing in the School of Tourism and Hospitality Management, Mugla University, Mugla, Turkey. He holds both Master's and PhD degrees in tourism. His research focuses on consumer behavior, benchmarking, performance measurement, destination management and marketing, and Mediterranean tourism. School of Tourism and Hospitality Management, Mugla University, 48170 Mugla, Turkey. E-mail: M.Kozak@superonline.com.

Xiang (Robert) Li is Assistant Professor at the School of Hotel, Restaurant, and Tourism Management at University of South Carolina, USA. He has conducted extensive research related to tourist behavior and psychology, destination marketing, and tourism knowledge development with special emphasis on customer loyalty, destination perception, and tourism in China. School of Hotel, Restaurant, and Tourism Management, University of South Carolina, Columbia, South Carolina, 29208, USA. E-mail: robertli@sc.edu.

Maria Månsson is a PhD candidate in service studies at Lund University/ Campus Helsingborg, Sweden. Her main research interest is tourism in relation to media and space with emphasis on tourist performances. Another research interest is gay destination marketing. Previously she worked in the tourism and hospitality industry and still she makes guest appearances as a guide. Department of Service Management, Lund University, Campus Helsingborg, P.O. Box 882, SE-251 08 Helsingborg, Sweden. E-mail: maria.mansson@msm.lu.se.

Miguel Moital is a Senior Lecturer in Events Management in the School of Services Management at Bournemouth University, UK. His current research interests include the consumer experience of events, leisure, and tourism, as well as event marketing and management. He has published in the *Services Industries Journal*, the *International Journal of Tourism Policy*, and the *Journal of Foodservice*. Centre for Event & Sport Research, School of Services Management, Bournemouth University, Dorset House, Talbot Campus, Fern Barrow, Poole, Dorset, BH1 2LS, UK. E-mail: mmoital@bournemouth.ac.uk.

Michael Morgan is Senior Lecturer in the School of Services Management, Bournemouth University, UK. His current research interests are in the area of consumer experience and experience management. With Pamela Watson he has recently published an online resource guide for teachers and students, *Resource Guide to Extraordinary Experiences*. HLST Network of the UK Higher Education Academy. School of Services Management, Bournemouth University, Fern Barrow, Poole BH12 5BB, UK. E-mail: mmorgan@bournemouth.ac.uk.

Gianna Moscardo is a Professor in the School of Business at James Cook University, Australia. Her background in psychology and sociology support her research interests in understanding the nature of relationships between destination community attitudes and tourism development and the nature of individual tourist experiences. School of Business, James Cook University, Townsville, QLD, 4811, Australia. E-mail: Gianna. Moscardo@jcu.edu.au.

Christine Petr is Assistant Professor of Marketing, CREM at Rennes University, France. She conducts research on leisure time consumer behavior. Her current works on tourism and e-tourism are supported by M@rsouin, a research federation, supported by the Breton Council, involving Social Science and Humanities Research Centre workforces dealing with the uses of interactive computer technologies. Center for Research in Economics and Management (CREM-UMR CNRS 6211), Institut d'Administration des Entreprises de Rennes (IGR-IAE), 11, rue Jean Macé, CS 70803, 35708 Rennes Cédex, France. E-mail: christine.petr@univ-rennes1.fr.

James F. Petrick is Associate Professor and Associate Department Head for Graduate Studies in the Department of Recreation, Park and Tourism Sciences at Texas A&M University, USA. His research explores the determinants of tourists' purchase behaviors. Pursuant to this interest, he has been examining the relationships between visitors' satisfaction, perceived value, and loyalty and their purchasing behavior. Department of Recreation, Park and Tourism Sciences, Texas A&M University, TAMU 2261, College Station, Texas 77843–2261, USA. E-mail: jpetrick@tamu.edu.

Yvette Reisinger is Associate Professor of Tourism in the School of Tourism and Hospitality Management, Temple University, USA. Her research activities focus on cross-cultural differences in tourist behavior. She is the founding member of the International Society of Culture, Tourism and Hospitality Research, and associate editor of the *International Journal of Tourism, Culture and Hospitality Research*. School of Tourism and Hospitality Management, Fox School of Business and Management, Temple University, 17000 N. Broad Street, Philadelphia, PA 19122, USA. E-mail: yvette.reisinger@temple.edu.

Karin Teichmann is Research and Teaching Assistant at the Institute for Tourism and Leisure Studies at the Wirtschaftsuniversität Wien, Austria, and currently works on her PhD focusing on factors that influence tourists' information-search behavior. Her research interests are in the area of tourist behavior research. She teaches marketing engineering and data collection methods in tourism and leisure sciences. Institute for Tourism and Leisure Studies, Wirtschaftsuniversität Wien, Austria. E-mail: karin.teichmann@wu-wien.ac.at.

Pamela Watson is a lecturer at Bournemouth University, UK. After a career in the travel industry in her native Australia, she worked in the International College of Tourism and Hotel Management of Macquarie University. She is currently researching the consumer experience of restaurants as revealed in online blogs and message boards. School of Services Management, Bournemouth University, Fern Barrow, Poole BH12 5BB, UK.

Andreas H. Zins is Associate Professor at the Institute for Tourism and Leisure Studies at the Wirtschaftsuniversität Wien (WU) and Full Professor of Tourism Management of MODUL University, both in Austria. His research interests are tourism behavior, marketing research, social impacts, Web-based interviewing, theme parks, and related leisure attractions. Institute for Tourism and Leisure Studies, Wirtschaftsuniversität Wien, Austria and Department of Tourism and Hospitality Management, MODUL University Vienna, Austria. E-mail: andreas.zins@wu-wien.ac.at.

Index

V
vacation planning. *See* trip planning
valence, 15, 17, 18–19, 21–22
value: co-creation of, 134, 230, 232;
    conspicuous, 18–19; emotional,
    20; hedonic, 19–20; perceived,
    18; quality, 19–20, 21; social,
    19–20; unique, 19–20
values, 182–183, 201–202; cultural,
    236–238, 242–243; individual,
    237
variation-in-behavior, 88
variety seeking, 81–82, 88–89, 90

Veblen effect, 18, 21
visitors, first-time vs. repeat, 57–59, 89
volitional process, 158, 166–167

W
Web 2.0, 213
websites, 120, 209, 211, 213, 214,
    217–220
wildlife-based tourism, 104, 110, 197
word of mouse, 38, 213
word of mouth (WOM), 23, 38–39, 50,
    86–87, 148, 152, 248
work, tourism as, 134, 139